H. T. Rogers, F. Max Müller

Buddhaghosha's Parables

H. T. Rogers, F. Max Müller

Buddhaghosha's Parables

ISBN/EAN: 9783743310834

Manufactured in Europe, USA, Canada, Australia, Japa

Cover: Foto ©Thomas Meinert / pixelio.de

Manufactured and distributed by brebook publishing software (www.brebook.com)

H. T. Rogers, F. Max Müller

Buddhaghosha's Parables

BUDDHAGHOSHA'S PARABLES:

TRANSLATED FROM BURMESE

By CAPTAIN T. ROGERS, R.E.

With an Introduction,

CONTAINING

BUDDHA'S DHAMMAPADA,

Or "PATH OF VIRTUE,"

TRANSLATED FROM PÂLI

By F. MAX MÜLLER, M.A.,

PROFESSOR OF COMPARATIVE PHILOLOGY AT OXFORD, FOREIGN MEMBER OF THE FRENCH INSTITUTE, ETC.

LONDON:
TRÜBNER AND CO., 60, PATERNOSTER ROW.
1870.

INTRODUCTION.

BY PROFESSOR MAX MÜLLER.

A FEW words seem required to explain the origin and history of this book. About the end of last year, Captain Rogers, after having spent some years in Burmah, returned to England, and as he had paid particular attention to the study of Burmese, he was anxious, while enjoying the leisure of his furlough, to translate some Burmese work that might be useful to Oriental students. He first translated 'The History of Prince Theemeewizaya,' being one of the former lives (gâtaka) of Buddha. Although this work contains many things that are of interest to the student of Buddhism, it was impossible to find a publisher for it. I then advised Captain Rogers to undertake a translation of the parables which are contained in Buddhaghosha's 'Commentary on the Dhammapada.' Many of these fables had been published in Pâli by Dr. Fausböll, at the end of his edition of the 'Dhammapada;' but as the MSS. used by him were very defective, the Pâli text of these parables had only excited, but had not satisfied the curiosity of Oriental scholars. It is well known that the Burmese look upon Buddhaghosha, not indeed as having introduced Buddhism into Burmah, but as having brought the most important works of Buddhist literature to the shores of the Gulf of Martaban, and I therefore hoped that the Burmese translation of Buddhaghosha's parables would be as trustworthy as the Pâli original. In this expectation, however, I was disappointed. When I received the first instalment of the translation by Captain Rogers, I saw at once that it gave a small number only of the stories contained in Buddhaghosha's Pâli original, and that the Burmese translation, though literal in some parts, was generally only a free rendering of the Pâli text. Nor does it seem as if the translator had always understood the text of Buddhaghosha correctly. Thus in the very first story, we read in the Pâli text that, when the wife of Mahâsva*nn*a had her first son, she called him Pâla; but when she had a second, she called the elder Mahâ-pâla, *i. e.* Great Pâla, and the second, *K*ulla-pâla, *i. e.* Little Pâla, In the translation all this is lost, and we simply read: " After ten months a son was born, to whom he gave the name of Mahâpâla, because he had obtained him through his prayers to the Nat. After this, another son was born, who received the name of *K*ullapâla."

Though, for a time, I thought that the Burmese version of these parables might be a shorter, and possibly a more original collection, yet passages like the one just quoted would hardly allow of such a view. On the contrary, the more I saw of the translation of the Burmese parables, the more I felt convinced that the Burmese text was an abstract of Buddhaghosha's work, giving only a certain number of Buddhaghosha's stories, and most of them considerably abridged, and sometimes altered. As Dr. Fausböll has given of many of these stories the titles only, it was impossible in every case to compare the Burmese version with the Pâli original. But, on the whole, I do not expect that the opinion which I have formed of the Burmese translation will be materially modified, when we have the whole of the Pâli text to compare with it; and we must wait till we receive from Burmese scholars an explanation of the extraordinary changes which Buddhaghosha's original has undergone in the hands of the Burmese translator. My own opinion is, that there must be a more complete and more accurate Burmese translation of Buddhaghosha's work, and that what we have now before us is only the translation of a popular edition of the larger work. Towards the end of the Burmese translation there are several additions, evidently from a different source; in one case, as stated (p. 174), from the 'Kammapabhedadîpa.'

By a strange coincidence, I received, at the very time when Captain Rogers had finished his translation, another translation of the same work by Captain Sheffield Grace. It was not intended for publication, but sent to me for my private use. I obtained Captain Sheffield Grace's permission to send his manuscript to Captain Rogers, who, as will be seen from his preface, derived much advantage from it while revising his own MS. for the press.

Although I felt disappointed at the character of the Burmese translation, yet I was most anxious that the labours of Captain Rogers and Captain Sheffield Grace should not have been in vain. Even such as they are, these parables are full of interest, not only for a study of Buddhism, but likewise for the history of fables and apologues in their migrations from East to West, or from West to East. This important chapter in the literary history of the ancient world, which since the days of Sylvestre de Sacy has attracted so much attention, and has of late been so ably treated by Professor Benfey and others, cannot be considered as finally closed without a far more exhaustive study of these Buddhist fables, many of them identically the same as the fables of the Pañkatantra, and as the fables of Æsop. Nay I thought that, if it were only to give to the world that one apologue of Kisâgotamî (p. 100), this small collection of Buddhist parables deserved to be published; and I hoped, moreover, that by the publication of this first instalment, an impulse would be given that might lead to a complete translation, either from Pâli or from Burmese, of all the fables contained in the 'Commentary on the Dhammapada.'

However, in spite of my pleading, no publisher, not even Mr. Trübner, who certainly has shown no lack of faith in Oriental literature, would undertake the risk of publishing this collection of parables, except on condition that I should write an introduction. Though my hands were full of work at the time, and my attention almost exclusively occupied with Vedic researches, yet I felt so reluctant to let this collection of Buddhistic fables remain unpublished, that I agreed to take my part in the work as soon as the first volume of my translation of the 'Rig Veda' should be carried through the press.

As the parables which Captain Rogers translated from Burmese, were originally written in Pâli, and formed part of Buddhaghosha's 'Commentary on the Dhammapada,' *i. e.* 'The Path of Virtue,' I thought that the most useful contribution that I could offer, by way of introduction, would be a translation of the original of the Dhammapada. The Dhammapada forms part of the Buddhistic canon, and consists of 423 verses,[1] which are believed to contain the utterances of Buddha himself. It is in explaining these verses that Buddhaghosha gives for each verse a parable, which is to illustrate the meaning of the verse, and is believed to have been uttered by Buddha, in his intercourse with his disciples, or in preaching to the multitudes that came to hear him. In translating these verses, I have followed the edition of the Pâli text, published in 1855 by Dr. Fausböll, and I have derived great advantage from his Latin translation, his notes, and his copious extracts from Buddhaghosha's commentary. I have also con-

---

[1] That there should be some differences in the exact number of these gâthâs, or verses, is but natural. In a short index at the end of the work, the number of chapters is given as twenty-six. This agrees with our text. The sum total, too, of the verses as there given, viz. 423, agrees with the number of verses which Buddhaghosha had before him, when writing his commentary, at the beginning of the fifth century of our era. It is only when the number of verses in each chapter is given that some slight differences occur. Cap. v. is said to contain 17 instead of 16 verses; cap. xii. 12 instead of 10; cap. xiv. 16 instead of 18; cap. xx. 16 instead of 17; cap. xxiv. 22 instead of 26; cap. xxvi. 40 instead of 41, which would give altogether five verses less than we actually possess. The cause of this difference may be either in the wording of the index itself (and we actually find in it a various reading, malavagge *ka* visati, instead of malavagg' ekavisati, see Fausböll, p. 435); or in the occasional counting of two verses as one, or of one as two. Thus in cap. v. we get 16 instead of 17 verses, if we take each verse to consist of two lines only, and not, as in vv. 74 and 75, of three. Under all circumstances the difference is trifling, and we may be satisfied that we possess in our MSS. the same text which Buddhaghosha knew in the fifth century of our era.

sulted translations, either of the whole of the Dhammapada, or of portions of it, by Weber, Gogerly,[1] Upham, Burnouf, and others. Though it will be seen that in many places my translation differs from those of my predecessors, I can only claim for myself the name of a very humble gleaner in the field of Pâli literature. The greatest credit is due to Dr. Fausböll, whose *editio princeps* of the Dhammapada will mark for ever an important epoch in the history of Pâli scholarship; and though later critics have been able to point out some mistakes, both in his text and in his translation, the value of their labours is not to be compared with that of the work accomplished singlehanded by that eminent Danish scholar.

On the Age of the Parables and of the Dhammapada.

The age of Buddhaghosha can be fixed with greater accuracy than most dates in the literary history of India, for not only his name, but the circumstances of his life and his literary activity are described in the Mahâvaṃsa, the history of Ceylon, by what may be called almost a contemporary witness. The Mahâvaṃsa, lit. the genealogy of the great,[2] or the great genealogy, is, up to the reign of Dhâtusena, the work of Mahânâma. It was founded on the Dîpavaṃsa, also called Mahâvaṃsa, a more ancient history of the

---

[1] "Several of the chapters have been translated by Mr. Gogerly, and have appeared in 'The Friend,' vol. iv. 1840." (Spence Hardy, 'Eastern Monachism,' p. 169.)

[2] See Mahânâma's own explanations given in the Tîkâ; 'Mâhavaṃsa,' Introduction, p. xxxi.

island of Ceylon, which ended with the reign of Mahâsena, who died 302 A.D. MSS. of the Dîpavaṃsa are said to exist, and there is a hope of its being published. Mahânâma, who lived during the reign of King Dhâtusena, 459–477, wrote the whole history of the island over again, and carried it on to his own time. He also wrote a commentary on this work, but that commentary extends only as far as the forty-eighth verse of the thirty-seventh chapter, i. e. as far as the reign of Mahâsena, who died in 302 A.D.[1] As it breaks off exactly where the older history, the Dîpavaṃsa, is said to have ended, it seems most likely that Mahânâma embodied in it the results of his own researches into the ancient history of Ceylon, while for his continuation of the work, from the death of Mahâsena to his own time, no such commentary was wanted. It is difficult to determine whether the thirty-eighth as well as the thirty-seventh chapter came from the pen of Mahânâma, for the Mahâvaṃsa was afterwards continued by different writers to the middle of the last century; but, taking into account all the circumstances of the case, it is most probable that Mahânâma carried on the history to his own time, to the death of Dhâtusena or Dâsen Kellîya, who died in 477.[2] This Dhâtusena was the nephew of the historian Mahânâma, and owed the throne to the protection of his uncle. Dhâtusena was in fact the restorer of a national dynasty, and after having defeated the foreign usurpers (the

[1] After the forty-eighth verse, the text, as published by Turnour, puts 'Mahâvaṃso niṭṭhito,' the Mahâvaṃsa is finished; and after a new invocation of Buddha, the history is continued with the forty-ninth verse. The title Mahâvaṃsa, as here employed, seems to refer to the Dîpavaṃsa.

[2] 'Mahâvaṃsa,' Introduction, p. xxxi.

Damilo dynasty) "he restored the religion which had been set aside by the foreigners."[1] Among his many pious acts, it is particularly mentioned that he gave a thousand, and ordered the Dîpava*n*sa to be promulgated.[2]

As Mahânâma was the uncle of Dhâtusena, who reigned from 459-477, he may be considered a trustworthy witness with regard to facts that occurred between 410 and 432. Now the literary activity of Buddhaghosha in Ceylon falls in that period, and this is what Mahânâma relates of him ('Mahâva*n*sa,' p. 250):

"A Brâhman youth, born in the neighbourhood of the terrace of the great Bo-tree (in Mâgadha), accomplished in the 'vijjá' (knowledge) and 'sippa' (art), who had achieved the knowledge of the three Vedas, and possessed great aptitude in attaining acquirements; indefatigable as a schismatic disputant, and himself a schismatic wanderer over *G*ambudîpa, established himself, in the character of a disputant, in a certain vihâra, and was in the habit of rehearsing, by night and by day with clasped hands, a discourse which he had learned, perfect in all its component parts, and sustained throughout in the same lofty strain. A certain mahâthera, Revata, becoming acquainted with him there, and (saying to himself), "This individual

---

[1] 'Mahâva*n*sa,' p. 256.

[2] Mahâv. p. 257, "And that he might also promulgate the contents of the 'Dîpava*n*sa,' distributing a thousand pieces, he caused it to be read aloud thoroughly." The text has, 'datvâ sahassa*m* dîpetu*m* Dîpava*n*sa*m* samâdisi,' having given a thousand, he ordered the Dîpava*n*sa to be rendered illustrious, or to be copied. (See Westergaard, 'Ueber den ältesten Zeitraum der Indischen Geschichte,' Breslau, 1862, p. 33; and 'Mahava*n*sa,' Introduction, p. xxxii. l. 2.)

is a person of profound knowledge, it will be worthy (of me) to convert him;" inquired, "Who is this who is braying like an ass?" The Brâhman replied to him, "Thou canst define, then, the meaning conveyed in the bray of asses." On the Thera rejoining, "I can define it;" he (the Brâhman) exhibited the extent of the knowledge he possessed. The Thera criticized each of his propositions, and pointed out in what respect they were fallacious. He who had been thus refuted, said, "Well, then, descend to thy own creed;" and he propounded to him a passage from the 'Abhidhamma' (of the Pitakattaya). He (the Brâhman) could not divine the signification of that passage, and inquired, "Whose manta is this?"—"It is Buddha's manta." On his exclaiming, "Impart it to me;" the Thera replied, "Enter the sacerdotal order." He who was desirous of acquiring the knowledge of the 'Pitakattaya,' subsequently coming to this conviction, "This is the sole road" (to salvation), became a convert to that faith. As he was as profound in his eloquence (ghosa) as Buddha himself, they conferred on him the appellation of Buddhaghosa (the voice of Buddha); and throughout the world he became as renowned as Buddha. Having there (in Gambudîpa) composed an original work called 'Nânodaya' (Rise of Knowledge), he, at the same time, wrote the chapter called "Atthasâlini, on the Dhammasanganî" (one of the Commentaries on the 'Abhidhamma').

"Revata Thera then observing that he was desirous of undertaking the compilation of a general commentary on the 'Pitakattaya,' thus addressed him: "The text alone of the 'Pitakattaya' has been preserved in this land, the 'Atthakathâ' are not extant here, nor is there any version to be found of the schisms (vâda) complete. The Singhalese 'Atthakathâ' are genuine. They were composed in the Singhalese language by the inspired and profoundly wise Mahinda, who had previously consulted the discourses of Buddha, authenticated at the thera-convocations, and the dissertations and arguments of Sâriputta and others, and they are extant among the Singhalese. Preparing for this, and studying the same, translate them according to the rules of the grammar of the Mâgadhas. It will be an act conducive to the welfare of the whole world."

"Having been thus advised, this eminently wise personage rejoicing therein, departed from thence, and visited this island in the reign of this monarch (*i. e.* Mahânâma). On reaching the Mahâvihâra (at Anurâdhapura), he entered the Mahâpadhâna hall, the most splendid of the apartments in the vihâra, and listened to the Singhalese Atthakathâ, and the Theravâda, from the beginning to the end, propounded by the thera Sanghapâla; and became thoroughly convinced that they conveyed the true meaning of the doctrines of the Lord of Dhamma. Thereupon paying reverential respect to the priesthood, he thus petitioned: "I am desirous of translating the 'Atthakathâ;' give me access to all your books." The priesthood, for the purpose of testing his qualifications, gave only two gâthâs, saying, "Hence prove thy qualification; having satisfied ourselves on this point, we will then let thee have all our books." From these (taking these gâthâ for his text), and consulting the 'Pitakattaya,' together with the 'Atthakathâ,' and condensing them into an abridged form, he composed the work called 'The Visuddhimagga.' Thereupon, having assembled the priesthood, who had acquired a thorough knowledge of the doctrines of Buddha, at the bo-tree, he commenced to read out the work he had composed. The devatâs, in order that they might make his (Buddhaghosa's) gifts of wisdom celebrated among men, rendered that book invisible. He, however, for a second and third time recomposed it. When he was in the act of producing his book for the third time, for the purpose of propounding it, the devatâs restored the other two copies also. The assembled priests then read out the three books simultaneously. In those three versions, neither in a signification nor in a single misplacement by transposition, nay even in the thera-controversies, and in the text (of the 'Pitakattaya') was there, in the measure of a verse or in the letter of a word, the slightest variation. Thereupon, the priesthood rejoicing, again and again fervently shouted forth, saying, "Most assuredly this is Metteya (Buddha) himself," and made over to him the books in which the 'Pitakattaya' were recorded, together with the 'Atthakathâ.' Taking up his residence in the secluded Ganthâkara vihâra, at Anurâdhapura, he translated, according to the grammatical rules of the Mâgadhas, which is the root of all languages, the whole of the Singhalese Atthakathâ (into Pâli). This proved an achievement of the utmost consequence to all languages spoken by the human race.

"All the theras and âchâriyas held this compilation in the same estimation as the text (of the 'Pitakattaya'). Thereafter, the objects of his mission having been fulfilled, he returned to Gambudîpa, to worship at the bo-tree (at Uruvelâya, or Uruvilvâ, in Mâgadha)."

Here we have a simple account of Buddhaghosha[1] and his literary labours written by a man, himself a priest, and who may well have known Buddhaghosha during his stay in Ceylon. It is true that the statement of his writing the same book three times over without a single various reading, partakes a little of the miraculous; but we find similar legends mixed up with accounts of translations of other sacred books, and we cannot contend that writers who believed in such legends are therefore unworthy to be believed as historical witnesses.

The next question which has to be answered is this, Did Buddhaghosha's Parables, and the whole of the commentary in which they are contained, form part of the 'Arthakathâ' which he translated from Singhalese into Pâli. The answer to this question depends on whether the Dhammapada formed part of the 'Pitakattaya' or not. If the verses of the Dham-

---

[1] The Burmese entertain the highest respect for Buddhaghosha. Bishop Bigandet, in his 'Life or Legend of Gaudama' (Rangoon, 1866), writes: "It is perhaps as well to mention here an epoch which has been, at all times, famous in the history of Budhism in Burma. I allude to the voyage which a Religious of Thaton, named Budhagosa, made to Ceylon, in the year of religion 943 = 400 A.C. The object of this voyage was to procure a copy of the scriptures. He succeeded in his undertaking. He made use of the Burmese, or rather Talaing characters, in transcribing the manuscripts, which were written with the characters of Magatha. The Burmans lay much stress upon that voyage, and always carefully note down the year it took place. In fact, it is to Budhagosa that the people living on the shores of the Gulf of Martaban owe the possession of the Budhist scriptures. From Thaton, the collection made by Budhagosa was transferred to Pagan, six hundred and fifty years after it had been imported from Ceylon."

mapada were contained in the canon, then they were also explained in the Singhalese 'Arthakathâ,' and consequently translated from it into Pâli by Buddhaghosha. Now it is true that the exact place of the Dhammapada in the Buddhistic canon has not yet been pointed out; but if we refer to Appendix iii., printed in Turnour's edition of the 'Mahavansa,' we there find in the third part of the canon, the Sûtra-pitaka, under No. 5, the Kshudraka-nikâya, containing fifteen subdivisions, the second of which is the Dhammapada.

We should, therefore, be perfectly justified in treating the parables contained in Buddhaghosha's Pâli translation of the 'Arthakathâ,' i. e. the commentary on the Dhammapada, as part of a much more ancient work, viz. the work of Mahinda, and it is only in deference to an over-cautious criticism that I have claimed no earlier date than that of Buddhaghosha for these curious relics of the fable-literature of India. I have myself on a former occasion[1] pointed out all the objections that can be raised against the authority of Buddhaghosha and Mahinda; but I do not think that scholars calling these parables the parables of Mahinda, if not of Buddha himself, and referring their date to the third century B.C., would expose themselves at present to any formidable criticism.

If we read the pages of the 'Mahâvansa' without prejudice, and make allowance for the exaggerations and superstitions of Oriental writers, we see clearly that the literary work of Buddhaghosha presupposes the existence, in some shape or other, not only of the canonical books, but also of their Singhalese commentary. The Buddhistic canon had been settled in seve-

[1] 'Chips from a German Workshop,' 2nd ed., vol. i. p. 197.

ral councils, whether two or three, we need not here inquire.[1] It had received its final form at the council held under Asoka in the year 246 B.C. We are further told in the 'Mahâvansa' that Mahinda, the son of Asoka, who had become a priest, learnt the whole of the Buddhist canon in three years (p. 37); and that at the end of the third council he was dispatched to Ceylon, in order to establish there the religion of Buddha (p. 71). The king of Ceylon, Devânâmpriya Tishya, was converted, and Buddhism soon became the dominant religion of the island. Next follows a statement which will naturally stagger those who are not acquainted with the power of memory if under strict discipline for literary purposes, but which exceeds by no means the limits of what is possible in times when the whole sacred literature of a people is preserved and lives by oral tradition only. The Pitakatraya, as well as the Arthakathâ, having been collected and settled at the third council in 246 B.C., were brought to Ceylon by Mahinda, who promulgated them orally;[2] the 'Pitakatraya' in Pâli, and the 'Arthakathâ' in Singhalese,[3] together with additional Arthakathâ of

---

[1] The question of these councils and of their bearing on Indian chronology has been discussed by me in my 'History of Ancient Sanskrit Literature,' p. 262 seq., 2nd ed.

[2] Cf. Bigandet, l. c. p. 387.

[3] Singhalese, being the language of the island, would naturally be adopted by Mahinda and his fellow-missionaries for communication with the natives. If he abstained from translating the canon also into Singhalese, this may have been on account of its more sacred character. At a later time, however, the canon, too, was translated into Singhalese, and, as late as the time of Buddhadâsa, who died 368 A.D., we read of a priest, profoundly versed in the doctrines, who translated the Sûtras, one of the three divi-

his own. It does not follow that Mahinda knew the whole of that enormous literature by heart, for, as he was supported by a number of priests, they may well have divided the different sections among them. The same applies to their disciples. But that to the Hindu mind there was nothing exceptional or incredible in such a statement, we see clearly from what is said by Mahânâma at a later period of his history. When he comes to the reign of Va*tt*agâmani,[1] 88–76 B.C., he states: "The profoundly wise priests had heretofore orally perpetuated the Pâli Pitakatraya and its Arthakathâ (commentaries). At this period these priests, foreseeing the perdition of the people (from the perversions of the true doctrines) assembled; and in order that the religion might endure for ages, recorded the same in books."[2]

Later than this date, even those who doubt the

sions of the Pitakatraya, into the Sihala language. (Mahâv. p. 247.) A note is added, stating that several portions of the other two divisions also of the Pitakatraya have been translated into the Singhalese language, and that these alone are consulted by the priests who are unacquainted with Pâli. On the other hand, it is stated that the Singhalese text of the Arthakathâ exists no longer (see Spence Hardy, 'Legends,' p. xxv., and p. 69). He states that the text and commentary of the Buddhist canon are believed to contain 29,368,000 letters. (*Ibid.* p. 66.)

[1] See Bigandet, l. c. p. 388.

[2] See also Spence Hardy, 'Legends,' p. 192. "After the Nirvâna of Buddha, for the space of 450 years, the text and commentaries, and all the works of the Tathâgata, were preserved and transmitted by wise priests, orally, mukha-pâ*tt*hena. But having seen the evils attendant upon this mode of transmission, five hundred and fifty arhats, of great authority, in the cave called Aloka (Alu) in the province of Malaya, in Lankâ, under the guardianship of the chief of that province, caused the (sacred) books to be written." (Extract from the 'Sâra-sangraha.')

powers of oral tradition have no right to place the final constitution of the Buddhistic canon and its commentaries in Ceylon, nor is there any reason to doubt that such as these texts existed in Ceylon in the first century B.C., they existed in the fifth century after Christ, when the commentaries were translated into Pâli by Buddhaghosha, and that afterwards they remained unchanged in the MSS. preserved by the learned priests of that island. It is easy to shrug one's shoulders, and shake one's head, and to disbelieve everything that can be disbelieved. Of course we cannot bring witnesses back from the grave, still less from the Nirvâna, into which, we trust, many of these ancient worthies have entered. But if we are asked to believe that all this was invented in order to give to the Buddhistic canon a fictitious air of antiquity, the achievement would, indeed, be one of consummate skill. When Asoka first met Nigrodha, who was to convert him to the new faith, we read (p. 25), that having refreshed the saint with food and beverage which had been prepared for himself, he interrogated the sâmanera on the doctrines propounded by Buddha. It is then said that the sâmanera explained to him the Apramâda-varga. Now this Apramâda-varga is the title of the second chapter of the Dhammapada. Its mention here need not prove that the Dhammapada existed previous to the Council of Asoka, 246 B.C., but only that Mahânâma believed that it existed before that time. But if we are to suppose that all this was put in on purpose, would it not be too deep-laid a scheme for the compiler of the Mahâvansa?[1]

And for what object could all this cunning have

[1] In the account given by Bishop Bigandet (p. 377) of the first

been employed? The Buddhists would have believed the most miraculous accounts that might be given of the origin and perpetuation of their sacred writings; why then tell the story so plainly, so baldly, so simply as a matter of fact? I have the greatest respect for really critical scepticism, but a scepticism without any arguments to support it is too cheap a virtue to deserve much consideration. Till we hear some reasons to the contrary, I believe we may safely say that we possess Buddhaghosha's translation of the Arthakathâ as it existed in the fifth century of our era; that the original was first reduced to writing in Ceylon in the first century before our era, having previously existed in the language of Magadha; and that our verses of the Dhammapada are the same which were recited to Asoka, and embodied in the canon of the third council, 246 B.C. This is enough for our purposes: the chronology previous to Asoka, or at least previous to his grandfather, Kandragupta, the ally of Seleucus, belongs to a different class of researches.

As, however, the antiquity and authenticity of the Buddhist literature have of late been called in question in a most summary manner, it may not seem superfluous to show, by one small fact at least, that the fables and parables of Buddhaghosha must have existed *in the very wording in which we possess them*, in the beginning at least of the sixth century of our era. It was at that time that Khosru Anushirván (531-579) ordered a collection of fables[1] to be translated from Sanskrit into the language of Persia, which

---

interview between Asoka and Nigrodha, the lines repeated by the priest to the king are likewise taken from the Apramádavarga.

[1] See Benfey, 'Pantschatantra,' vol. i. p. 6.

translation became in turn the source of the Arabic and the other numerous translations of that ancient collection of apologues. These Sanskrit fables, as collected in the Pañkatantra, have been proved by Prof. Benfey to have been borrowed from Buddhistic sources; and I believe we may go even a step further and maintain, that not only the general outlines of these fables, but in some cases the very words, were taken over from Pâli into Sanskrit.

We read in the Pañkatantra, ii. 10, the following verse:

> Gâlam âdâya gakkhanti sahasâ[1] pakshino 'py amî,
> Yâvak ka vivadishyante patishyanti na samsayah.

"Even these birds fly away quickly taking the net; and when they shall quarrel, they will fall, no doubt."

This verse recapitulates the story of the birds which are caught in a net, but escape the fowler by agreeing to fly up together at the same moment. The same story is told in the Hitopadesa, i. 36 (32):

> Samhatâs tu haranty ete mama gâlam vihamgamâh,
> Yadâ tu nipatishyanti vasam eshyanti me tadâ.

"Combined indeed do these birds take away my net; but when they fall down, they will then fall into my power."

The first thing that should be pointed out is, that of these two versions of the same idea, neither is borrowed from the other, neither that of the Hitopadesa from the Pañkatantra, nor *vice versâ*.[2] They presup-

---

[1] If we read 'samhatâh' instead of 'sahasâ,' we have to translate, "Holding together even these birds fly away, taking the net."

[2] A third version is found in the Mahâbhârata, Udyoga-parva,'

pose a common source from which they are derived, thus sharing together certain terms in common, and following an independent course in other respects. This common source is a Pâli verse which occurs in the Vattaka-*g*âtaka, and is quoted by Buddhaghosha in his commentary on the Sûtra-nipâta.[1]

    Sa*m*modamânâ ga*kkh*anti *g*âlam âdâya pakkhino,
    Yadâ te vivadissanti tadâ ehinti me vasa*m*.

"The birds fly away, taking the net while they are happy together; when they shall quarrel, then they will come into my power."

If we mark these three verses by the letters P., H., and V., we see that P. takes from V. the words '*g*âlam âdâya ga*kkh*anti pakshi*nah*' and 'vivadishyante,' while H. takes from V. the words 'vasam eshyanti me tadâ.' For the rest, H. and P. follow each their own way in transforming the Pâli verse, as best they can, into a Sanskrit verse, and H. with more success than P. The words 'apy amî' in P. are mere expletives, 'patishyanti' is a poor rendering, and 'na sa*m*saya*h*' again is added only in order to fill the verse. Without calling H.

v. 2461, where a similar story is told of two birds being caught and escaping from the fowler by agreeing to fly up together. Here we read:—

    Pâsam ekam ubhâv etam sahitau harato mama,
    Yatra vai vivadishyete tatra me vasam eshyata*h*.

"These two united carry off this one net of mine; when they shall quarrel, then they will fall into my power."

[1] This extract from the commentary was published by Dr. Fausböll in the 'Indische Studien,' v. p. 412, and the similarity was pointed out between the verse of Buddhaghosha and the corresponding verses in the 'Hitopadesa' and 'Pañ*k*atantra.' Further comparisons may be seen in Benfey, 'Pañ*k*atantra,' i. p. 305; ii. pp. 450, 540. See also 'Les Avadânas traduits par Stanislas Julien,' vol. i. p. 155.

and P. together a faithful copy of V., I think we may safely say that it would be impossible to explain both the points on which H. and P. differ and those on which they agree, without admitting that both had before them the Pâli verse in the very wording in which we find it in Buddhaghosha's commentary, and which, according to Buddhaghosha, was taken from one of the *G*âtakas, a portion of the Buddhistic canon. And this would prove, though one could hardly have thought that, after the labours of Burnouf and Lassen and Julien,[1] such proof was still needed, that the Buddhist canon and its commentary existed in the very wording in which we now possess them, previous at least to 500 after Christ.

On the Importance of the Dhammapada.

If we may consider the date of the Dhammapada firmly established, and treat its verses, if not as the utterances of Buddha, at least as what were believed by the members of the Council under Asoka, in 246 B.C., to have been the utterances of the founder of their religion, its importance for a critical study of the history of Buddhism must be very considerable, for we can hardly ever expect to get nearer to Buddha himself and to his personal teaching. I shall try to illustrate this by one or two examples.

I pointed out on a former occasion[2] that if we derive our ideas of Nirvâ*n*a from the Abhidharma, *i. e.*

---

[1] On Buddhist books carried to China and translated there previous to the beginning of our era, see M. M.'s 'Chips from a German Workshop,' 2nd ed., vol. i. p. 258, *seq.*

[2] On the meaning of Nirvâ*n*a, in 'Chips from a German Workshop,' 2nd ed., vol. i. p. 280.

the metaphysical portion of the Buddhistic canon, we cannot escape the conclusion that it meant perfect annihilation. Nothing has been brought forward to invalidate Burnouf's statements on this subject, much has since been added, particularly by M. Barthélemy St. Hilaire, to strengthen and support them, and the latest writer on Buddhism, Bishop Bigandet, the Vicar Apostolic of Ava and Pegu, in his 'Life and Legend of Gaudama, the Buddha of the Burmese,' arrives at exactly the same conclusion. No one could suspect the bishop of any prejudice against Buddhism, for he is most candid in his praises of whatever is praiseworthy in that ancient system of religion. Thus he says (p. 494), "The Christian system and the Buddhistic one, though differing from each other in their respective objects and ends as much as truth from error, have, it must be confessed, many striking features of an astonishing resemblance. There are many moral precepts equally commanded and enforced in common by both creeds. It will not be considered rash to assert that most of the moral truths prescribed by the gospel are to be met with in the Buddhistic scriptures." And again (p. 495), "In reading the particulars of the life of the last Budha Gautama, it is impossible not to feel reminded of many circumstances relating to our Saviour's life, such as it has been sketched by the Evangelists." Yet, in spite of all these excellences, Bishop Bigandet, too, sums up dead against Buddhism, as a religion culminating in atheism and nihilism. "It may be said in favour of Buddhism," he writes (p. viii.), "that no philosophico-religious system has ever upheld, to an equal degree, the notions of a saviour and deliverer, and the necessity of his mission for procuring the salvation, in a Buddhist sense, of man. The *rôle* of Buddha, from beginning to end, is that of a deliverer, who preaches a law designed to procure to man the deliverance from all the miseries he is labouring under. By an inexplicable and deplorable eccentricity, the pretended saviour, after having taught man the way to deliver himself from the tyranny of his passions, leads him, after all, into the bottomless gulf of 'total annihilation.'"

That Buddha was an atheist, at least in one sense of the word, cannot be denied, but whether he believed in a total annihilation of the soul as the highest goal of religion, is a different question. The gods whom he found worshipped by the multitude, were the gods of the Vedas and the Brâhmaṇas, such as Indra, Agni, and Yama, and in the divinity of such deities, Buddha certainly did not believe. He never argues against their existence; on the contrary, he treats the old gods as superhuman beings, and promises his followers who have not yet reached the highest knowledge, but have acquired merit by a virtuous life, that after death they shall be born again in the world of the gods, and enjoy divine bliss in company with these deities. Similarly he threatens the wicked that after death they shall meet with their punishment in the subterranean abodes and hells, where Asuras, Sarpas, Pretas, and other spirits dwell. The belief in these beings was so firmly rooted in the popular belief and language that even the founder of a new religion could not have dared to reason them away, and there was so little in the doctrine of Buddha that appealed to the senses or lent itself to artistic representation, whether in painting or sculpture, that nothing remained to Buddhist artists but to fall back for their own purposes on the old mythology, or at least on the popular superstition, the fairy and snake-tales of the people.[1]

The gods, in general, are frequently mentioned in the Dhammapada:—

V. 177. The uncharitable do not go to the world of the gods.

V. 224. Speak the truth, do not yield to anger; give, if thou art asked, from the little thou hast; by those steps thou wilt go near the gods.

V. 417. He who, after leaving all bondage to men, has risen above all bondage to the gods, him I call indeed a Brâhmana.

In vv. 44 and 45 three worlds are mentioned, the earth, the world of Yama (the lord of the departed), and the world of the gods; and in v. 126 we find hell (niraya), earth, heaven (svarga), and Nirvâna.

In v. 56 it is said that the odour of excellent

---

[1] This may be seen from the curious ornamentations of Buddhist temples, some of which were lately published by Mr. Fergusson. Those of the Sanchi tope are taken from drawings executed for the late East-India Company by Lieutenant (now Lieut.-Colonel) Maisey, and from photographs by Lieutenant Waterhouse; those of the Amravatî tope are photographed from the sculptured slabs sent home by Colonel Mackenzie, formerly exhibited in the Museum of the East-India Company, and from another valuable collection sent home by Sir Walter Elliot. Architectural evidence is supposed to fix the date of the Sanchi topes from about 250–100 B.C.; that of the gateways in the first century A.D.; while the date of the Amravatî buildings is referred to the fourth century A.D. No one would venture to doubt Mr. Fergusson's authority within the sphere of architectural chronology, but we want something more than mere affirmation when he says (p. 56), "that the earliest of the (Buddhist) scriptures we have were not reduced to writing in their present form before the fifth century after Christ."

people rises up to the gods; in vv. 94 and 181, that the gods envy him whose senses have been subdued; in v. 366, that they praise a Bhikshu who is contented, pure, and not slothful (cf. v. 230); in v. 224, that good people go near the gods; in v. 236, that a man who is free from guilt will enter into the heavenly world of the elect (the ariya); while in v. 187 we read of heavenly pleasures that fail to satisfy the disciples of Buddha.

Individual deities, too, are mentioned. Of Indra, who is called Maghavan, it is said in v. 30, that by perseverance he rose to the lordship of the gods.[1] In vv. 107 and 392 the worship of Agni, or fire, is spoken of as established among the Brahmans. Yama, as the lord of the departed, occurs in vv. 44, 237, and he seems to be the same as Ma*kk*urâga, the king of death, mentioned in vv. 45, 170. The men or messengers of Yama are spoken of in v. 235; death itself is represented as Antaka, vv. 48, 288, or as Ma*kk*u; in v. 46 the king of death (ma*kk*urâga) is mentioned together with Mâra; in v. 48 he seems to be identified with Mâra, the tempter (v. 48, note).

This Mâra, the tempter, the great antagonist of Buddha, as well as of his followers, is a very important personage in the Buddhist scriptures. He is in many places the representative of evil, the evil spirit, or, in Christian terminology, the devil, conquered by Buddha, but not destroyed by him. In the Dhammapada his character is less mythological than in other Buddhist writings. His retinue is, however, mentioned (v. 175), and his flower-pointed arrow (v. 46) reminds

---

[1] There is a curious story of Buddha dividing his honours with Sakka (Sakra) or Indra on p. 162 of the Parables.

one of the Hindu god of love. We read that Mâra will overcome the careless, but not the faithful (vv. 7, 8, 57); that men try to escape from his dominion (v. 34), and his snares (vv. 37, 276, 350); that he should be attacked with the weapon of knowledge (v. 40); that the wise, who have conquered him, are led out of this world (v. 175). In vv. 104 and 105 we find a curious climax, if it is intended as such, from a god to a Gândharva, thence to Mâra, and finally to Brahman, all of whom are represented as powerless against a man who has conquered himself. In v. 230, too, Brahman is mentioned, and, as it would seem, as a being superior to the gods.

But although these gods and demons were recognized in the religion of Buddha, and had palaces, gardens, and courts assigned to them, hardly inferior to those which they possessed under the old *régime*, they were deprived of all their sovereign rights. Although, according to the Buddhists, the worlds of the gods last for millions of years, they must perish at the end of every kalpa with the gods and with the spirits who, in the circle of births, have raised themselves to the world of the gods. Indeed, the reorganization of the spirit-world in the hands of Buddha goes further still. Already before Buddha, the Brahmans had left the low stand-point of mythological polytheism, and had risen to the conception of the Brahman, as the absolute divine, or super-divine being. To this Brahman also, who, in the Dhammapada, already appears as superior to the gods, a place is assigned in the Buddhist demonology. Over and above the world of the gods with its six paradises, the sixteen Brahma-worlds are erected,—worlds, not to be attained through virtue, and piety only, but through inner contemplation, through knowledge and enlightenment.

The dwellers in these Brahma-worlds are more than gods; they are spiritual beings, without body, without weight, without desires. Nay, even this is not sufficient, and as the Brahmans had imagined a higher Brahman, without form and without suffering (tato yad uttarataram tad arûpam anâmayam, *S*vet. Up. 3, 10), the Buddhists too, in their ideal dreams, imagined four other worlds towering high above the worlds of Brahman, which they call Arûpa, the worlds of the Formless. All these worlds are open to man, after he has divested himself of all that is human, and numberless beings are constantly ascending and descending in the circle of time, according to the works they have performed, and according to the truths they have discovered. But in all these worlds the law of change prevails; in none is there exemption from birth, age, and death. The world of the gods will perish like that of men; the world of Brahman will vanish like that of the gods; nay, even the world of the Formless will not last for ever; but the Buddha, the enlightened and truly free, stands higher, and will not be affected or disturbed by the collapse of the universe, *Si fractus illabatur orbis, impavidum ferient ruinæ.*

Here, however, we meet with a vein of irony, which one would hardly have expected in Buddha. Gods and devils he has located, to all mythological and philosophical acquisitions of the past he had done justice as far as possible. Even fabulous beings, such as Nâgas, Gandharvas, and Garu*d*as, had escaped the process of dissolution and sublimization which was to reach them later at the hands of comparative mythologists. There is only one idea, the idea of a personal Creator, in regard to which Buddha seems merciless. It is not only denied, but even its origin, like that of an ancient myth, is carefully explained by him with the minutest detail. The Rev. D. J. Gogerly, in his numerous articles published in the local journals of Ceylon, has collected and translated the most important passages from the Buddhist canon bearing on this subject. The Rev. Spence Hardy,[1] too, another distinguished missionary in Ceylon, has several times touched on this point—a point, no doubt, of great practical importance to Christian missionaries. They dwell on such passages as when Buddha said to Upâsaka, an ascetic, who inquired who was his teacher and whose doctrine he embraced, " I have no teacher; there is no one who resembles me. In the world of the gods I have no equal. I am the most noble in the world, being the irrefutable teacher, the sole, all-perfect Buddha." In the Pârâgika section of the Vinaya Pitaka, a conversation is recorded between Buddha and a Brahman, who accused him of not honouring aged Brahmans, of not rising in their presence, and of not inviting them to be seated. Buddha replied, "Brahman, I do not see any one in the heavenly worlds nor in that of Mâra, nor among the inhabitants of the Brahma-worlds, nor among gods or men, whom it would be proper for me to honour, or in whose presence I ought to rise up, or whom I ought to request to be seated. Should the Tathâgata (Buddha) thus act towards any one, that person's head would fall off."

Such doctrines, as Gogerly points out, are irrecon-

[1] 'Legends and Theories of the Buddhists,' 1866, p. 171.

cilable with the doctrine of a universal Creator, who must necessarily be superior to all the beings formed and supported by him. But the most decisive passage on the subject is one taken from the Brahma-*g*âla-sûtra,[1] the first in the Dîrgha nikâya, which is itself the first work of the Sûtra Pitaka. It was translated by Gogerly, whose translation I follow, as the text has not yet been published. In the Brahma-*g*âla-sûtra, Buddha discourses respecting the sixty-two different sects; among whom four held the doctrine both of the pre-existence of the soul, and of its eternal duration through countless transmigrations. Others believed that some souls have always existed, whilst others have had a commencement of existence. Among these one sect is described as believing in the existence of a Creator, and it is here that Buddha brings together his arguments against the correctness of this opinion. "There is a time," he says, "O Bhikshus, when, after a very long period, this world is destroyed. On the destruction of the world very many beings obtained existence in the Âbhâsvara[2] Brahmaloka, which is

---

[1] See J. D'Alwis's 'Pâli Grammar,' p. 88, note; Turnour, 'Mahâva*n*sa,' Appendix iii. p. lxxv.

[2] The Âbhâsvara gods, âbhâssarâ in Pâli, are mentioned already in the Dhammapada, v. 200, but none of the minute details, describing the six worlds of the gods, and the sixteen worlds of Brahman, and the four of Arûpa, are to be found there. The universe is represented (v. 126) as consisting of hell (niraya), earth, heaven (svarga), and Nirvâ*n*a. In v. 44 we find the world of Yama, the earth, and the world of the gods; in v. 104 we read of gods, Gandharvas, Mâra, and Brahman. The ordinary expression, too, which occurs in almost all languages, viz. in this world and in the next, is not avoided by the author of the Dhammapada. Thus we read in v. 168, 'ami*m* loke paramhi *k*a,' in this world and

THE IMPORTANCE OF THE DHAMMAPADA.   xxxiii

the sixth in the series, and in which the term of life never exceeds eight kalpas. They are there spiritual beings (having purified bodies, uncontaminated with evil passions, or with any corporeal defilement); they in the next (cf. vv. 242, 410); we find in v. 20 'idhâ vâ huram vâ,' here or there; in v. 15-18 we find 'idha' and 'pekkha,' here and yonder; pekka, i.e. pretya, meaning literally, 'after having died,' cf. vv. 131, 306. We also find 'idh'eva,' here, v. 402, and 'idha lokasmin,' here in the world (v. 247), or simply 'loke,' in this world (v. 89); and 'parattha' for 'paratra,' yonder, or in the other world.

A very characteristic expression, too, is that of v. 176, where as one of the greatest crimes is mentioned, the scoffing at another world.

The following is a sketch of the universe and its numerous worlds, according to the later systems of the Buddhists. There are differences, however, in different schools.

1. The infernal regions:
   (1) Nyaya, hell.
   (2) The abode of animals.
   (3) The abode of Pretas, ghosts.
   (4) The abode of Asuras, demons.
2. The earth:
   (1) Abode of men.
3. The worlds of the gods:
   (1) Katur-mahârâga (duration, 9,000,000 years).
   (2) Trayastrimsa (duration, 36,000,000 years).
   (3) Yâma (duration, 144,000,000 years).
   (4) Tushita (duration, 576,000,000 years).
   (5) Nirmâna rati (duration, 2,304,000,000 years).
   (6) Paranirmita-vasavartin (duration, 9,216,000,000 years).
4. The worlds of Brahman:
   (a) First Dhyâna:
   (1) Brahma-parishadya (duration, $\frac{1}{3}$ kalpa).
   (2) Brahma-purohita (duration, $\frac{1}{2}$ kalpa).
   (3) Mahâbrahman (duration, one kalpa).
   (b) Second Dhyâna:
   (4) Parîttâbha (duration, two kalpas).
   (5) Apramânâbha (duration, four kalpas).

c

have intellectual pleasures, are self-resplendent, traverse the atmosphere without impediment, and remain for a long time established in happiness. After a very long period this mundane system is reproduced, and the world named Brahma-vimâna (the third of the Brahmalokas) comes into existence, but uninhabited."

"At that time a being, in consequence either of the period of residence in Âbhâsvara being expired, or in consequence of some deficiency of merit preventing him from living there the full period, ceased to exist in Âbhâsvara, and was reproduced in the uninhabited

   (6) Âbhâsvara (duration, eight kalpas).
     (c) Third Dhyâna:
   (7) Parîttasubha (duration, sixteen kalpas).
   (8) Apramânasubha (duration, thirty-two kalpas).
   (9) Subhakritsna (duration, sixty-four kalpas).
     (d) Fourth Dhyâna:
        (Anabhraka, of Northern Buddhism.)
        (Punya-prasava, of Northern Buddhism.)
  (10) Vrihat-phala (500 kalpas).
  (11) Arangisattvas or Asangisattvas, of Nepal; Asanyasatya, of Ceylon (500 kalpas).
     (e) Fifth Dhyâna:
  (12) Avriha (1000 kalpas).
  (13) Atapa (2000 kalpas).
  (14) Sudrisa (4000 kalpas).
  (15) Sudarsana (8000 kalpas).
        (Sumukha, of Nepal.)
  (16) Akanishtha (16,000 kalpas).
5. The world of Arûpa:
   (1) Âkâsânantyâyatanam (20,000 kalpas).
   (2) Vignânânantyâyatanam (40,000 kalpas).
   (3) Akinkanyâyatanam (60,000 kalpas).
   (4) Naivasangnânâsangnâyatanam (80,000 kalpas).

Cf. Burnouf, 'Introduction,' p. 599 *seq.*; Lotus, p. 811 *seq.*; Hardy, 'Manual,' p. 25 *seq.*; Bigandet, p. 449.

Brahma-vimâna. He was there a spiritual being; his pleasures were intellectual; he was self-resplendent, traversed the atmosphere, and, for a long time, enjoyed uninterrupted felicity. After living there a very long period in solitude, a desire of having an associate is felt by him, and he says, 'Would that another being were dwelling in this place.' At that precise juncture another being ceasing to exist in Âbhâsvara, comes into existence in the Brahma-vimâna, in the vicinity of the first one. They are both of them spiritual beings, have intellectual pleasures, are self-resplendent, traverse the atmosphere, and are, for a long time, in the enjoyment of happiness. Then the following thoughts arose in him who was the first existent in that Brahma-loka: 'I am Brahma, the Great Brahma, the Supreme, the Invincible, the Omniscient, the Governor of all things, the Lord of all. I am the Maker, the Creator of all things; I am the Chief, the disposer and controller of all, the Universal Father. This being was made by me. How does this appear? Formerly I thought, Would that another being were in this place, and upon my volition this being came here. Those beings also, who afterwards obtained an existence there, thought, this illustrious Brahma is the Great Brahma, the Supreme, the Invincible, the Omniscient, the Ruler, the Lord, the Creator of all. He is the Chief, the Disposer of all things, the Controller of all, the Universal Father. We were created by him, for we see that he was first here, and that we have since then obtained existence. Furthermore, he who first obtained existence there lives during a very long period, exceeds in beauty, and is of immense power, but those who followed him are short-lived, of inferior beauty and of little power.'"

"It then happens, that one of those beings ceasing to exist there, is born in this world, and afterwards retires from society and becomes a recluse. He subjects his passions, is persevering in the practice of virtue, and by profound meditation he recollects his immediately previous state of existence, but none prior to that; he therefore says, that illustrious Brahma is the Great Brahma, the Supreme, the Invincible, the Omniscient, the Ruler, the Lord, the Maker, the Creator of all. He is the Chief, the Disposer of all things, the Controller of all, the Universal Father. That Brahma by whom we were created is ever enduring, immutable, eternal, unchangeable, continuing for ever the same. But we, who have been created by this illustrious Brahma, are mutable, short-lived, and mortal."

There is, it seems to me, an unmistakable note of irony in this argumentation against the belief in a personal Creator; and to any one acquainted with the language of the Upanishads, the pointed allusions to expressions occurring in those philosophical and religious treatises of the Brahmans are not to be mistaken. If then it is true, as Gogerly remarks, that many who call themselves Buddhists acknowledge the existence of a Creator, the question naturally arises, whether the point-blank atheism of the Brahma-gâla was the doctrine of the founder of Buddhism or not?

This is, in fact, but part of the problem so often started, whether it is possible to distinguish between Buddhism and the personal teaching of Buddha. We possess the Buddhist canon, and whatever is found in that canon, we have a right to consider as the orthodox Buddhist doctrine. But as there has been no lack of efforts in Christian theology to distinguish between the doctrine of the founder of our religion and that of the writers of the Gospels, to go beyond the canon of the New Testament, and to make the λόγια of the Master the only solid rule of our faith, so the same want was felt at a very early period among the followers of Buddha. King Asoka, the Indian Constantine, had to remind the assembled priests at the great council which had to settle the Buddhist canon, that '*what had been said by Buddha, that alone was well said.*'[1] Works attributed to Buddha, but declared to be apocryphal, or even heterodox, existed already at that time (246 B.C.). Thus we are by no means without authority for distinguishing between Buddhism and the teaching of Buddha; the only question is, whether in our time such a separation is still practicable?

My belief is that, in general, all honest inquirers must oppose a No to this question, and confess that it is useless to try to cast a glance beyond the boundaries of the Buddhist canon. What we find in the canonical books in the so-called 'Three Baskets,' is orthodox Buddhism and the doctrine of Buddha, similarly as we must accept in general whatever we find in the four gospels as orthodox Christianity and the doctrine of Christ.

Still, with regard to certain doctrines and facts, the question, I think, ought to be asked again and again whether it may not be possible to advance a step fur-

---

[1] M. M.'s 'Chips from a German Workshop,' 2nd ed., vol. i. p. xxiv.

ther, even with the conviction that we cannot arrive at results of apodictic certainty? If it happens that on certain points we find in different parts of the canon, not only doctrines differing from each other, but plainly contradictory to each other, it follows, surely, that one only of these can have belonged to Buddha personally. In such a case, therefore, I believe we have a right to choose, and I believe we shall be justified in accepting that view as the original one, the one peculiar to Buddha himself, which harmonizes *least* with the later system of orthodox Buddhism.

As regards the denial of a Creator, or atheism in the ordinary acceptation of the word, I do not think that any one passage from the books of the canon known to us, can be quoted which contravenes it, or which in any way presupposes the belief in a personal God or Creator. All that might be urged are the words said to have been spoken by Buddha at the time when he became the Enlightened, the Buddha. They are as follows:—" Without ceasing shall I run through a course of many births, looking for the maker of this tabernacle,—and painful is birth again and again. But now, maker of the tabernacle, thou hast been seen; thou shalt not make up this tabernacle again. All thy rafters are broken, thy ridge-pole is sundered; the mind, being sundered, has attained to the extinction of all desires."

Here in the maker of the tabernacle, *i.e.* the body, one might be tempted to see a creator. But he who is acquainted with the general run of thought in Buddhism, soon finds that this architect of the house is only a poetical expression, and that whatever meaning may underlie it, it evidently signifies a force subordinate to the Buddha, the Enlightened.

But whilst we have no ground for exonerating the Buddha personally from the accusation of atheism, the matter stands very differently as regards the charge of nihilism. The Buddhist nihilism has always been much more incomprehensible than mere atheism. A kind of religion is still conceivable, when there is something firm somewhere, when a something, eternal and self-dependent, is recognized, if not *without* and *above* man, at least *within* him. But if, as Buddhism teaches, the soul after having passed through all the phases of existence, all the worlds of the gods and of the higher spirits, attains finally Nirvâna as its highest aim and last reward, *i.e.* becomes utterly extinct, then religion is not any more what it is meant to be—a bridge from the finite to the infinite, but a trap-bridge hurling man into the abyss at the very moment when he thought he had arrived at the stronghold of the Eternal. According to the metaphysical doctrine of Buddhism, the soul cannot dissolve itself in a higher being, or be absorbed in the absolute substance, as was taught by the Brahmans, and other mystics of ancient and modern times; for Buddhism knew not the Divine, the Eternal, the Absolute; and the soul even as the I, or as the mere Self, the Âtman, as called by the Brahmans, was represented in the orthodox metaphysics of Buddhism as transient, as futile, as a mere phantom.

No person who reads with attention the metaphysical speculations on the Nirvâna contained in the third part of the Buddhist canon, can arrive at any other conviction than that expressed by Burnouf, viz.

that Nirvâṇa, the highest aim, the *summum bonum* of Buddhism, is the absolute nothing.

Burnouf adds, however, that this doctrine appears in its crude form in the third part only of the canon, the so-called Abhidharma, but not in the first and second parts, in the Sûtras, the sermons, and the Vinaya, the ethics, which together bear the name of Dharma, or Law. He next points out that, according to some ancient authorities, this entire part of the canon was designated as not "pronounced by Buddha."[1] These are, at once, two important limitations. I add a third, and maintain that sayings of Buddha occur in the Dhammapada, which are in open contradiction to this metaphysical nihilism.

Now, first, as regards the soul, or the self, the existence of which, according to the orthodox metaphysics, is purely phenomenal,[2] a sentence attributed to the Buddha (Dhammapada, v. 160) says, "Self is the Lord of Self, who else could be the Lord?" And again (v. 323), "A man who controls himself enters the untrodden land through his own self-controlled self." But this untrodden land is the Nirvâṇa.

Nirvâṇa certainly means extinction, whatever its later arbitrary interpretations[3] may have been, and

---

[1] Max Müller's 'Chips,' 2nd ed., vol. i. p. 285, note.

[2] See "Wassiljew, 'Der Buddhismus,' p. 296, (269); and Bigandet's 'Life of Gaudama,' p. 479. "The things that I see and know, are not myself, nor from myself, nor to myself. What seems to be myself is in reality neither myself nor belongs to myself."

[3] See Bastian, 'Die Völker des östlichen Asien,' vol. iii. p. 354. The learned abbot who explained the meaning of Nirvâṇa to Dr. Bastian was well versed in the old grammatical terminology. He distinguishes the causal meaning, called hetumat, of the verb 'vâ,' to cause to blow out, from the intransitive meaning,

seems therefore to imply, even etymologically, a real blowing out or passing away. But Nirvâṇa occurs also in the Brahmanic writings as synonymous with Moksha,[1] Nirvṛitti,[1] and other words, all designating the highest stage of spiritual liberty and bliss, but not annihilation. Nirvâṇa may mean the extinction of many things—of selfishness, desire, and sin, without going so far as the extinction of subjective consciousness. Further, if we consider that Buddha himself, after he had already seen Nirvâṇa, still remains on earth until his body falls a prey to death; that in the legends Buddha appears to his disciples even after his death, it seems to me that all these circumstances are hardly reconcilable with the orthodox metaphysical doctrine of Nirvâṇa.

But I go even further and maintain that, if we look in the Dhammapada at every passage where Nirvâṇa is mentioned, there is not one which would require that its meaning should be annihilation, while most, if not all, would become perfectly unintelligible if we assigned to the word Nirvâṇa the meaning which it has in the Abhidharma or the metaphysical portions of the canon.

What does it mean, when Buddha, v. 21, calls reflection the path to immortality, thoughtlessness the path of death? Buddhaghosha does not hesitate to explain immortality by Nirvâṇa, and that the same

to go out. He also distinguishes between the verb as expressing the state of vanishing, 'bhâvasâdhana,' (cf. Pâṇ. ii. 3, 37; iii. 4, 69), or the place of vanishing, 'adhikaraṇasâdhana' (Pâṇ. i. 4, 45). How place and act become one in the conception of Buddhists, is better seen by the four dhyânas, originally meditations, than the places reached by these meditations.

[1] See Dhammapada, v. 92, 89.

idea was connected with it in the mind of Buddha is clearly proved by a passage immediately following, v. 23: "The wise people, meditative, steady, always possessed of strong powers, attain to Nirvâna, the highest happiness." In the last verse, too, of the same chapter we read, "A Bhikshu who delights in reflection, who looks with fear on thoughtlessnes, will not go to destruction,—he is near to Nirvâna." If the goal at which the followers of Buddha have to aim had been in the mind of Buddha perfect annihilation, 'amata,' *i.e.* immortality, would have been the very last word he could have chosen as its name.

In several passages of the Dhammapada, Nirvâna occurs in the purely ethical sense of rest, quietness, absence of passion; *e.g.*, v. 134, "If, like a trumpet trampled underfoot, thou utter not, then thou hast reached Nirvâna; anger is not known in thee." In v. 184 long-suffering (titikshâ) is called the highest Nirvâna. While in v. 202 we read that there is no happiness like rest (sânti) or quietness, we read in the next verse that the highest happiness is Nirvâna. In v. 285, too, 'sânti' seems to be synonymous with Nirvâna, for the way that leads to 'sânti,' or peace, leads also to Nirvâna, as shown by Buddha. In v. 369 it is said, "When thou hast cut off passion and hatred, thou wilt go to Nirvâna;" and in v. 225 the same thought is expressed, only that instead of Nirvâna we have the expression of unchangeable place:—"The sages who injure nobody, and who always control their body, they will go to the unchangeable place, where, if they have gone, they will suffer no more."

In other passages Nirvâna is described as the result of right knowledge. Thus we read, v. 203, "Hunger is the worst of diseases, the body the greatest of pains; if one knows this truly, that is Nirvâna, the highest happiness."

A similar thought seems contained in v. 374: "As soon as a man has perceived the origin and destruction of the elements of the body (khandha), he finds happiness and joy, which belong to those who know the immortal (Nirvâna); or which is the immortality of those who know it, viz. the transitory character of the body." In v. 372 it is said that he who has knowledge and meditation is near unto Nirvâna.

Nirvâna is certainly more than heaven or heavenly joy. "Some people are born again" (on earth), says Buddha, v. 126, "evildoers go to hell; righteous people go to heaven; those who are free from all worldly desires enter Nirvâna." The idea that those who had reached the haven of the gods were still liable to birth and death, and that there is a higher state in which the power of birth and death is broken, existed clearly at the time when the verses of the Dhammapada were composed. Thus we read, v. 238, "When thy impurities are blown away, and thou art free from guilt, thou wilt not enter again into birth and decay." And in the last verse the highest state that a Brâhmana can reach is called "the end of births," *gâti-kshaya*.

There are many passages in the Dhammapada where we expect Nirvâna, but where, instead of it, other words are used. Here, no doubt, it might be said that something different from Nirvâna is intended, and that we have no right to use such words as throwing light on the original meaning of Nirvâna. But, on the other hand, these words, and the passages where they occur, must mean something definite; they cannot mean heaven or the world of the gods, for reasons stated above; and if they do not mean Nirvâ*n*a, they would have no meaning at all. There may be some doubt whether 'pâra,' the shore, and particularly the other shore, stands always for Nirvâ*n*a, and whether those who are said to have reached the other shore, are to be supposed to have entered Nirvâ*n*a. It may possibly not have that meaning in verses 384 and 385, but it can hardly have another in places such as vv. 85, 86, 347, 348, 355, 414. There is less doubt, however, that other words are used distinctly as synonyms of Nirvâ*n*a. Such words are, the quiet place (sânta*m* padam, v. 368, 381); the changeless place (a*k*yuta*m* sthânam, v. 225, compared with v. 226); the immortal place (amatam padam, v. 114); also simply that which is immortal, v. 374. In v. 411 the expression occurs that the wise dives into the immortal.

Though, according to Buddha, everything that has been made, everything that was put together, resolves itself again into its component parts and passes away, (v. 277, sarve sa*m*skârâ anityâ*h*), he speaks nevertheless of that which is not made, *i.e.* the uncreated and eternal, and uses it, as it would seem, synonymously with Nirvâ*n*a (v. 97). Nay, he says (v. 383), "When you have understood the destruction of all that was made, you will understand that which was not made." This surely shows that even for Buddha a something existed which is not made, and which, therefore, is imperishable and eternal.

On considering such sayings, to which many more might be added, one recognizes in them a conception

of Nirvâna, altogether irreconcilable with the nihilism
of the third part of the Buddhist canon. It is not a
question of more or less, but of *aut—aut*. Nirvâna cannot,
in the mind of one and the same person, mean
black and white, nothing and something. If these sayings,
as recorded in the Dhammapada, have maintained
themselves, in spite of their being in open contradiction
to orthodox metaphysics, the only explanation, in my
opinion is, that they were too firmly fixed in the tradition
which went back to Buddha and his disciples.
What Bishop Bigandet and others represent as the
popular view of Nirvâna, in contradistinction to that
of the Buddhist divines, was, in my opinion, the conception
of Buddha and his disciples. It represented
the entrance of the soul into rest, a subduing of all
wishes and desires, indifference to joy and pain, to
good and evil, an absorption of the soul in itself, and
a freedom from the circle of existences from birth to
death, and from death to a new birth. This is still
the meaning which educated people attach to it, whilst
to the minds of the larger masses[1] Nirvâna suggests
rather the idea of a Mohammedan paradise or of blissful
Elysian fields.

Only in the hands of the philosophers, to whom
Buddhism owes its metaphysics, the Nirvâna, through
constant negations carried to an indefinite degree,
through the excluding and abstracting of all that is
not Nirvâna, at last became an empty Nothing, a philosophical
myth. There is no lack of such philosophical
myths either in the east or in the west. What has
been fabled by philosophers of a Nothing, and of the

[1] Bigandet, 'The Life of Gaudama,' p. 320, note; Bastian, 'Die
Völker des östlichen Asien,' vol. iii. p. 353.

terrors of a Nothing, is as much a myth as the myth of Eos and Tithonus. There is no more a Nothing than there is an Eos or a Chaos. All these are sickly, dying, or dead words, which, like shadows and ghosts, continue to haunt language, and succeed in deceiving for a while even the healthiest intellect.

Even modern philosophy is not afraid to say that there is a Nothing. We find passages in the German mystics, such as Eckhart and Tauler, where the abyss of the Nothing is spoken of quite in a Buddhist style. If Buddha had said, like St. Paul, "that what no eye hath seen, nor ear heard, neither has it entered into the heart of man," was prepared in the Nirvâna for those who had advanced to the highest degree of spiritual perfection, such expressions would have been quite sufficient to serve as a proof to the philosophers by profession that this Nirvâna, which could not become an object of perception by the senses, nor of conception by the categories of the understanding,—the anâkkhâta, the ineffable, as Buddha calls it (v. 218)—could be nothing more nor less than the Nothing. Could we dare with Hegel to distinguish between a Nothing (*Nichts*) and a Not (*Nicht*), we might say that the Nirvâna had, through a false dialectical process, been driven from a relative Nothing to an absolute Not. This was the work of the theologians and of the orthodox philosophers. But a religion has never been founded by such teaching, and a man like Buddha, who knew mankind, must have known that he could not, with such weapons, overturn the tyranny of the Brahmans. Either we must bring ourselves to believe that Buddha taught his disciples two diametrically opposed doctrines on Nirvâna, say an exoteric and esoteric one, or we must allow *that* view of Nirvâṇa to have been the original view of the founder of this marvellous religion, which we find recorded in the verses of the Dhammapada, and which corresponds best with the simple, clear, and practical character of Buddha.

On the Title of the Dhammapada.

I have still to say a few words on the title of the Dhammapada. This title was first rendered by Gogerly, 'The Footsteps of Religion;' by Spence Hardy, 'The Paths of Religion,' and this, I believe, is in the main a correct rendering. 'Dharma,' or, in Pâli, 'dhamma,' has many meanings. Under one aspect, it means religion, in so far, namely, as religion is the law that is to be accepted and observed. Under another aspect 'dharma' is virtue, in so far, namely, as virtue is the realization of that law. Thus 'dharma' can be rendered by law, by religion, more particularly Buddha's religion, or by virtue.

'Pada,' again, may be rendered by footsteps, but its more natural rendering is path. Thus we read in verse 21, 'appamâdo amatapadam,' reflection is the path of immortality, *i.e.* the path that leads to immortality. Again, 'pamâdo maććuno padam,' thoughtless is the path of death, *i.e.* the path that leads to death. The commentator explains 'padam' here by 'amatasya adhigamupâya,' the means of obtaining immortality, *i.e.* Nirvâṇa, or simply by 'upâyo' and 'magga,' the way.[1] In the same manner 'dhammapadam' would

[1] If we compare verses 92 and 93, and again 254 and 255, we see that 'padam' is used synonymously with 'gati,' going.

mean 'the path of virtue,' *i. e.* the path that leads to virtue, a very appropriate title for a collection of moral precepts. In this sense 'dhammapadam' is used in verses 44 and 45, as I have explained in my notes to these verses.

Gogerly, though not to be trusted in all his translations, may generally be taken as a faithful representative of the tradition of the Buddhists in Ceylon, and we may therefore take it for granted that the priests of that island take Dhammapada to mean, as Gogerly translates it, the vestiges of religion, or, from a different point of view, the path of virtue.

It is well known, however, that the learned editor of the Dhammapada, Dr. Fausböll, proposed a different rendering. On the strength of verses 44 and 102, he translated 'dhammapada' by 'collection of verses on religion.' But though 'pada' may mean a verse, I doubt whether 'pada' in the singular could ever mean a collection of verses. In verse 44 'padam' cannot mean a collection of verses, for reasons I have explained in my notes; and in verse 102 we have, it seems to me, the best proof that, in Buddhist phraseology, 'dhammapada' is not to be taken in a collective sense, but means a law-verse, a wise saw. For there we read, "Though a man recite a hundred Gâthâs made up of senseless words, one 'dhammapada,' *i. e.* one single word or line of the law, is better, which if a man hears, he becomes quiet." If the Buddhist wish to speak of many law-verses, they use the plural, dhammapadâni.[1] Thus Buddhaghosha says,[2] "Be it known that the Gâthâ

---

[1] 'Pada' by itself forms the plural 'padâ,' as in v. 243, *k*aturo padâ.

[2] D'Alwis, 'Pâli Grammar,' p. 61.

consists of the Dhammapadâni, Theragâthâ, Therigâthâ, and those unmixed (detached) Gâthâ not comprehended in any of the above-named Suttantâ."

Unless, therefore, it can be proved that in Pâli, 'padam' in the singular can be used in a collective sense, so as to mean a collection of words or sayings, and this has never been done, it seems to me that we must retain the translation of Gogerly, 'Footsteps of Religion,' though we may with advantage make it more intelligible in English by rendering it "The Path of Virtue." The idea of representing life, and particularly the life of the faithful, as a path of duty or virtue leading to deliverance (in Sanskrit, dharmapatha) is very familiar to the Buddhists. The four great truths[1] of their religion consist in the recognition, 1, that there is suffering; 2, that there is a cause of that suffering; 3, that such cause can be removed; 4, that there is a way of deliverance, *viz.* the doctrine of Buddha. This way, this mârga, is then fully described as consisting of eight stations,[2] and leading in the end to Nirvâṇa.[3] The faithful advances on that road, 'padât padam,' step by step, and it is therefore called paṭipadâ, lit. the step by step.[4]

---

[1] Spence Hardy, 'Manual,' p. 496.   [2] *Ibid.*

[3] Burnouf, 'Lotus,' p. 520. " Ajoutons, pour terminer ce que nous trouvons à dire sur le mot *magga*, quelque commentaire qu'on en donne d'ailleurs, que suivant une définition rapportée par Turnour, le *magga* renferme une sous-division que l'on nomme *patipadá*, en sanscrit *pratipad*. Le *magga*, dit Turnour, est la voie qui conduit au Nibbâna, le paṭipadâ, littéralement 'la marche pas à pas, ou le degré,' est la vie de rectitude qu'on doit suivre, quand on marche dans la voie de *magga*."

[4] See Spence Hardy, 'Manual,' p. 496. Should not 'ḱaturvidha-

The only way in which Dhammapadam could possibly be defended in the sense of 'Collection of verses of the Law,' would be if we took it for an aggregate compound. But such aggregate compounds, in Sanskrit at least, are possibly only with numerals, as, for instance, Tri-bhuvanam, the three worlds, *k*aturyugam, the four ages.[1] It might, therefore, be possible to form in Pâli also such compounds as dasapadam, a collection of ten padas, a work consisting of ten padas, a 'decamerone'; but it would in no way follow that we could attempt such a compound as Dhammapadam, in the sense of collection of law-verses.

I find that Dr. Köppen has been too cautious to adopt Dr. Fausböll's rendering, while Professor Weber, of Berlin, not only adopts that rendering without any misgivings, but in his usual way blames me for my backwardness.[2]

In conclusion, I have to say a few words on the spelling of technical terms which occur in the translation of the Dhammapada and in my introduction. It is very difficult to come to a decision on this subject; and I have to confess that I have not been consistent

---

dharma-pada,' mentioned on p. 497, be translated by 'the fourfold path of the Law'? It can hardly be the fourfold word of the Law.

[1] See M. M.'s 'Sanskrit Grammar,' § 519.

[2] "Dies ist eben auch der Sinn, der dem Titel unseres Werkes zu geben ist (nicht, 'Footsteps of the Law,' wie *neuerdings noch* M. Müller will, s. dessen 'Chips from a German Workshop,' i. 200.) The fact is that on page 200 of my 'Chips' there is no mention of the Dhammapada at all, while on page 220 I had simply quoted from Spence Hardy, and given the translation of Dhammapada, 'Footsteps of the Law' between inverted commas.

throughout in following the rule which, I think, ought to be followed. Most of the technical terms employed by Buddhist writers come from Sanskrit; and in the eyes of the philologist the various forms which they have assumed in Pâli, in Burmese, in Tibetan, in Chinese, in Mongolian, are only so many corruptions of the same original form. Everything, therefore, would seem to be in favour of retaining the Sanskrit forms throughout, and of writing, for instance, Nirvâna instead of the Pâli Nibbâna, the Burmese Niban or Nepbhân, the Siamese Niruphan, the Chinese Nipan. The only hope, in fact, that writers on Buddhism will ever arrive at a uniform and generally intelligible phraseology seems to lie in their agreeing to use throughout the Sanskrit terms in their original form, instead of the various local disguises and disfigurements which they present in Ceylon, Burmah, Siam, Tibet, China, and Mongolia. But against this view another consideration is sure to be urged, viz. that many Buddhist words have assumed such a strongly marked local or national character in the different countries and in the different languages in which the religion of Buddha has found a new home, that to translate them back into Sanskrit would seem as affected, nay prove in certain cases as misleading, as if, in speaking of *priests* and *kings*, we were to speak of *presbyters* and *cynings*. Between the two alternatives of using the original Sanskrit forms or adopting their various local varieties, it is sometimes difficult to choose, and the rule by which I have been mainly guided has been to use the Sanskrit forms as much as possible; in fact, everywhere except where it seemed affected to do so. I have therefore written Buddhaghosha instead of the Pâli Buddhaghosa, because the name of that famous theologian, "the Voice of Buddha," seemed to lose its significance if turned into Buddhaghosa. But I am well aware what may be said on the other side. The name of Buddhaghosha, "Voice of Buddha," was given him after he had been converted from Brahmanism to Buddhism, and it was given to him by people to whom the Pâli word *ghosa* conveyed the same meaning as *ghosha* does to us. On the other hand, I have retained the Pâli *Dhammapada* instead of Dharmapada, simply because, as the title of a Pâli book, it has become so familiar that to speak of it as Dharmapada seemed like speaking of another work. We are accustomed to speak of Samanas instead of Sramanas, for even in the days of Alexander's conquest, the Sanskrit word Sramana had assumed the prakritized or vulgar form which we find in Pâli, and which alone could have been rendered by the later Greek writers (first by Alexander Polyhistor, 80–60, B.C.) by σαμαναῖοι.[1] As a Buddhist term, the Pâli form Samana has so entirely supplanted that of Sramana that, even in the Dhammapada (v. 388) we find an etymology of Samana as derived from 'sam,' to be quiet, and not from 'sram,' to toil. But though one might bring oneself to speak of Samanas, who would like to introduce Bâhmana instead of Brâhmana? And yet this word, too, had so entirely been replaced by bâhmana, that in the Dhammapada, it is derived from a root

---

[1] See Lassen, 'Indische Alterthumskunde,' vol. ii. p. 700, note. That Lassen is right in taking the Σαρμᾶναι, mentioned by Megasthenes, for Brahmanic, not for Buddhist ascetics, might be proved also by their dress. Dresses made of the bark of trees are not Buddhistic. On page lxxix, note, read Alexander Polyhistor instead of Bardesanes.

'vah,' to remove, to separate, to cleanse.¹ My own conviction is that it would be best if writers on Buddhist literature and religion were to adopt Sanskrit throughout as the *lingua franca*. For an accurate understanding of the original meaning of most of the technical terms of Buddhism a knowledge of their Sanskrit form is indispensable; and nothing is lost, while much would be gained, if, even in the treating of Southern Buddhism, we were to speak of the town of Srâvasti instead of Sâvatthi in Pâli, Sevet in Singhalese; of Tripitaka, 'the three baskets,' instead of Pitakattaya in Pâli, Tunpitaka in Singhalese; of Arthakathâ, 'commentary,' instead of Atthakathâ in Pâli, Atuwâva in Singhalese; and therefore also of Dharmapada, 'the path of virtue,' instead of Dhammapada.

MAX MÜLLER.

Düsternbrook, near Kiel, in the summer of 1869.

---

¹ See 'Dhammapada,' v. 388; Bastian, 'Völker des östlichen Asien,' vol. iii. p. 412: "Ein buddhistischer Mönch erklärte mir, dass die Brahmanen ihren Namen führten, als Leute, die ihre Sünden abgespült hätten." See also 'Lalita-vistara,' p. 551, line 1; p. 553, line 7.

CHAPTER I.

THE TWIN-VERSES.

1.

All that we are is the result of what we have thought: it is founded on our thoughts, it is made up of our thoughts. If a man speaks or acts with an evil thought, pain follows him, as the wheel follows the foot of him who draws the carriage.

(1.) 'Dharma,' though clear in its meaning, is difficult to translate. It has different meanings in different systems of philosophy, and its peculiar application in the phraseology of Buddhism has been fully elucidated by Burnouf, 'Introduction à l'Histoire du Buddhisme,' p. 41 *seq*. He writes: "Je traduis ordinairement ce terme par *condition*, d'autres fois par *lois*, mais aucune de ces traductions n'est parfaitement complète; il faut entendre par 'dharma' ce qui fait qu'une chose est ce qu'elle est, ce qui constitue sa nature propre, comme l'a bien montré Lassen, à l'occasion de la célèbre formule, 'Ye dharmâ hetuprabhavâ.' Etymologically the Latin *for-ma* expresses the same general idea which was expressed by 'dhar-ma.' See also Burnouf, 'Lotus de la bonne Loi,' p. 524. Fausböll translates: "Naturæ a mente principium ducunt," which shows that he understood 'dharma' in the Buddhist sense. Gogerly and D'Alwis translate: Mind precedes action, which, if not wrong, is at all events wrongly expressed; while Professor Weber's rendering, "Die Pflichten aus dem Herz folgern," is quite inadmissible.

2.

All that we are is the result of what we have thought: it is founded on our thoughts, it is made up of our thoughts. If a man speaks or acts with a pure thought, happiness follows him, like a shadow that never leaves him.

3.

"He abused me, he beat me, he defeated me, he robbed me,"—hatred in those who harbour such thoughts will never cease.

4.

"He abused me, he beat me, he defeated me, he robbed me,"—hatred in those who do not harbour thoughts will cease.

5.

For hatred does not cease by hatred at any time: hatred ceases by love, this is an old rule.

6.

And some do not know that we must all come to an end here;—but others know it, and hence their quarrels cease.

(3.) On 'akko*kkh*i,' see Ka*kkh*âyana, vi. 4, 17. D'Alwis, 'Pâli Grammar,' p. 38, note. "When akko*kkh*i means 'abused,' it is derived from 'kuusa,' not from 'kudha.'"

(6.) It is necessary to render this verse freely, because literally translated it would be unintelligible. 'Pare' is explained by fools, but it has that meaning by implication only. There is an opposition between 'pare *k*a' and 'ye *k*a,' which I have rendered by 'some' and 'others.' Yamâmase, a 1 pers. plur. imp. âtm., but really a Le*t* in Pâli. (See Fausböll, 'Five *G*âtakas,' p. 38.)

7.

He who lives looking for pleasures only, his senses uncontrolled, immoderate in his enjoyments, idle, and weak, Mâra (the tempter) will certainly overcome him, as the wind throws down a weak tree.

(7.) 'Mâra' must be taken in the Buddhist sense of tempter, or evil spirit. See Burnouf, 'Introduction,' p. 76: "Mâra est le démon de l'amour, du péché et de la mort; c'est le tentateur et l'ennemi de Buddha." As to the definite meaning of 'vîrya,' see Burnouf, 'Lotus,' p. 548.

'Kusîta,' idle, is evidently the Pâli representative of the Sanskrit 'kusîda.' In Sanskrit 'kusîda,' slothful, is supposed to be derived from 'sad,' to sit, and even in its other sense, viz. a loan, it may have been intended originally for a pawn, or something that lies inert. In the Buddhistical Sanskrit, 'kusida' is the exact counterpart of the Pâli 'kusîta;' see Burnouf, 'Lotus,' p. 548. But supposing 'kusîda' to be derived from 'sad,' the d would be organic, and its phonetic change to t in Pâli, against all rules. I do not know of any instance where an original Sanskrit d, between two vowels, is changed to t in Pâli. The Pâli 'dandham' (Dhammap. v. 116) has been identified with 'tandram,' lazy; but here the etymology is doubtful, and 'dandra' may really be a more correct dialectic variety, *i.e.* an intensive form of a root 'dram' (dru) or 'drâ.' Anyhow the change here affects an initial, not a medial d, and it is supposed to be a change of Sanskrit t to Pâli d, not *vice versâ*. Professor Weber supposed 'pithîyati' in v. 173, to stand for Sk. 'pidhîyate,' which is impossible. (See Ka*kk*ayana's 'Grammar,' iv. 21.) Dr. Fausböll had identified it rightly with Sk. 'apistîryati.' Comparisons such as Pâli 'alâpu' (v. 149) with Sk. 'alâbu,' and Pâli 'pabba*g*a' (v. 345) with Sk. 'bâlba*g*a,' prove nothing whatever as to a possible change of Sk. d to Pâli t, for they refer to words the organic form of which is doubtful, and to labials instead of dentals.

A much better instance was pointed out to me by Mr. R. C. Childers, viz. the Pâli 'pâtu,' Sk. 'prâdus,' clearly, openly. Here, however, the question arises, whether 'pâtu' may not be due to dialectic variety, instead of phonetic decay. If 'pâtu' is connected

8.

He who lives without looking for pleasures, his senses well controlled, in his enjoyments moderate, faithful and strong, Mâra will certainly not overcome

---

with 'prâtar,' before, early, 'prâdus' would be a peculiar Sanskrit corruption, due to a mistaken recollection of 'dus,' while the Pâli 'pâtu' would have preserved the original t.

Anyhow, we require far stronger evidence before we can admit a medial t in Pâli as a phonetic corruption of a medial d in Sanskrit. We might as well treat the O. H. G. t as a phonetic corruption of Gothic d. The only way to account for the Pâli form 'kusîta' instead of 'kusîda,' is by admitting the influence of popular etymology. Pâli has in many cases lost its etymological consciousness. It derives 'samana' from a root 'sam,' 'b(r)âhmana' from 'bâh;' see v. 388. Now as 'sîta' in Pâli means cold, apathetic, but in a good sense, 'kusîta' may have been formed in Pâli to express apathetic in a bad sense.

Further, we must bear in mind that the Sanskrit etymology of 'kusîda' from 'sad,' though plausible, is by no means certain. If, on the one hand, 'kusîda' might have been misinterpreted in Pâli, and changed to 'kusîta,' it is equally possible that 'kusîta,' supposing this to have been the original form, was misinterpreted in Sanskrit, and changed there to 'kusîda.' 'Sai' is mentioned as a Sk. root in the sense of *tabescere*; from it 'kusîta' might possibly be derived in the sense of idle. 'Sîta' in Sanskrit is what is sown, 'sîtâ,' the furrow; from it 'kusîta' might mean a bad labourer. These are merely conjectures, but it is certainly remarkable that there is an old Vedic proper name Kushîta-ka, the founder of the Kaushîtakas, whose Brâhmana, the Kaushîtaki-brâhmana, belongs to the Rig-Veda. An extract from it was translated in my 'History of Ancient Sanskrit Literature,' p. 407.

Lastly, it should be mentioned, that while 'kusîta' is the Pâli counterpart of 'kusîda,' the abstract name in Pâli is 'kosagga,' Sanskrit 'kausîdya,' and not 'kosakka,' as it would have been if derived from 'kusîta.'

him, any more than the wind throws down a rocky mountain.

9.

He who wishes to put on the sacred orange-coloured dress without having cleansed himself from sin, who disregards also temperance and truth, is unworthy of the orange-coloured dress.

10.

But he who has cleansed himself from sin, is well grounded in all virtues, and regards also temperance and truth, is indeed worthy of the orange-coloured dress.

(9.) The saffron dress, of a reddish-yellow or orange colour, the Kásáva or Káshâya, is the distinctive garment of the Buddhist priests. The play on the words 'anikkasávo kásávam,' or in Sanskrit, 'anishkashâyah kâshâyam,' cannot be rendered in English. 'Kashâya' means, impurity, 'nish-kashâya,' free from impurity, 'a-nish-kashâya,' not free from impurity, while 'kâshâya' is the name of the orange-coloured or yellowish Buddhist garment. The pun is evidently a favourite one, for, as Fausböll shows, it occurs also in the Mahâbhârata, xii. 568:

"Anishkashâye kâshâyam îhârtham iti viddhi tam,
Dharmadhvagânâm mundânâm vrittyartham iti me matih."

Know that this orange-coloured garment on a man who is not free from impurity, serves only for the purpose of cupidity; my opinion is, that it is meant to supply the means of living to those men with shaven heads, who carry their virtue like a flag.

(I read 'vrittyartham,' according to the Bombay edition, instead of 'kritârtham,' the reading of the Calcutta edition.)

With regard to 'sîla,' virtue, see Burnouf, 'Lotus,' p. 547.

On the exact colour of the dress, see Bishop Bigandet, 'The Life or Legend of Gaudama, the Budha of the Burmese,' Rangoon, 1866; p. 504.

11.

They who imagine truth in untruth, and see untruth in truth, never arrive at truth, but follow vain desires.

12.

They who know truth in truth, and untruth in untruth, arrive at truth, and follow true desires.

13.

As rain breaks through an ill-thatched house, passion will break through an unreflecting mind.

14.

As rain does not break through a well-thatched house, passion will not break through a well-reflecting mind.

15.

The evil-doer mourns in this world, and he mourns in the next; he mourns in both. He mourns, he suffers when he sees the evil of his own work.

(11–12.) 'Sâra,' which I have translated by truth, has many meanings in Sanskrit. It means the sap of a thing, then essence or reality; in a metaphysical sense, the highest reality; in a moral sense, truth. It is impossible in a translation to do more than indicate the meaning of such words, and in order to understand them fully, we must know not only their definition, but their history.

(15.) 'Kilittha' is 'klishta,' a participle of 'klis.' It means literally, what is spoilt. The abstract noun 'klesa,' evil or sin, is constantly employed in Buddhist works; see Burnouf, 'Lotus,' p. 413. Possibly the words were intended to be separated, 'kamma kilittham,' and not to be joined like 'kamma-visuddhim' in the next verse.

16.

The virtuous man delights in this world, and he delights in the next; he delights in both. He delights, he rejoices, when he sees the purity of his own work.

17.

The evildoer suffers in this world, and he suffers in the next; he suffers in both. He suffers when he thinks of the evil he has done; he suffers more when going on the evil path.

18.

The virtuous man is happy in this world, and he is happy in the next; he is happy in both. He is happy when he thinks of the good he has done; he is still more happy when going on the good path.

19.

The thoughtless man, even if he can recite a large portion (of the law), but is not a doer of it, has no share in the priesthood, but is like a cowherd counting the cows of others.

(16.) Like 'klish/a' in the preceding verse, 'visuddhi' in the present has a technical meaning. One of Buddhaghosha's most famous works is called 'Visuddhi magga.' (See Burnouf, 'Lotus,' p. 844.)

(17–18.) 'The evil path and the good path' are technical expressions for the descending and ascending scale of worlds through which all beings have to travel upward or downward, according to their deeds. (See Bigandet, 'Life of Gaudama,' p. 5, note 4, and p. 449; Burnouf, Introduction, p. 599; 'Lotus,' p. 865, l. 7; l. 11.)

(19.) In taking 'sahitam' in the sense of 'samhitam' or 'samhitâ,' I follow the commentator who says, "Tepi/akassa Buddhava/anass'

20.

The follower of the law, even if he can recite only a small portion (of the law), but, having forsaken passion and hatred and foolishness, possesses true knowledge and serenity of mind, he, caring for nothing in this world, or that to come, has indeed a share in the priesthood.

---

etam nâmam," but I cannot find another passage where the Tripiṭaka, or any portion of it, is called Sahita. 'Samhita' in vv. 100–102, has a different meaning. The fact that some followers of Buddha were allowed to learn short portions only of the sacred writings by heart, and to repeat them, while others had to learn a larger collection, is shown by the story of 'Kakkhupâla,' p. 3, of 'Mahâkâla,' p. 26, etc.

'Sâmañña,' which I have rendered by 'priesthood,' expresses all that belongs to, or constitutes a real samaña or sramaña, this being the Buddhist name corresponding to the brâhmaña, or priest, of the orthodox Hindus. Buddha himself is frequently called the Good Samaña. Fausböll takes the abstract word 'sâmañña' as corresponding to the Sanskrit 'sâmânya,' community, but Weber has well shown that it ought to be taken as representing 'srâmañya.' He might have quoted the 'Sâmañña phala sutta' of which Burnouf has given such interesting details in his 'Lotus,' p. 449 seq. Fausböll also, in his notes on v. 332, rightly explains 'sâmaññatâ' by 'srâmañyatâ.'

'Anupâdiyâno,' which I have translated by 'caring for nothing,' has a technical meaning. It is the negative of the fourth Nidâna, the so-called Upâdâna, which Köppen has well explained by 'Anhänglichkeit,' taking to the world, loving the world. (Köppen, 'Die Religion des Buddha,' p. 610.)

CHAPTER II.

ON REFLECTION.

21.

REFLECTION is the path of immortality, thoughtlessness the path of death. Those who reflect do not die, those who are thoughtless are as if dead already.

22.

Having understood this clearly, those who are

(21.) 'Apramâda,' which Fausböll translates by *vigilantia*, Gogerly by *religion*, expresses literally the absence of that giddiness or thoughtlessness which characterizes the state of mind of worldly people. It is the first entering into oneself, and hence all virtues are said to have their root in 'apramâda.' (Ye keki kusalâ dhammâ sabbe te appamâdamûlakâ.) I have translated it by 'reflection,' sometimes by 'earnestness.' Immortality, 'amrita,' is explained by Buddhagosha as Nirvâna. 'Amrita' is used, no doubt, as a synonym of Nirvâna, but this very fact shows how many conceptions entered from the very first into the Nirvâna of the Buddhists.

If it is said that those who reflect do not die, this may be understood of spiritual death. The commentator, however, takes it in a technical sense, that they are free from the two last stages of the so-called Nidânas, viz. the Garâmarana (decay and death) and the Gâti (new birth). (See Köppen, 'Die Religion des Buddha,' p. 609.)

advanced in reflection, delight in reflection, and rejoice in the knowledge of the Ariyas (the Elect).

23.

These wise people, meditative, steady, always possessed of strong powers, attain to Nirvâna, the highest happiness.

24.

If a reflecting person has roused himself, if he is not forgetful, if his deeds are pure, if he acts with consideration, if he restrains himself, and lives according to law,—then his glory will increase.

25.

By rousing himself, by reflection, by restraint and control, the wise man may make for himself an island which no flood can overwhelm.

26.

Fools follow after vanity, men of evil wisdom. The wise man possesses reflection as his best jewel.

27.

Follow not after vanity, nor after the enjoyment of love and lust! He who reflects and meditates, obtains ample joy.

28.

When the learned man drives away vanity by re-

---

(22). The Ariyas, the noble or elect, are those who have entered on the path that leads to Nirvâna. (See Köppen, p. 396.) Their knowledge and general status is minutely described. (See Köppen, p. 436.)

flection, he, the wise, having reached the repose of wisdom, looks down upon the fools, far from toil upon the toiling crowd, as a man who stands on a hill looks down on those who stand on the ground.

29.

Reflecting among the thoughtless, awake among the sleepers, the wise man advances like a racer leaving behind the hack.

30.

By earnestness did Maghavan (Indra) rise to the lordship of the gods. People praise earnestness; thoughtlessness is always blamed.

31.

A Bhikshu (mendicant) who delights in reflection, who looks with fear on thoughtlessness, moves about like fire, burning all his fetters, small or large.

32.

A Bhikshu (mendicant) who delights in reflection, who looks with fear on thoughtlessness, will not go to destruction—he is near to Nirvâna.

(31.) Instead of 'saham,' which Dr. Fausböll translates by *vincens*, Dr. Weber by 'conquering,' I think we ought to read '*d*aham,' burning, which was evidently the reading adopted by Buddhaghosha. Mr. R. C. Childers, whom I requested to see whether the MS. at the India Office gives 'saham' or '*d*aham,' writes that the reading '*d*aham' is as clear as possible in that MS. The fetters are meant for the senses. (See Sûtra 370.)

CHAPTER III.

THOUGHT.

33.

As a fletcher makes straight his arrow, a wise man makes straight his trembling and unsteady thought, which is difficult to keep, difficult to turn.

34.

As a fish taken from his watery home and thrown on the dry ground, our thought trembles all over in order to escape the dominion of Mâra (the tempter).

35.

It is good to tame the mind, which is difficult to hold in and flighty, rushing wherever it listeth; a tamed mind brings happiness.

36.

Let the wise man guard his thoughts, for they are difficult to perceive, very artful, and they rush wherever they list: thoughts well guarded bring happiness.

(34.) On Mâra, see verses 7 and 8.

37.

Those who bridle their mind which travels far, moves about alone, is without a body, and hides in the chamber (of the heart), will be free from the bonds of Mâra (the tempter).

38.

If a man's thoughts are unsteady, if he does not know the true law, if his peace of mind is troubled, his knowledge will never be perfect.

39.

If a man's thoughts are not dissipated, if his mind

(39.) Fausböll traces 'anavassuta,' dissipated, back to the Sanskrit root 'syai,' to become rigid; but the participle of that root would be 'sîta,' not 'syuta.' Professor Weber suggests that 'anavassuta' stands for the Sanskrit 'anavasruta,' which he translates 'unbefleckt,' unspotted. If 'avasruta' were the right word, it might be taken in the sense of 'not fallen off, not fallen away,' but it could not mean 'unspotted;' cf. 'dhairyam no susruvat,' our firmness ran away. I have little doubt, however, that 'avassuta' represents the Sk. 'avasruta,' and is derived from the root 'sru' here used in its technical sense, peculiar to the Buddhist literature, and so well explained by Burnouf in his Appendix XIV. ('Lotus,' p. 820.) He shows that, according to Hemakandra and the Gina alankâra, âsravakshaya, Pâli âsavasamkhaya, is counted as the sixth abhignâ, wherever six of these intellectual powers are mentioned, instead of five. The Chinese translate the term in their own Chinese fashion by stillationis finis, but Burnouf claims for it the definite sense of destruction of faults or vices. He quotes from the Lalita-vistara (Adhyâya xxii., ed. Râjendra Lal Mittra, p. 448) the words uttered by Buddha when he arrived at his complete Buddha-hood:—

"sushkâ âsravâ na puna*h* sravanti"
The vices are dried up, they will not flow again,

and he shows that the Pâli dictionary, the 'Abhidhânappadîpikâ,'

is not perplexed, if he has ceased to think of good or evil, then there is no fear for him while he is watchful.

---

explains 'âsava' simply by 'kâma,' love, pleasure of the senses. In the Mahâparinibbâna sutta, three classes of âsava are distinguished, the kâmâsavâ, the bhavâsavâ, and the avig*g*âsavâ. See also Burnouf, 'Lotus,' p. 665.

Burnouf takes 'âsrava' at once in a moral sense, but though it has that sense in the language of the Buddhists, it may have had a more material sense in the beginning. That 'sru' means, to run, and is in fact a merely dialectic variety of 'sru,' is admitted by Burnouf. The noun 'âsrava,' therefore, would have meant originally, a running, and the question is, did it mean a running, *i.e.* a *lapsus*, or did it mean a running, *i.e.* an impetuous desire, or, lastly did it signify originally a bodily ailment, a running sore, and assume afterwards the meaning of a moral ailment? The last view might be supported by the fact that 'âsrâva' in the sense of flux or sore occurs in the Atharva-veda, i. 2, 4, "tad âsrâvasya bheshaga*m* tadu rogam anînasat," this is the medicine for the sore, this destroyed the illness. But if this was the original meaning of the Buddhist 'âsava,' it would be difficult to explain such a word as 'anâsava,' faultless, nor could the participle 'avasuta' or 'avassuta' have taken the sense of sinful or faulty, or, at all events, engaged in worldly thoughts, attached to mundane interests. In order to get that meaning, we must assign to 'âsrava' the original meaning of running towards or attending to external objects (like sa*n*ga, âlaya,' etc.) while 'avasruta' would mean, carried off towards external objects, deprived of inward rest. This conception of the original purport of 'â+sru' or 'ava-sru' is confirmed by a statement of Colebrooke's, who, when treating of the *G*ainas, writes (Miscellaneous Essays, i. 382): "Âsrava is that which directs the embodied spirit (âsravayati purusham) towards external objects. It is the occupation and employment (v*r*itti or prav*r*itti) of the senses or organs on sensible objects. Through the means of the senses it affects the embodied spirit with the sentiment of taction, colour, smell, and taste. Or it is the association or connection of body with right and wrong deeds. It comprises all the karmas, for they (âsravayanti) pervade, influence, and attend the doer, following him or attaching

40.

Knowing that this body is (fragile) like a jar, and making this thought firm like a fortress, one should attack Mâra (the tempter) with the weapon of knowledge, one should watch him when conquered, and should never cease (from the fight).

41.

Before long, alas! this body will lie on the earth, despised, without understanding, like a useless log.

42.

Whatever a hater may do to a hater, or an enemy

---

to him. It is a misdirection (mithyâ-pravritti) of the organs, for it is vain, a cause of disappointment, rendering the organs of sense and sensible objects subservient to fruition. Samvara is that which stops (samvrinoti) the course of the foregoing, or closes up the door or passage to it, and consists in self-command or restraint of organs internal and external, embracing all means of self-control and subjection of the senses, calming and subduing them."

For a full account of the âsravas, see also Lalita-vistara, ed. Calc. pp. 445 and 552, where Kshînâsrava is given as a name of Buddha.

(40.) 'Anivesana' has no doubt a technical meaning, and may signify, one who has left his house, his family and friends, to become a monk. A monk shall not return to his home, but travel about; he shall be anivesana, homeless, anâgâra, houseless. But I doubt whether this can be the meaning of 'anivesana' here, as the sentence, let him be an anchorite, would come in too abruptly. I translate it therefore in a more general sense, let him not return or turn away from the battle, let him watch Mâra, even after he is vanquished, let him keep up a constant fight against the adversary.

to an enemy, a wrongly-directed mind will do us greater mischief.

43.

Not a mother, not a father will do so much, nor any other relative; a well-directed mind will do us greater service.

CHAPTER IV.

FLOWERS.

44.

Who shall overcome this earth, and the world of Yama (the lord of the departed), and the world of the gods? Who shall find out the plainly shown path of virtue, as a clever man finds out the (right) flower?

45.

The disciple will overcome the earth, and the world of Yama, and the world of the gods. The disciple will find out the plainly shown path of virtue, as a clever man finds out the (right) flower.

(44, 45.) If I differ from the translation of Fausböll and Weber, it is because the commentary takes the two verbs, 'vigessati' and 'pakessati,' to mean in the end the same thing, i.e. 'sakkhi-karissati' he will perceive. I have not ventured to take 'vigessate' for 'viganissati,' but it should be remembered that the overcoming of the earth and of the worlds below and above, as here alluded to, is meant to be achieved by means of knowledge. 'Pakessati,' he will gather (cf. vi-ki, 'Indische Sprüche,' 4560), means also, like to gather in English, he will perceive or understand, and the 'dhammapada,' or path of virtue, is distinctly explained by Buddhagosha as consisting of the thirty-seven states or stations which lead to Bodhi. (See Burnouf, 'Lotus,' p. 430; Hardy, Manual, p. 497.) 'Dhamma-

46.

He who knows that this body is like froth, and has learnt that it is as unsubstantial as a mirage, will break the flower-pointed arrow of Mâra, and never see the King of Death.

47.

Death carries off a man who is gathering flowers and whose mind is distracted, as a flood carries off a sleeping village.

---

pada' might, no doubt, mean also 'a law-verse,' but 'sudesita' can hardly mean 'well delivered,' while, as applied to a path, it means 'well pointed out' (v. 285). Buddha himself is called 'Mârgadarsaka' and 'Mârga-desika' (cf. Lal. Vist. p. 551). Nor could one well say that a man collects one single law-verse. Hence Fausböll naturally translates *versus legis bene enarratos*, and Weber gives 'Lehrsprüche' in the plural, but the original has 'dhammapadam,' in the sing. (47-48). There is a curious similarity between these verses and verses 6540-41, and 9939 of the Sânti-parva;

"Pushpâṇiva viḱinvantam anyatragatamanasam,
 Anavâpteshu kâmeshu mṛityur abhyeti mânavam."

Death approaches man like one who is gathering flowers, and whose mind is turned elsewhere, before his desires have been fulfilled.

"Suptam vyâghram mahaugho vâ mṛityur âdâya gaḱḱhati,
 Samḱinvânakam evainam kâmânâm avitṛiptikam."

As a stream (carries off) a sleeping tiger, death carries off this man who is gathering flowers, and who is not satiated in his pleasures.

This last verse, particularly, seems to me clearly a translation from Pâli, and the 'kam' of 'samḱinvânakam' looks as if put in *metri causâ*.

(46.) The flower-arrows of Mâra, the tempter, are borrowed from Kâma, the Hindu god of love. For a similar expression see Lalita-vistara, ed. Calc., p. 40, l. 20, "mâyâmarîḱisadṛisâ vidyutphenopamâs ḱapalâh." It is on account of this parallel passage that I prefer to translate 'mariḱi' by mirage, and not by sunbeam, as Fausböll, or by solar atom, as Weber proposes.

48.

Death subdues a man who is gathering flowers, and whose mind is distracted, before he is satiated in his pleasures.

49.

As the bee collects nectar and departs without injuring the flower, or its colour and scent, so let the sage dwell on earth.

50.

Not the failures of others, not their sins of commission or omission, but his own misdeeds and negligences should the sage take notice of.

51.

Like a beautiful flower, full of colour, but without scent, are the fine but fruitless words of him who does not act accordingly.

52.

But, like a beautiful flower, full of colour and full of scent, are the fine and fruitful words of him who acts accordingly.

53.

As many kinds of wreaths can be made from a heap of flowers, so many good things may be achieved by a mortal if once he is born.

54.

The scent of flowers does not travel against the

(48.) 'Antaka,' death, is given as an explanation of 'Mâra' in the Amarakosha and Abhidhânappadîpika (cf. Fausböll, p. 210).

wind, nor (that of) sandal-wood, or of a bottle of Tagara oil; but the odour of good people travels even against the wind; a good man pervades every place.

55.

Sandal-wood or Tagara, a lotus flower, or a Vassikî, the scent of their excellence is peerless when their fragrance is out.

56.

But mean is the scent that comes from Tagara and sandal-wood;—the odour of excellent people rises up to the gods as the highest.

57.

Of the people who possess these excellencies, who live without thoughtlessness, and who are emancipated through true knowledge, Mâra, the tempter, never finds the way.

58–59.

As on a heap of rubbish cast upon the highway the lily will grow full of sweet perfume and delightful, thus the disciple of the truly enlightened Buddha shines forth by his knowledge among those who are like rubbish, among the people that walk in darkness.

(54.) 'Tagara' a plant from which a scented powder is made. 'Mallaka' or 'mallikâ,' according to Benfey, is an oil vessel. Hence 'tagaramallikâ' is probably meant for a bottle holding aromatic powder, or oil made of the Tagara.

CHAPTER V.

THE FOOL.

60.

Long is the night to him who is awake; long is a mile to him who is tired; long is life to the foolish who do not know the true law.

61.

If a traveller does not meet with one who is his better, or his equal, let him firmly keep to his solitary journey; there is no companionship with a fool.

62.

"These sons belong to me, and this wealth belongs to me," with such thoughts a fool is tormented. He himself does not belong to himself; how much less sons and wealth?

63.

The fool who knows his foolishness, is wise at least

(60.) Life, samsâra, is the constant revolution of birth and death which goes on for ever until the knowledge of the true law or the true doctrine of Buddha enables a man to free himself from samsâra, and to enter into Nirvâna. (See Parable xix., p. 134.)

so far. But a fool who thinks himself wise, he is called a fool indeed.

64.

If a fool be associated with a wise man all his life, he will perceive the truth as little as a spoon perceives the taste of soup.

65.

If an intelligent man be associated for one minute only with a wise man, he will soon perceive the truth, as the tongue perceives the taste of soup.

66.

Fools of little understanding have themselves for their greatest enemies, for they do evil deeds which must bear bitter fruits.

67.

That deed is not well done of which a man must repent, and the reward of which he receives crying and with a tearful face.

68.

No, that deed is well done of which a man does not repent, and the reward of which he receives gladly and cheerfully.

69.

As long as the evil deed done does not bear fruit, the fool thinks it is like honey; but when it ripens, then the fool suffers grief.

70.

Let a fool month after month eat his food (like an

ascetic) with the tip of a blade of Kusa grass, yet is he not worth the sixteenth particle of those who have well weighed the law.

71.

An evil deed does not turn suddenly, like milk; smouldering it follows the fool, like fire covered by ashes.

72.

And when the evil deed, after it has become known, brings sorrow to the fool, then it destroys his bright lot, nay it cleaves his head.

73.

Let the fool wish for a false reputation, for prece-

(70.) The commentator clearly takes 'sa*m*khâta' in the sense of 'samkhyâta,' not of 'samskrita,' for he explains it by 'ñâtadhammâ tulitadhammâ.' The eating with the tip of Kusa-grass has reference to the fastings performed by the Brahmans, but disapproved of, except as a moderate discipline, by the followers of Buddha. This verse seems to interrupt the continuity of the other verses which treat of the reward of evil deeds, or of the slow but sure ripening of every sinful act.

(71.) I am not at all certain of the simile, unless '*mukk*ati,' as applied to milk, can be used in the sense of changing or turning sour. In Manu iv. 172, where a similar sentence occurs, the commentators are equally doubtful: Nâdharmas *k*arito loke sadya*h* phalati gaur iva,—for an evil act committed in the world does not bear fruit at once, like a cow; or like the earth (in due season).

(72.) I take 'ñattam' for '*g*ñapitam,' the causative of '*g*ñâtam,' for which in Sanskrit, too, we have the form without i, '*g*ñaptam.' This '*g*ñaptam,' made known, revealed, stands in opposition to the '*kh*anna,' covered, hid, of the preceding verse. 'Sukka*m*sa,' which Fausböll explains by '*s*uklânsa,' has probably a more technical and special meaning.

dence among the Bhikshus, for lordship in the convents, for worship among other people!

74.

"May both the layman and he who has left the world think that this is done by me; may they be subject to me in everything which is to be done or is not to be done," thus is the mind of the fool, and his desire and pride increase.

75.

"One is the road that leads to wealth, another the road that leads to Nirvâna;" if the Bhikshu, the disciple of Buddha, has learnt this, he will not yearn for honour, he will strive after separation from the world.

(75.) 'Viveka,' which in Sanskrit means chiefly understanding, has with the Buddhists the more technical meaning of separation, whether separation from the world and retirement to the solitude of the forest (kâya viveka), or separation from idle thoughts (kitta viveka), or the highest separation and freedom (Nirvâna).

CHAPTER VI.

THE WISE MAN.

76.

If you see an intelligent man who tells you where true treasures are to be found, who shows what is to be avoided, and who administers reproofs, follow that wise man; it will be better, not worse, for those who follow him.

77.

Let him admonish, let him command, let him hold back from what is improper!—he will be beloved of the good, by the bad he will be hated.

78.

Do not have evil-doers for friends, do not have low people: have virtuous people for friends, have for friends the best of men.

79.

He who drinks in the Law lives happily with a

(78.) It is hardly possible to take 'mitte kalyâne' in the technical sense of 'kalyâna-mitra,' 'ein geistlicher Rath,' a spiritual guide. Burnouf (Introd. p. 281) shows that in the technical sense 'kalyâna-mitra' was widely spread in the Buddhist world.

(79.) The commentator clearly derives 'piti' from 'pâ,' to drink;

serene mind: the sage rejoices always in the Law, as preached by the elect.

80.

Well-makers lead the water (wherever they like); fletchers bend the arrow; carpenters bend a log of wood; wise people fashion themselves.

81.

As a solid rock is not shaken by the wind, wise people falter not amidst blame and praise.

82.

Wise people, after they have listened to the laws, become serene, like a deep, smooth, and still lake.

83.

Good people walk on whatever befall, the good do not murmur, longing for pleasure; whether touched by happiness or sorrow wise people never appear elated or depressed.

---

if it were derived from 'prî,' as Professor Weber seems to suppose, we should expect a double p. 'Ariya,' elect, venerable, is explained by the commentator as referring to Buddha and other teachers.

(80.) See verse 33, and 145, the latter being a mere repetition of our verse. The 'nettikâs,' to judge from the commentary and from the general purport of the verse, are not simply water-carriers, but builders of canals and aqueducts, who force the water to go where it would not go by itself.

(83.) The first line is very doubtful. I have adopted, in my translation, a suggestion of Mr. Childers, who writes, "I think it will be necessary to take 'sabbattha' in the sense of 'everywhere,' or 'under every condition;' 'pañkakhandâdibhedesu, sabba-dhammesu,' says Buddhaghosha. I do not think we need assume

CHAPTER VI.

84.

If, whether for his own sake, or for the sake of others, a man wishes neither for a son, nor for wealth, nor for lordship, and if he does not wish for his own success by unfair means, then he is good, wise, and virtuous.

85.

Few are there among men who arrive at the other shore; the other people here run up and down the shore.

86.

But those who, when the Law has been well preached to them, follow the Law, will pass across the dominion of death, however difficult to overcome.

---

that B. means the word 'vigahanti' to be a synonym of 'vaganti.' I would rather take the whole sentence together as a gloss upon the word 'vaganti':—'vagantîti arahattañânena apaka*ddh*antâ *kh*andarâga*m* vigahanti;' 'vaganti' means that, ridding themselves of lust by the wisdom which Arhat-ship confers, they cast it away." I am inclined to think the line means 'the righteous walk on (unmoved) in all the conditions of life.' 'Nindâ, pasa*m*sâ, sukha*m*, dukkha*m*,' are four of the eight lokadhammas, or earthly conditions; the remaining lokadhammas are 'lâbha, alâbha, yasa, ayasa."

In v. 245, 'passatâ,' by a man who sees, means, by a man who sees clearly or truly. In the same manner 'vra*g*' and 'pravra*g*' may mean, not simply to walk, but to walk properly.

(86.) 'The other shore' is meant for Nirvâna, 'this shore' for common life. On reaching Nirvâna, the dominion of death is overcome. The commentator supplies 'târitvâ,' having crossed, in order to explain the accusative 'ma*kk*udheyya*m*.' Possibly 'pâra*m* essanti' should here be taken as one word, in the sense of overcoming.

87, 88.

A wise man should leave the dark state (of ordinary life), and follow the bright state (of the Bhikshu). After going from his home to a homeless state, he should in his retirement look for enjoyment where there seemed to be no enjoyment. Leaving all pleasures behind, and calling nothing his own, the wise man should free himself from all the troubles of the mind.

89.

Those whose mind is well grounded in the elements of knowledge, who have given up all attachments, and

---

(87, 88.) Leaving one's home is the same as joining the clergy, or becoming a mendicant, without a home or family, an 'anâgâra,' or anchorite. A man in that state of 'viveka,' or retirement (see v. 75, note), sees, that where before there seemed to be no pleasure there real pleasure is to be found, or *vice versâ*. A similar idea is expressed in verse 99. (See Burnouf, 'Lotus,' p. 474, where he speaks of 'Le plaisir de la satisfaction, né de la distinction.')

The five troubles or evils of the mind are passion, anger, ignorance, arrogance, pride. (See Burnouf, 'Lotus,' p. 360, and p. 443.) As to 'pariyodapeyya,' see verse 183, and 'Lotus,' pp. 523, 528; as to 'akim*k*ano,' see Mahâbh. xii. 6568; 1240.

89. The elements of knowledge are the seven Sambodhyaṅgas,' on which see Burnouf, 'Lotus,' p. 796. 'Khînâsavâ,' which I have translated by, they whose frailties have been conquered, may also be taken in a more metaphysical sense, as explained in the note to v. 39. The same applies to the other terms occurring in this verse, such as 'âdâna, anupâdâya,' etc. Dr. Fausböll seems inclined to take 'âsava' in this passage, and in the other passages where it occurs, as the Pâli representative of 'âsraya.' But 'âsraya,' in Buddhist phraseology, means rather the five organs of sense with 'manas,' the soul, and these are kept distinct from the 'âsavas,' the inclinations, the frailties, passions, or vices. The

rejoice without clinging to anything, those whose frailties have been conquered, and who are full of light, are free (even) in this world.

---

commentary on the Abhidharma, when speaking of the Yogâ-*k*âras, says, "En réunissant ensemble les réceptacles (âsraya), les choses reçues (âsrita) et les supports (âlambana), qui sont chacun composés de six termes, on a dix-huit termes qu'on appelle 'Dhâtus' ou contenants. La collection des six réceptacles, ce sont les organes de la vue, de l'ouïe, de l'odorat, du goût, du toucher, et le 'manas' (ou l'organe du cœur), qui est le dernier. La collection des six choses reçues, c'est la connaissance produite par la vue et par les autres sens jusqu'au 'manas' inclusivement. La collection des six supports, ce sont la forme et les autres attributs sensibles jusqu'au 'Dharma' (la loi ou l'être) inclusivement." (See Burnouf, Introduction, p. 449.)

'Parinibbuta' is again a technical term, the Sanskrit 'parinivrita' meaning, freed from all worldly fetters, like 'vimukta.' (See Burnouf, Introduction, p. 590.)

CHAPTER VII.

THE VENERABLE.

90.

There is no suffering for him who has finished his journey, and abandoned grief, who has freed himself on all sides, and thrown off all fetters.

91.

They depart with their thoughts well-collected, they are not happy in their abode; like swans who have left their lake, they leave their house and home.

92.

They who have no riches, who live on authorized food, who have perceived the Void, the Unconditioned,

---

(91.) 'Satimanto,' Sansk. 'smritimantaḥ,' possessed of memory, but here used in the technical sense of 'sati,' the first of the Bodhyaṅgas. (See Burnouf, Introduction, p. 797.) Clough translates it by intense thought, and this is the original meaning of 'smar,' even in Sanskrit. (See 'Lectures on the Science of Language,' ii. p. 332.)

Uyyuñganti which Buddhaghosha explains by 'they exert themselves,' seems to me to signify in this place 'they depart,' *i. e.* they leave their family, and embrace an ascetic life. (See note to verse 235.)

(92.) 'Suññato' (or -tâ), 'animitto,' and 'vimokho' are three dif-

the Absolute, their way is difficult to understand, like that of birds in the ether.

93.

He whose passions are stilled, who is not absorbed in enjoyment, who has perceived the Void, the Unconditioned, the Absolute, his path is difficult to understand, like that of the birds in the ether.

94.

The gods even envy him whose senses have been subdued, like horses well broken in by the driver, who is free from pride, and free from frailty.

95.

Such a one who does his duty is tolerant like the earth, like Indra's bolt; he is like a lake without mud; no new births are in store for him.

---

ferent aspects of Nirvâna. (See Burnouf, Introd. 442, 462, on sûnya.) Nimitta is cause in the most general sense, what causes existence to continue. The commentator explains it chiefly in a moral sense: "râgâdinimittâbhâvena animittam, tehi ka vimuttan ti animitto vimokho," *i.e.* 'owing to the absence of passion and other causes, without causation; because freed from these causes, therefore it is called freedom without causation.'

The simile is intended to compare the ways of those who have obtained spiritual freedom to the flight of birds, it being difficult to understand how the birds move on without putting their feet on anything. This, at least, is the explanation of the commentator. The same metaphor occurs Mahâbh. xii. 6763. 'Goḱara,' which has also the meaning of food, forms a good opposition to 'bhoǵana.'

(95.) Without the hints given by the commentator, we should probably take the three similes of this verse in their natural sense, as illustrating the imperturbable state of an Arahanta, or venerable person. The earth is always represented as an emblem of patience; the bolt of Indra, if taken in its technical sense, as

96.

His thought is quiet, quiet are his word and deed, when he has obtained freedom by true knowledge, when he has thus become a quiet man.

97.

The man who is free from credulity, but knows the Uncreated, who has cut all ties, removed all temptations, renounced all desires, he is the greatest of men.

98.

In a hamlet or in a forest, in the deep water or on

---

the bolt of a gate, might likewise suggest the idea of firmness; while the lake is a constant representative of serenity and purity. The commentator, however, suggests that what is meant is, that the earth, though flowers are cast on it, does not feel pleasure, nor the bolt of Indra displeasure, although less savoury things are thrown upon it, and that in like manner a wise person is indifferent to honour or dishonour.

(96.) That this very natural threefold division, thought, word, and deed, the 'trividha dvâra' or the three doors of the Buddhists (Hardy, 'Manual,' p. 494), was not peculiar to the Buddhists or unknown to the Brahmans, has been proved against Dr. Weber by Professor Köppen in his 'Religion des Buddha,' i. p. 445. He particularly called attention to Manu xii. 4-8; and he might have added Mahâbh. xii. 4059, 6512, 6549, 6554; xiii. 5677, etc. Dr. Weber has himself afterwards brought forward a passage from the Atharva-veda, vi. 96, 3 (' yak kakshushâ manasâ yak ka vâkâ upârima'), which, however, has a different meaning. A better one was quoted by him from the Taitt. Ar. x. 1, 12 (yan me manasâ, vâkâ, karmanâ vâ dushkritam kritam.) Similar expressions have been shown to exist in the Zendavesta, and among the Manichæans (Lassen, 'Indische Alterthumskunde,' iii. p. 414; see also Boehtlingk's Dictionary, s. v. kâya). There was no ground, therefore, for supposing that this formula had found its way into the Christian Liturgy from Persia, for, as Professor Cowell remarks, Greek

CHAPTER VII.

the dry land, wherever venerable persons (Arahanta) dwell, that place is delightful.

99.

Forests are delightful; where the world finds no delight, there the passionless will find delight, for they look not for pleasures.

---

writers, such as Plato, employ very similar expressions, *e.g.* Protag. p. 318, 30, πρὸς ἅπαν ἔργον καὶ λόγον καὶ διανόημα. In fact, the opposition between words and deeds occurs in almost every writer, from Homer downwards; and the further distinction between thoughts and words is clearly implied in such expressions as, 'they say in their heart.' That the idea of sin committed by thought was not a new idea, even to the Jews, may be seen from Prov. xxiv. 9, 'the thought of foolishness is sin.' In the Apastamba-sûtras, lately edited by Professor Bühler, we find the expression, 'atho yatkim*k*a manasâ vâ*k*â *k*akshushâ vâ sa*m*kalpayan dhyâyaty âhâbhivipasyati vâ tathaiva tad bhavatîty upadisanti;' They say that whatever a Brahman intending with his mind, voice, or eye, thinks, says, or looks, that will be. This is clearly a very different division, and it is the same which is intended in the passage from the Atharva-veda, quoted above. In the mischief done by the eye, we have the first indication of the evil eye. (Mahâbh. xii. 3117. See Dhammapada, v. 231-234.)

CHAPTER VIII.

THE THOUSANDS.

100.

Even though a speech be a thousand (of words), but made up of senseless words, one word of sense is better, which if a man hears, he becomes quiet.

101.

Even though a Gâthâ (poem) be a thousand (of words), but made up of senseless words, one word of a Gâthâ is better, which if a man hears, he becomes quiet.

102.

Though a man recite a hundred Gâthâs made up of senseless words, one word of the law is better, which if a man hears, he becomes quiet.

103.

If one man conquer in battle a thousand times thousand men, and if another conquer himself, he is the greatest of conquerors.

(100.) 'Vâkâ' is to be taken as a nom. sing. fem., instead of the Sk. 'vâk.'

CHAPTER VIII.

104, 105.

One's own self conquered is better than all other people; not even a god, a Gandharva, not Mâra with Brahman could change into defeat the victory of a man who has vanquished himself, and always lives under restraint.

106.

If a man for a hundred years sacrifice month after month with a thousand, and if he but for one moment pay homage to a man whose soul is grounded (in true knowledge), better is that homage than a sacrifice for a hundred years.

(104.) 'Gitam,' according to the commentator, stands for *gito* (liṅgavipallâso, *i.e.* viparyâsa); 'have' is an interjection.

The Devas (gods), Gandharvas (fairies), and other fanciful beings of the Brahmanic religion, such as the Nâgas, Sarpas, Garuḍas, etc., were allowed to continue in the traditional language of the people who had embraced Buddhism. See the pertinent remarks of Burnouf, Introduction, p. 134 *seq.*, 184. On Mâra, the tempter, see v. 7. Sástram Aiyar, 'On the Gaina Religion,' p. xx, says:—"Moreover as it is declared in the Gaina Vedas that all the gods worshipped by the various Hindu sects, viz. Siva, Brahma, Vishṇu, Gaṇapati, Subramaniyan, and others, were devoted adherents of the above-mentioned Tirthankaras, the Gainas therefore do not consider them as unworthy of their worship; but as they are servants of Arugan, they consider them to be deities of their system, and accordingly perform certain pûgâs in honour of them, and worship them also." The case is more doubtful with orthodox Buddhists. "Orthodox Buddhists," as Mr. D'Alwis writes (Attanagalu-vansa, p. 55) "do not consider the worship of the Devas as being sanctioned by him who disclaimed for himself and all the devas any power over man's soul. Yet the Buddhists are everywhere idol-worshippers. Buddhism, however, acknowledges the existence of some of the Hindu deities, and from the various friendly offices which those Devas are said to have rendered to Gotama, Buddhists evince a respect for their idols." See also 'Parables,' p. 162.

107.

If a man for a hundred years worship Agni (fire) in the forest, and if he but for one moment pay homage to a man whose soul is grounded (in true knowledge), better is that homage than sacrifice for a hundred years.

108.

Whatever a man sacrifice in this world as an offering or as an oblation for a whole year in order to gain merit, the whole of it is not worth a quarter; reverence shown to the righteous is better.

109.

He who always greets and constantly reveres the aged, four things will increase to him, viz. life, beauty, happiness, power.

110.

But he who lives a hundred years, vicious and unrestrained, a life of one day is better if a man is virtuous and reflecting.

(109.) Dr. Fausböll, in a most important note, called attention to the fact that the same verse, with slight variations, occurs in Manu. We there read, ii. 121:—

"Abhivâdanasîlasya nityam vriddhopasevinah,
*K*atvâri sampravardhante: âyur vidyâ yaso balam."

Here the four things are, life, knowledge, glory, power.

In the Âpastamba-sûtras, 1, 2, 5, 15, the reward promised for the same virtue is 'svargam âyus *k*a,' heaven and long life. It seems, therefore, as if the original idea of this verse came from the Brahmans, and was afterwards adopted by the Buddhists. How largely it spread is shown by Dr. Fausböll from the 'Asiatic Researches,' xx. p. 259, where the same verse of the Dhammapada is mentioned as being in use among the Buddhists of Siam.

111.

And he who lives a hundred years, ignorant and unrestrained, a life of one day is better, if a man is wise and reflecting.

112.

And he who lives a hundred years, idle and weak, a life of one day is better, if a man has attained firm strength.

113.

And he who lives a hundred years, not seeing beginning and end, a life of one day is better if a man sees beginning and end.

114.

And he who lives a hundred years, not seeing the immortal place, a life of one day is better if a man sees the immortal place.

115.

And he who lives a hundred years, not seeing the highest law, a life of one day is better, if a man sees the highest law.

(112.) On 'kusito' and 'hinaviriyo,' see note to v. 7.

CHAPTER IX.

EVIL.

116.

If a man would hasten towards the good, he should keep his thought away from evil; if a man does what is good slothfully, his mind delights in evil.

117.

If a man commits a sin, let him not do it again; let him not delight in sin: pain is the outcome of evil.

118.

If a man does what is good, let him do it again; let him delight in it: happiness is the outcome of good.

119.

Even an evildoer sees happiness as long as his evil deed has not ripened; but when his evil deed has ripened, then does the evildoer see evil.

120.

Even a good man sees evil days, as long as his good

deed has not ripened; but when his good deed has ripened, then does the good man see happy days.

121.

Let no man think lightly of evil, saying in his heart, It will not come near unto me. Even by the falling of water-drops a water-pot is filled; the fool becomes full of evil, even if he gathers it little by little.

122.

Let no man think lightly of good, saying in his heart, It will not benefit me. Even by the falling of water-drops a water-pot is filled; the wise man becomes full of good, even if he gather it little by little.

123.

Let a man avoid evil deeds, as a merchant if he has few companions and carries much wealth avoids a dangerous road; as a man who loves life avoids poison.

124.

He who has no wound on his hand, may touch poison with his hand; poison does not affect one who has no wound; nor is there evil for one who does not commit evil.

125.

If a man offend a harmless, pure, and innocent per-

(124.) This verse, taken in connection with what precedes, can only mean that no one suffers evil but he who has committed evil, or sin; an idea the very opposite of that pronounced in Luke xiii. 1–5.

son, the evil falls back upon that fool, like light dust thrown up against the wind.

126.

Some people are born again; evildoers go to hell; righteous people go to heaven; those who are free from all worldly desires enter Nirvâna.

127.

Not in the sky, not in the midst of the sea, not if we enter into the clefts of the mountains, is there known a spot in the whole world where a man might be freed from an evil deed.

128.

Not in the sky, not in the midst of the sea, not if we enter into the clefts of the mountains, is there known a spot in the whole world where death could not overcome (the mortal).

(125.) Cf. 'Indische Sprüche,' 1582; Kathâsaritsâgara, 49, 222.

(126.) For a description of hell and its long, yet not endless sufferings, see 'Parables,' p. 132. The pleasures of heaven, too, are frequently described in these Parables and elsewhere. Buddha, himself, enjoyed these pleasures of heaven, before he was born for the last time. It is probably when good and evil deeds are equally balanced, that men are born again as human beings; this, at least, is the opinion of the *G*ainas. (Cf. Chintâmani, ed. H. Bower, Introd. p. xv.)

CHAPTER X.

PUNISHMENT.

129.

All men tremble at punishment, all men fear death; remember that you are like unto them, and do not kill nor cause slaughter.

(129.) One feels tempted, no doubt, to take 'upamâ' in the sense of the nearest (der Nächste), the neighbour, and to translate, having made oneself one's neighbour, *i.e.* 'loving one's neighbour as oneself.' But as 'upamâm,' with a short a, is the correct accusative of 'upamâ,' we must translate 'having made oneself the likeness, the image of others,' 'having placed oneself in the place of others.' This is an expression which occurs frequently in Sanskrit (cf. Hitopadesa, i. 11).

"Prâṇâ yathâtmano 'bhishṭâ bhûtânâm api te tathâ,

Âtmaupamyena bhûteshu dayâm kurvanti sâdhavaḥ."

'As life is dear to oneself, it is dear also to other living beings: by comparing oneself with others, good people bestow pity on all beings.'

See also Hit. i. 12; Râm. v. 23, 5, 'âtmânam upamâm kritvâ sveshu dâreshu ramyatâm,' 'Making oneself a likeness, *i.e.* putting oneself in the position of other people, it is right to love none but one's own wife.' Dr. Fausböll has called attention to similar passages in the Mahâbhârata, xiii. 5569 *seq.*

130.

All men tremble at punishment, all men love life; remember that thou art like unto them, and do not kill, nor cause slaughter.

131.

He who for his own sake punishes or kills beings longing for happiness, will not find happiness after death.

132.

He who for his own sake does not punish or kill beings longing for happiness, will find happiness after death.

133.

Do not speak harshly to anybody; those who are spoken to will answer thee in the same way. Angry speech is painful, blows for blows will touch thee.

134.

If, like a trumpet trampled underfoot, thou utter

(131.) Dr. Fausböll points out the striking similarity between this verse and two verses occurring in Manu and the Mahâbhârata:

Manu, v. 45:
"Yo ˚himsakâni bhûtâni hinasty âtmasukhekkhayâ
    Sa gîvams ka mritas kaiva na kvakit sukham edhate."
Mahâbh. xiii. 5568:
"Ahimsakâni bhûtâni dandena vinihanti yah
    Âtmanah sukham ikkhan sa pretya naiva sukhî bhavet."
If it were not for 'ahimsakâni,' in which Manu and the Mahâbhârata agree, I should say that the verses in both were Sanskrit modifications of the Pâli original. The verse in the Mahâbhârata presupposes the verse of the Dhammapada.

(133.) See 'Mahâbhârata,' xii. 4056.

135.

As a cowherd with his staff gathers his cows into the stable, so do Age and Death gather the life of man.

136.

A fool does not know when he commits his evil deeds: but the wicked man burns by his own deeds, as if burnt by fire.

137.

He who inflicts pain on innocent and harmless persons, will soon come to one of these ten states:

138.

He will have cruel suffering, loss, injury of the body, heavy affliction, or loss of mind,

139.

Or a misfortune of the king, or a fearful accusation, or loss of relations, or destruction of treasures,

---

(136.) The metaphor of 'burning' for 'suffering' is very common in Buddhist literature. Everything burns, *i.e.* 'everything suffers,' was one of the first experiences of Buddha himself. See v. 146.

(138.) 'Cruel suffering is explained by 'sisaroga,' headache, etc. 'Loss' is taken for loss of money. 'Injury of the body' is held to be the cutting off of the arm, and other limbs. 'Heavy afflictions' are, again, various kinds of diseases.

(139.) 'Misfortune of the king' may mean, a misfortune that happened to the king, defeat by an enemy, and therefore conquest of the country. 'Upasarga' means accident, misfortune. Dr. Fausböll translates 'râgato va upassaggam' by 'ful-

140.

Or lightning-fire will burn his houses; and when his body is destroyed, the fool will go to hell.

141.

Not nakedness, not platted hair, not dirt, not fasting, or lying on the earth, not rubbing with dust, not sitting motionless, can purify a mortal who has not overcome desires.

---

gentis (lunae) defectionem;' Dr. Weber, by 'Bestrafung vom König.' 'Abbhakkhânam,' Sansk. 'abhyâkhyânam' is a heavy accusation for high-treason, or similar offences.

The 'destruction of pleasures or treasures' is explained by gold being changed to coals (see 'Parables,' p. 98), pearls to cotton-seed, corn to potsherds, and by men and cattle becoming blind, lame, etc.

(141.) Dr. Fausböll has pointed out that the same or a very similar verse occurs in a legend taken from the Divyâvadâna, and translated by Burnouf (Introduction, p. 313 *seq.*). Burnouf translates the verse: " Ce n'est ni la coutume de marcher nu, ni les cheveux nattés, ni l'usage d'argile, ni le choix des diverses espèces d'aliments, ni l'habitude de coucher sur la terre nue, ni la poussière, ni la malpropreté, ni l'attention à fuir l'abri d'un toit, qui sont capables de dissiper le trouble dans lequel nous jettent les désirs non-satisfaits; mais qu'un homme, maître de ses sens, calme, recueilli, chaste, évitant de faire du mal à aucune créature, accomplisse la Loi, et il sera, quoique paré d'ornements, un Brâhmane, un Çramana, un Religieux."

Walking naked, and the other things mentioned in our verse, are outward signs of a saintly life, and these Buddha rejects because they do not calm the passions. Nakedness he seems to have rejected on other grounds too, if we may judge from the 'Sumâgadhâ-avadâna:' "A number of naked friars were assembled in the house of the daughter of Anâtha-pindika. She called her daughter-in-law, Sumâgadhâ, and said, 'Go and see those highly respectable persons.' Sumâgadhâ, expecting to see some

142.

He who, though dressed in fine apparel, exercises tranquillity, is quiet, subdued, restrained, chaste, and has ceased to find fault with all other beings, he indeed is a Brâhmana, an ascetic (Sramana), a friar (bhikshu).

143.

Is there in this world any man so restrained by humility that he does not mind reproof, as a well-trained horse the whip?

144.

Like a well-trained horse when touched by the

---

of the saints, like Sâriputra, Maudgalyâyana, and others, ran out full of joy. But when she saw these friars with their hair like pigeon wings, covered by nothing but dirt, offensive, and looking like demons, she became sad. 'Why are you sad?' said her mother-in-law. Sumâgadhâ replied, 'O, mother, if these are saints, what must sinners be like?'"

Burnouf (Introd. p. 312) supposed that the Gainas only, and not the Buddhists, allowed nakedness. But the Gainas, too, do not allow it universally. They are divided into two parties, the Svetambaras and Digambaras. The Svetambaras, clad in white, are the followers of Parsvanâtha, and wear clothes. The Digambaras, i. e. sky-clad, disrobed, are followers of Mahâvira, and resident chiefly in Southern India. At present they, too, wear clothing, but not when eating. (See Sâstram Aiyar, p. xxi.)

The 'gatâ,' or the hair platted and gathered up in a knot, was a sign of a Saiva ascetic. The sitting motionless is one of the postures assumed by ascetics. Clough explains 'ukkutika' as the act of sitting on the heels; Wilson gives for 'utkatukâsana,' 'sitting on the hams.' (See Fausböll, note on verse 140.)

(142.) As to 'dandanidhâna,' see Mahâbh. xii. 6559.

(143, 144.) I am very doubtful as to the real meaning of these verses. I think their object is to show how reproof or punish-

whip, be ye active and lively, and by faith, by virtue, by energy, by meditation, by discernment of the law you will overcome this great pain (of reproof), perfect in knowledge and in behaviour, and never forgetful.

145.

Well-makers lead the water (wherever they like), fletchers bend the arrow; carpenters break a log of wood; wise people fashion themselves.

---

ment should be borne. I therefore take 'bhadra assa' in the sense of a well-broken or well-trained, not in the sense of a spirited horse. 'Hrî,' no doubt, means generally 'shame,' but it also means 'humility,' or 'modesty.' However, I give my translation as conjectural only, for there are several passages in the commentary which I do not understand.

(145.) The same as verse 80.

CHAPTER XI.

OLD AGE.

146.

How is there laughter, how is there joy, as this world is always burning? Why do you not seek a light, ye who are surrounded by darkness?

147.

Look at this dressed-up lump, covered with wounds, joined together, sickly, full of many thoughts, which has no strength, no hold!

148.

This body is wasted, full of sickness, and frail; this heap of corruption breaks to pieces, the life in it is death.

149.

Those white bones, like gourds thrown away in the autumn, what pleasure is there in looking at them?

(146.) Dr. Fausböll translates 'semper exardescit recordatio;' Dr. Weber, 'da's doch beständig Kummer giebt.' The commentator explains, 'as this abode is always lighted by passion and the other fires.' (Cf. Hardy, 'Manual,' p. 495.)

150.

After a frame has been made of the bones, it is covered with flesh and blood, and there dwell in it old age and death, pride and deceit.

151.

The brilliant chariots of kings are destroyed, the body also approaches destruction, but the virtues of good people never approach destruction, thus do the good say to the good.

152.

A man who has learnt little, grows old like an ox; his flesh grows, but his knowledge does not grow.

153, 154.

Without ceasing shall I run through a course of many births, looking for the maker of this tabernacle,—and painful is birth again and again. But now, maker of the tabernacle, thou hast been seen; thou shalt not make up this tabernacle again. All thy rafters are broken, thy ridge-pole is sundered; the mind, being sundered, has attained to the extinction of all desires.

(150.) The expression 'ma*m*salohitalepanam' is curiously like the expression used in Manu, vi. 76, 'mâ*m*sasonitalepanam,' and in several passages of the Mahâbhârata, xii. 12462, 12053, as pointed out by Dr. Fausböll.

(153, 154.) These two verses are famous among Buddhists, for they are the words which the founder of Buddhism is supposed to have uttered at the moment he attained to Buddhahood. (See Spence Hardy, 'Manual,' p. 180.) According to the Lalita-vistara, the words uttered on that solemn occasion were those quoted in the note to verse 39. Though the purport of both is

155.

Men who have not observed proper discipline, and have not gained wealth in their youth, they perish like old herons in a lake without fish.

156.

Men who have not observed proper discipline, and have not gained wealth in their youth; they lie like broken bows, sighing after the past.

---

the same, the tradition preserved by the Southern Buddhists shows greater vigour than that of the North.

'The maker of the tabernacle' is explained as a poetical expression for the cause of new births, at least according to the views of Buddha's followers, whatever his own views may have been. Buddha had conquered Mâra, the representative of worldly temptations, the father of worldly desires, and as desires (tanhâ) are, by means of 'upâdâna' and 'bhava,' the cause of 'gâti,' or birth, the destruction of desires and the defeat of Mâra are really the same thing, though expressed differently in the philosophical and legendary language of the Buddhists. Tanhâ, thirst or desire, is mentioned as serving in the army of Mâra. ('Lotus,' p. 443.) There are some valuable remarks of Mr. D'Alwis on these verses in the 'Attanugaluvansa,' p. cxxviii. This learned scholar points out a certain similarity in the metaphors used by Buddha, and some verses in Manu, vi. 76-77. (See also Mahâbh. xii. 12463-4.) Mr. D'Alwis' quotation, however, from 'Pânini,' iii. 2, 112, proves in no way that 'sandhavissan,' or any other future can, if standing by itself, be used in a past sense. Pânini speaks of 'bhûtaanadyatana,' and he restricts the use of the future in a past sense to cases where the future follows verbs expressive of recollection, etc.

(155.) On 'ghâyanti,' i.e. 'kshâyanti,' see Dr. Bollensen's learned remarks, 'Zeitschrift der Deutschen Morgenl. Gesellschaft,' xviii. 834, and Boehtlingk-Roth, s. v. 'kshâ.'

CHAPTER XII.

SELF.

157.

If a man hold himself dear, let him watch himself carefully; during one at least out of the three watches a wise man should be watchful.

158.

Let each man first direct himself to what is proper, then let him teach others; thus a wise man will not suffer.

159.

Let each man make himself as he teaches others to be; he who is well subdued may subdue (others); one's own self is difficult to subdue.

160.

Self is the lord of self, who else could be the lord? With self well-subdued, a man finds a lord such as few can find.

(157.) The three watches of the night are meant for the three stages of life.

161.

The evil done by oneself, self-begotten, self-bred, crushes the wicked, as a diamond breaks a precious stone.

162.

He whose wickedness is very great brings himself down to that state where his enemy wishes him to be, as a creeper does with the tree which it surrounds.

163.

Bad deeds, and deeds hurtful to ourselves, are easy to do; what is beneficial and good, that is very difficult to do.

164.

The wicked man who scorns the rule of the venerable (Arahat), of the elect (Ariya), of the virtuous, and follows false doctrine, he bears fruit to his own destruction, like the fruits of the Ka*tt*aka reed.

165.

By oneself the evil is done, by oneself one suffers; by oneself evil is left undone, by oneself one is purified. Purity and impurity belong to oneself, no one can purify another.

(164.) The reed either dies after it has borne fruit, or is cut down for the sake of its fruit.

'Di*tth*i,' literally view, is used even by itself, like the Greek 'hairesis' in the sense of heresy (see Burnouf, 'Lotus,' p. 441). In other places a distinction is made between 'mikkhâdi*tth*i' (v. 167, 316) and 'sammâdi*tth*i' (v. 319). If 'arahatam ariyânam' are used in their technical sense, we should translate 'the reverend Arhats,'—'Arhat' being the highest degree of the four orders of Ariyas, viz. Srotaâpanna, Sakridâgâmin, Anâgâmin, and Arhat. See note to v. 178.

166.

Let no one forget his own duty for the sake of another's, however great; let a man, after he has discerned his own duty, be always attentive to his duty.

(166.) 'Attha,' lit. 'object,' must be taken in a moral sense, as 'duty' rather than as 'advantage.' The story which Buddhaghosha tells of the 'Thera Attadattha' gives a clue to the origin of some of his parables, which seem to have been invented to suit the text of the Dhammapada rather than *vice versâ*. A similar case occurs in the commentary to verse 227.

CHAPTER XIII.

THE WORLD.

167.

Do not follow the evil law! Do not live on in thoughtlessness! Do not follow false doctrine! Be not a friend of the world.

168.

Rouse thyself! do not be idle! Follow the law of virtue! The virtuous lives happily in this world and in the next.

169.

Follow the law of virtue; do not follow that of sin. The virtuous lives happily in this world and in the next.

170.

Look upon the world as a bubble, look upon it as a mirage: the king of death does not see him who thus looks down upon the world.

171.

Come, look at this glittering world, like unto a royal chariot; the foolish are immersed in it, but the wise do not cling to it.

172.

He who formerly was reckless and afterwards became sober, brightens up this world, like the moon when freed from clouds.

173.

He whose evil deeds are covered by good deeds, brightens up this world, like the moon when freed from clouds.

174.

This world is dark, few only can see here; a few only go to heaven, like birds escaped from the net.

175.

The swans go on the path of the sun, they go through the ether by means of their miraculous power; the wise are led out of this world, when they have conquered Mâra and his train.

176.

If a man has transgressed one law, and speaks lies, and scoffs at another world, there is no evil he will not do.

177.

The uncharitable do not go to the world of the gods; fools only do not praise liberality; a wise man rejoices in liberality, and through it becomes blessed in the other world.

(175.) 'Hamsa' may be meant for the bird, whether flamingo, or swan, or ibis (see Hardy, 'Manual,' p. 17), but it may also, I believe, be taken in the sense of saint. As to 'iddhi,' magical power, *i.e.* 'riddhi,' see Burnouf, 'Lotus,' p. 310; Spence Hardy, 'Manual,' pp. 498 and 504; 'Legends,' pp. 55, 177. See note to verse 254.

CHAPTER XIII.

178.

Better than sovereignty over the earth, better than going to heaven, better than lordship over all worlds, is the reward of the first step in holiness.

(178.) 'Sotâpatti,' the technical term for the first step in the path that leads to Nirvâna. There are four such steps, or stages, and on entering each, a man receives a new title:—

1. The 'Srota âpanna,' lit. he who has got into the stream. A man may have seven more births before he reaches the other shore, *i.e.* 'Nirvâna.'

2. 'Sakridâgâmin,' lit. he who comes back once, so called because, after having entered this stage, a man is born only once more among men or gods.

3. 'Anâgâmin,' lit. he who does not come back, so called because, after this stage, a man cannot be born again in a lower world, but can only enter a Brahman world before he reaches Nirvâna.

4. 'Arhat,' the venerable, the perfect, who has reached the highest stage that can be reached, and from which Nirvâna is perceived (sukkhavipassanâ, 'Lotus,' p. 849). See Hardy, 'Eastern Monachism,' p. 280, Burnouf, Introduction, p. 209; Köppen, p. 398; D'Alwis, Attanugaluvansa, p. cxxiv.

CHAPTER XIV.

THE AWAKENED (BUDDHA).

179.

He whose conquest is not conquered again, whose conquest no one in this world escapes, by what path can you lead him, the Awakened, the Omniscient, into a wrong path?

180.

He whom no desire with its snares and poisons can lead astray, by what path can you lead him, the Awakened, the Omniscient, into a wrong path?

(179-180.) These two verses, though their general meaning seems clear, contain many difficulties which I do not at all pretend to solve. 'Buddha,' the Awakened, is to be taken as an appellative rather than as the proper name of the 'Buddha.' It means, anybody who has arrived at complete knowledge. 'Anantagokaram' I take in the sense of, possessed of unlimited knowledge. 'Apadam,' which Dr. Fausböll takes as an epithet of Buddha and translates by *non investigabilis*, I take as an accusative governed by 'nessatha,' and in the sense of wrong place (uppatha, v. 309, p. 396, l. 2) or sin.

The second line of verse 179 is most difficult. The commentator seems to take it in the sense of "in whose conquest nothing is wanting," "who has conquered all sins and all passions." In that case we should have to supply 'kileso' (masc.) or 'râgo,' or take 'koki' in the sense of any enemy. Cf. v. 105.

CHAPTER XIV.

181.

Even the gods envy those who are awakened and not forgetful, who are given to meditation, who are wise, and who delight in the repose of retirement (from the world).

182.

Hard is the conception of men, hard is the life of mortals, hard is the hearing of the True Law, hard is the birth of the Awakened (the attainment of Buddhahood).

183.

Not to commit any sin, to do good, and to purify one's mind, that is the teaching of the Awakened.

184.

The Awakened call patience the highest penance,

(183.) This verse is again one of the most solemn verses among the Buddhists. According to Csoma de Körös, it ought to follow the famous Âryâ stanza, 'Ye dhammâ' ('Lotus,' p. 522), and serve as its complement. But though this may be the case in Tibet, it was not so originally. Burnouf has fully discussed the metre and meaning of our verse on pp. 527, 528 of his 'Lotus.' He prefers 'sakittaparidamanam,' which Csoma translated by "the mind must be brought under entire subjection" (svakittaparidamanam), and the late Dr. Mill by "proprii intellectus subjugatio." But his own MS. of the 'Mahâpadhâna sutta' gave likewise 'sakittapariyodapanam,' and this is no doubt the correct reading. (See D'Alwis, 'Attanugaluvansa,' cxxix.) We found 'pariyodappeya' in verse 88, in the sense of freeing oneself from the troubles of thought. The only question is whether the root 'dâ,' with the prepositions 'pari' and 'ava,' should be taken in the sense of cleansing oneself from, or cutting oneself out from. I prefer the former conception, the same which in Buddhist literature has given rise to the name Avadâna, a legend, originally a pure and virtuous act, an ἀπύρταια, afterwards a sacred story, and possibly a story the hearing of which purifies the mind. See Boehtlingk-Roth, s. v. 'avadâna.'

long-suffering the highest Nirvâna; for he is not an anchorite (Pravragita) who strikes others, he is not an ascetic (Sramana) who insults others.

185.

Not to blame, not to strike, to live restrained under the law, to be moderate in eating, to sleep and eat alone, and to dwell on the highest thoughts,—this is the teaching of the Awakened.

186.

There is no satisfying lusts, even by a shower of gold pieces; he who knows that lusts have a short taste and cause pain, he is wise.

187.

Even in heavenly pleasures he finds no satisfaction, the disciple who is fully awakened delights only in the destruction of all desires.

(185.) 'Pâtimokkhe,' under the law, *i.e.* according to the law, the law which leads to 'Moksha,' or freedom. 'Prâtimoksha' is the title of the oldest collection of the moral laws of the Buddhists (Burnouf, Introduction, p. 300; Bigandet, 'The Life of Gaudama,' p. 439), and as it was common both to the Southern and the Northern Buddhists, 'pâtimokkhe' in our passage may possibly be meant, as Professor Weber suggests, as the title of that very collection. The commentator explains it by '*getth*akasîla' and 'pâtimokkhasîla.' I take 'sayanâsam' for 'sayanâsanam;' see Mahâb. xii. 6684. In xii. 9978, however, we find also 'sayyâsane.'

(187.) There is a curious similarity between this verse and verse 6503 (9919) of the Sântiparva:

'Ya*k k*a kâmasukha*m* loke, ya*k k*a divyam mahat sukham,
Trishnâkshayasukhasyaite nârhata*h* sho*d*asîm kalâm;'

And whatever delight of love there is on earth, and whatever is the great delight in heaven, they are not worth the sixteenth part of the pleasure which springs from the destruction of all desires.

188.

Men, driven by fear, go to many a refuge, to mountains and forests, to groves and sacred trees.

189.

But that is not a safe refuge, that is not the best refuge; a man is not delivered from all pains after having gone to that refuge.

190.

He who takes refuge with Buddha, the Law, and the Church; he who, with clear understanding, sees the four holy truths:—

191.

Viz. Pain, the origin of pain, the destruction of pain, and the eightfold holy way that leads to the quieting of pain;—

192.

That is the safe refuge, that is the best refuge; having gone to that refuge, a man is delivered from all pain.

(188–192.) These verses occur in Sanskrit in the 'Prâtihârya-sûtra,' translated by Burnouf, Introduction, pp. 162–189; see p. 186. Burnouf translates 'rukkhaketyâni' by 'arbres consacrés;' properly, sacred shrines under or near a tree.

(190.) Buddha, Dharma, and Saṅgha are called the 'Trisarana' (cf. Burnouf, Introd. p. 630). The four holy truths are the four statements that there is pain in this world, that the source of pain is desire, that desire can be annihilated, that there is a way (shown by Buddha) by which the annihilation of all desires can be achieved, and freedom be obtained. That way consists of eight parts. (See Burnouf, Introduction, p. 630.) The eightfold way forms the subject of chapter xviii. (See also 'Chips from a German Workshop,' 2nd ed. vol. i. p. 251 seq.)

193.

A supernatural person is not easily found, he is not born everywhere. Wherever such a sage is born, that race prospers.

194.

Happy is the arising of the Awakened, happy is the teaching of the True Law, happy is peace in the church, happy is the devotion of those who are at peace.

195, 196.

He who pays homage to those who deserve homage, whether the awakened (Buddha) or their disciples, those who have overcome the host (of evils), and crossed the flood of sorrow, he who pays homage to such as have found deliverance and know no fear, his merit can never be measured by anybody.

CHAPTER XV.

HAPPINESS.

197.

Let us live happily then, not hating those who hate us! let us dwell free from hatred among men who hate!

198.

Let us live happily then, free from ailments among the ailing! let us dwell free from ailments among men who are ailing!

199.

Let us live happily then, free from greed among the greedy! let us dwell free from greed among men who are greedy!

200.

Let us live happily then, though we call nothing

(198.) The ailment here meant is moral rather than physical. Cf. Mahábh. xii. 9924, 'samprasânto nirâmayaḥ;' 9925, 'yo saupránântiko rogas tâm trishnâm tyagataḥ sukham.'

(200.) The words placed in the mouth of the king of Videha, while his residence Mithilâ was in flames, are curiously like our verse; cf. Mahábh. xii. 9917,

'Susukham vata gívámi yasya me násti kimkana.
Mithiláyâm pradiptâyâm na me dahyati kimkana;'

our own! We shall be like the bright gods, feeding on happiness!

201.

Victory breeds hatred, for the conquered is unhappy. He who has given up both victory and defeat, he, the contented, is happy.

202.

There is no fire like passion; there is no unlucky die like hatred; there is no pain like this body; there is no happiness like rest.

203.

Hunger is the worst of diseases, the body the

I live happily, indeed, for I have nothing; while Mithilâ is in flames, nothing of mine is burning.

The 'âbhassara,' *i. e.* 'âbhâsvara,' the bright gods, are frequently mentioned. (Cf. Burnouf, Introd. p. 611.)

(202.) I take 'kali' in the sense of an unlucky die which makes a player lose his game. A real simile seems wanted here, as in v. 252, where, for the same reason, I translate 'graha' by 'shark,' not by 'captivitas,' as Dr. Fausböll proposes. The same scholar translates 'kali' in our verse by 'peccatum.' If there is any objection to translating 'kali' in Pâli by unlucky die, I should still prefer to take it in the sense of the age of depravity, or the demon of depravity.

'Body' for 'khandha' is a free translation, but it is difficult to find any other rendering. According to the Buddhists each sentient being consists of five 'khandha' (skandha), or branches, the organized body (rûpa khandha) with its four internal capacities of sensation (vedanâ), perception (samgñâ), conception (samskâra), knowledge (vigñâna). See Burnouf, Introd. pp. 589, 634; 'Lotus,' p. 335.

(203.) It is difficult to give an exact rendering of 'samskâra,' which I have translated sometimes by 'body' or 'created things,' sometimes by 'natural desires.' 'Samskâra' is the fourth of

greatest of pains; if one knows this truly, that is Nirvâna, the highest happiness.

204.

Health is the greatest of gifts, contentedness the best riches; trust is the best of relatives, Nirvâna, the highest happiness.

205.

He who has tasted the sweetness of solitude and tranquillity, is free from fear and free from sin, while he tastes the sweetness of drinking in the Law.

---

the five 'khandhas,' but the commentator takes it here, as well as in v. 255, for the five 'khandhas' together, in which case we can only translate it by body, or created things. There is, however, another 'samskâra,' that which follows immediately upon 'avidyâ,' ignorance, as the second of the 'nidânas,' or causes of existence, and this too might be called the greatest pain, considering that it is the cause of birth, which is the cause of all pain. Burnouf, 'Lotus,' pp. 109, 827, says, "l'homme des Buddhistes qui, doué intérieurement de l'idée de la forme, voit au dehors des formes, et, après les avoir vaincues, se dit: je connais, je vois, ressemble singulièrement au 'sujet victorieux de chaque objectivité qui demeure le sujet triomphant de toutes choses.'"

'Samskâra' seems sometimes to have a different and less technical meaning, and be used in the sense of conceptions, plans, desires, as, for instance, in v. 368, where 'samkhârânam khayam' is used much like 'tamhâkhaya.' Desires, however, are the result of 'samkhâra,' and if the samkhâras are destroyed, desires cease; see v. 154, 'visamkhâragatam kittam tamhânam khayam ayghagâ.' Again, in his comment on v. 75, Buddhaghosha says, 'upadhiviveko samkhârasamganikam vinodeti;' and again, 'upadhiviveko ka nirupadhînâm puggalânam visamkhâragatânâm.'

For a similar sentiment, see Stanislas Julien, 'Les Avadânas,' vol. i. p. 40, "Le corps est la plus grande source de souffrance," etc. I should say that 'khandha' in v. 202, and 'samkhârâ' in v. 203, are nearly, if not quite, synonymous. I should prefer to

206.

The sight of the elect (Arya) is good, to live with them is always happiness; if a man does not see fools, he will be truly happy.

207.

He who walks in the company of fools suffers a long way; company with fools, as with an enemy, is always painful; company with the wise is pleasure, like meeting with kinsfolk.

208.

Therefore, one ought to follow the wise, the intelligent, the learned, the much enduring, the dutiful, the elect; one ought to follow a good and wise man, as the moon follows the path of the stars.

---

read 'gigakkhâ-paramâ' as a compound. 'Gigakkhâ,' or as it is written in one MS., 'digakkhâ,' (Sk. 'gighatsâ') means not only hunger, but appetite, desire.

(208.) I should like to read 'sukho ka dhîrasamvâso.'

CHAPTER XVI.

PLEASURE.

209.

He who gives himself to vanity, and does not give himself to meditation, forgetting the real aim (of life) and grasping at pleasure, will in time envy him who has exerted himself in meditation.

210.

Let no man ever look for what is pleasant, or what is unpleasant. Not to see what is pleasant is pain, and it is pain to see what is unpleasant.

211.

Let, therefore, no man love anything; loss of the beloved is evil. Those who love nothing, and hate nothing, have no fetters.

212.

From pleasure comes grief, from pleasure comes fear; he who is free from pleasure knows neither grief nor fear.

213.

From affection comes grief, from affection comes

fear; he who is free from affection knows neither grief nor fear.

214.

From lust comes grief, from lust comes fear; he who is free from lust knows neither grief nor fear.

215.

From love comes grief, from love comes fear; he who is free from love knows neither grief nor fear.

216.

From greed comes grief, from greed comes fear; he who is free from greed knows neither grief nor fear.

217.

He who possesses virtue and intelligence, who is just, speaks the truth, and does what is his own business, him the world will hold dear.

218.

He in whom a desire for the Ineffable (Nirvâna) has sprung up, who is satisfied in his mind, and whose thoughts are not bewildered by love, he is called Ûrdhvamsrotas (carried upwards by the stream).

(218.) 'Ûrdhvamsrotas,' or 'uddhamsoto,' is the technical name for one who has reached the world of the 'Avrihas' (Aviha), and is proceeding to that of the 'Akanishthas' (Akanittha). This is the last stage before he reaches the formless world, the 'Arûpa-dhâtu. (See Parables, p. 123; Burnouf, Introd. 599.) Originally 'ûrdhvamsrotas' may have been used in a less technical sense, meaning one who swims against the stream, and is not carried away by the vulgar passions of the world.

CHAPTER XVI.

219.

Kinsfolk, friends, and lovers salute a man who has been long away, and returns safe from afar.

220.

In like manner his good works receive him who has done good, and has gone from this world to the other;—as kinsmen receive a friend on his return.

CHAPTER XVII.

ANGER.

221.

Let a man leave anger, let him forsake pride, let him overcome all bondage! No sufferings befall the man who is not attached to either body or soul, and who calls nothing his own.

222.

He who holds back rising anger like a rolling chariot, him I call a real driver; other people are but holding the reins.

223.

Let a man overcome anger by love, let him overcome evil by good; let him overcome the greedy by liberality, the liar by truth!

224.

Speak the truth, do not yield to anger; give, if

(221.) 'Body and soul' is the translation of 'nâma-rûpa,' lit. 'name and form,' the ninth of the Buddhist Nidânas. (Cf. Burnouf, Introd. p. 501; see also Gogerly, Lecture on Buddhism, and Bigandet, 'The Life of Gaudama,' p. 454.)

(223.) Mahâbh. xii. 3550, 'asâdhum sadhunâ gayet.'

thou art asked, from the little thou hast; by those steps thou wilt go near the gods.

225.

The sages who injure nobody, and who always control their body, they will go to the unchangeable place (Nirvâna), where if they have gone, they will suffer no more.

226.

Those who are always watchful, who study day and night, and who strive after Nirvâna, their passions will come to an end.

227.

This is an old saying, O Atula, this is not only of to-day: "They blame him who sits silent, they blame him who speaks much, they also blame him who says little; there is no one on earth who is not blamed.

228.

There never was, there never will be, nor is there

(227.) It appears from the commentary that 'porânam' and 'ayyatanam' are neuters, referring to what happened formerly and what happens to-day, and that they are not to be taken as adjectives referring to 'âsînam,' etc. The commentator must have read 'atula' instead of 'atulam,' and he explains it as the name of a pupil whom Gautama addressed by that name. This may be so (see note to verse 166); but 'atula' may also be taken in the sense of incomparable (Mahâbh. xiii. 1937), and in that case we ought to supply, with Professor Weber, some such word as 'saw' or 'saying.'

now, a man who is always blamed, or a man who is always praised.

229, 230.

But he whom those who discriminate praise continually day after day, as without blemish, wise, rich in knowledge and virtue, who would dare to blame him, like a coin made of gold from the *G*ambû river? Even the gods praise him, he is praised even by Brahman.

231.

Beware of bodily anger, and control thy body! Leave the sins of the body, and with thy body practise virtue!

232.

Beware of the anger of the tongue, and control thy tongue! Leave the sins of the tongue, and practise virtue with thy tongue!

233.

Beware of the anger of the mind, and control thy mind! Leave the sins of the mind, and practise virtue with thy mind!

234.

The wise who control their body, who control their tongue, the wise who control their mind, are indeed well controlled.

(230.) The Brahman worlds are higher than the Deva worlds as the Brahman is higher than a Deva; (see Hardy, 'Manual,' p. 25; Burnouf, Introduction, pp. 134, 184.)

CHAPTER XVIII.

IMPURITY.

235.

Thou art now like a sear leaf, the messengers of Death (Yama) have come near to thee; thou standest at the door of thy departure, and thou hast no provision for thy journey.

236.

Make thyself an island, work hard, be wise! When thy impurities are blown away, and thou art free from guilt, thou wilt enter into the heavenly world of the Elect (Ariya).

237.

Thy life has come to an end, thou art come near to Death (Yama), there is no resting-place for thee

---

(235.) 'Uyyoga' seems to mean 'departure.' (See Buddhaghosha's commentary on verse 152, p. 319, l. 1; Fausböll, 'Five Gâtakas,' p. 35.

(236.) An 'island,' for a drowning man to save himself. (See verse 25.) 'Dipamkara' is the name of one of the former Buddhas, and it is also used as an appellative of the Buddha.

on the road, and thou hast no provision for thy journey.

238.

Make thyself an island, work hard, be wise! When thy impurities are blown away, and thou art free from guilt, thou wilt not enter again into birth and decay.

239.

Let a wise man blow off the impurities of his soul, as a smith blows off the impurities of silver, one by one, little by little, and from time to time.

240.

Impurity arises from the iron, and, having arisen from it, it destroys it; thus do a transgressor's own works lead him to the evil path.

241.

The taint of prayers is non-repetition; the taint of houses, non-repair; the taint of the body is sloth, the taint of a watchman thoughtlessness.

242.

Bad conduct is the taint of woman, greediness the taint of a benefactor; tainted are all evil ways, in this world and in the next.

243.

But there is a taint worse than all taints, ignorance is the greatest taint. O mendicants! throw off that taint, and become taintless!

244.

Life is easy to live for a man who is without shame, a crow hero, a mischief-maker, an insulting, bold, and wretched fellow.

245.

But life is hard to live for a modest man, who always looks for what is pure, who is disinterested, quiet, spotless, and intelligent.

246.

He who destroys life, who speaks untruth, who takes in this world what is not given him, who takes another man's wife;

247.

And the man who gives himself to drinking intoxicating liquors, he, even in this world, digs up his own root.

248.

O man, know this, that the unrestrained are in a bad state; take care that greediness and vice do not bring thee to grief for a long time!

(244.) 'Pakkhandin' is identified by Dr. Fausböll with 'praskandin,' one who jumps forward, insults, or, as Buddhaghosha explains it, one who meddles with other people's business, an interloper. At all events, it is a term of reproach, and, as it would seem, of theological reproach.

(246.) On the five principal commandments which are recapitulated in verses 246 and 247, see Parables, p. 153.

(248.) Cf. Mahábhárata, xii. 4055, 'yeshām vrittis ka samyatá.' See also v. 307.

249.

The world gives according to their faith or according to their pleasure: if a man frets about the food and the drink given to others, he will find no rest either by day or by night.

250.

He in whom that feeling is destroyed, and taken out with the very root, finds rest by day and by night.

251.

There is no fire like passion, there is no shark like hatred, there is no snare like folly, there is no torrent like greed.

252.

The fault of others is easily perceived, but that of oneself is difficult to perceive; the faults of others one lays open as much as possible, but one's own fault one hides, as a cheat hides the bad die from the gambler.

(249.) This verse has evidently regard to the feelings of the Bhikshus or mendicants who receive either much or little, and who are exhorted not to be envious if others receive more than they themselves. Several of the Parables illustrate this feeling.

(251.) Dr. Fausböll translates 'gaho' by 'captivitas,' Dr. Weber by 'fetter.' I take it in the same sense as 'gráha' in Manu, vi. 78; and Buddhaghosha does the same, though he assigns to 'gráha' a more general meaning, viz. anything that seizes, whether an evil spirit (yakkha), a serpent (a*g*agara), or a crocodile (kumbhíla).

Greed or thirst is represented as a river in 'Lalita-vistara,' ed. Calc. p. 482, 'trish*n*á-nadi tivegá prasoshitá me *gñ*ánasúryena,' the wild river of thirst is dried up by the sun of my knowledge.

253.

If a man looks after the faults of others, and is always inclined to detract, his own weaknesses will grow, and he is far from the destruction of weakness.

254.

There is no path through the air, a man is not a Sramana by outward acts. The world delights in vanity, the Tathâgatas (the Buddhas) are free from vanity.

(253.) As to 'âsava,' 'weakness,' see note to v. 39.

(254.) I have translated this verse very freely, and not in accordance with Buddhagosha's commentary. Dr. Fausböll proposed to translate: 'No one who is outside the Buddhist community can walk through the air, but only a Sramana;' and the same view is taken by Professor Weber, though he arrives at it by a different construction. Now it is perfectly true that the idea of magical powers (riddhi) which enable saints to walk through the air, etc., occurs in the Dhammapada, see v. 175, note. But the Dhammapada may contain earlier and later verses, and in that case our verse might be an early protest on the part of Buddha against the belief in such miraculous powers. We know how Buddha himself protested against his disciples being called upon to perform vulgar miracles. "I command my disciples not to work miracles,' he said, 'but to hide their good deeds, and to show their sins." (Burnouf, Introd. p. 170.) It would be in harmony with this sentiment if we translated our verse as I have done. As to 'bahira,' I should take it in the sense of 'external,' as opposed to 'adhyâtmika,' or 'internal;' and the meaning would be, a 'Sramana is not a Sramana by outward acts, but by his heart.'

'Prapanka,' which I have here translated by 'vanity,' seems to include the whole host of human weaknesses; cf. v. 196, where it is explained by 'tamhâditthimânapapañka;' in our verse by 'tamhâdisu papañkesu.' (Cf. Lal. Vist. p. 564, 'anâlayam nishprapañkam anutpâdam asambhavam (dharmakakram).') As to 'Tathâgata,' a name of Buddha, cf. Burnouf, Introd. p. 75.

255.

There is no path through the air, a man is not a *S*ramana by outward acts. No creatures are eternal; but the awakened (Buddha) are never shaken.

(259.) 'Sa*m*khârâ' for 'sa*m*skâra;' cf. note to v. 203.

CHAPTER XIX.

THE JUST.

256, 257.

A man is not a just judge if he carries a matter by violence; no, he who distinguishes both right and wrong, who is learned and leads others, not by violence, but by law and equity, he who is a guardian of the law and intelligent, he is called Just.

258.

A man is not learned because he talks much; he who is patient, free from hatred and fear, he is called learned.

259.

A man is not a supporter of the law because he talks much; even if a man has learnt little, but sees the law bodily, he is a supporter of the law, a man who never neglects the law.

(259.) Buddhaghosha here takes law (dhamma) in the sense of the four great truths, see note to v. 190. Could 'dhammam kâyena passati' mean, he observes the law in his acts? Hardly, if we compare expressions like 'dhammam vipassato,' v. 373.

260.

A man is not an elder because his head is grey; his age may be ripe, but he is called 'Old-in-vain.'

261.

He in whom there is truth, virtue, love, restraint, moderation, he who is free from impurity and is wise, he is called an 'Elder.'

262.

An envious, greedy, dishonest man does not become respectable by means of much talking only, or by the beauty of his complexion.

263.

He in whom all this is destroyed, taken out with the very root, he, freed from hatred and wise, is called 'Respectable.'

264.

Not by tonsure does an undisciplined man who speaks falsehood, become a *Sramana*; can a man be a *Sramana* who is still held captive by desire and greediness?

265.

He who always quiets the evil, whether small or large, he is called a *Sramana* (a quiet man), because he has quieted all evil.

(265.) This is a curious etymology, because it shows that at the time when this verse was written, the original meaning of '*sramana*' had been forgotten. '*Sramana*' meant originally, in the language of the Brahmans, a man who performed hard penances, from '*sram*,' to work hard, etc. When it became the name

266.

A man is not a mendicant (Bhikshu), simply because he asks others for alms; he who adopts the whole law is a Bhikshu, not he who only begs.

267.

He who is above good and evil, who is chaste, who with knowledge passes through the world, he indeed is called a Bhikshu.

268, 269.

A man is not a Muni because he observes silence (mona, *i.e.* mauna), if he is foolish and ignorant; but the wise who, taking the balance, chooses the good and avoids evil, he is a 'Muni,' and is a 'Muni' thereby; he who in this world weighs both sides is called a 'Muni.'

270.

A man is not an Elect (Ariya) because he injures living creatures; because he has pity on all living creatures, therefore is a man called 'Ariya.'

---

of the Buddhist ascetics, the language had changed, and 'sramana' was pronounced 'samana.' Now there is another Sanskrit root, 'sam,' to quiet, which in Páli becomes likewise 'sam,' and from this root 'sam,' to quiet, and not from 'sram,' to tire, did the popular etymology of the day and the writer of our verse derive the title of the Buddhist priests. The original form 'sramana' became known to the Greeks as Σαρμᾶναι, that of 'samana' as Σαμαναῖοι; the former through Megasthenes, the latter through Bardesanes, 80 60 B.C. (See Lassen, 'Indische Alterthumskunde,' ii. 700.) The Chinese 'Shamen' and the Tungusian 'Shamen' come from the same source, though the latter is sometimes doubted.

(266-270.) The etymologies here given of the ordinary titles of

271, 272.

Not only by discipline and vows, not only by much learning, not by entering into a trance, not by sleeping alone, do I earn the happiness of release which no worldling can know. A Bhikshu receives confidence when he has reached the complete destruction of all desires!

---

the followers of Buddha are entirely fanciful, and are curious only as showing how the people who spoke Pâli had lost the etymological consciousness of their language. A 'Bhikshu' is a beggar, *i.e.* a Buddhist friar who has left his family and lives entirely on alms. 'Muni' is a sage, hence 'Sâkya-muni,' the name of Gautama. 'Muni' comes from 'man,' to think, and from 'muni' comes 'mauna,' silence. 'Ariya,' again, is the general name of those who embrace a religious life. It meant originally 'respectable, noble.' In v. 270 it seems as if the writer wished to guard against deriving 'ariya' from 'ari,' enemy. See note to v. 22.

(272.) The last line is obscure, because the commentary is imperfect.

CHAPTER XX.

THE WAY.

273.

The best of ways is the Eightfold; the best of truths the Four Words; the best of virtues passionlessness; the best of men he who has eyes to see.

274.

This is the way, there is no other that leads to the purifying of intelligence. Go ye on this way! Everything else is the deceit of Mâra (the tempter).

275.

If you go on this way, you will make an end of pain!

(273.) The eight-fold or eight-membered way is the technical term for the way by which Nirvâna is attained. (See Burnouf, 'Lotus,' 519.) This very way constitutes the fourth of the Four Truths, or the four words of truth, viz. Duḥkha, pain; Samudaya, origin; Nirodha, destruction; Mârga, road. ('Lotus,' p. 517.) See note to v. 178. For another explanation of the Mârga, or way, see Hardy, 'Eastern Monachism,' p. 280.

(275.) The 'salyas,' arrows or thorns, are the 'sokasalya,' the arrows of grief. Buddha himself is called 'mahâsalya-hartâ,' the great remover of thorns. (Lalita-vistara, p. 550; Mahâbh. xii. 5616.)

The way was preached by me, when I had understood the removal of the thorns (in the flesh).

276.

You yourself must make an effort. The Tathâgatas (Buddhas) are only preachers. The thoughtful who enter the way are freed from the bondage of Mâra.

277.

'All created things perish,' he who knows and sees this becomes passive in pain; this is the way to purity.

278.

'All creatures are grief and pain,' he who knows and sees this becomes passive in pain; this is the way to purity.

279.

'All forms are unreal,' he who knows and sees this becomes passive in pain; this is the way to purity.

280.

He who does not rise when it is time to rise, who, though young and strong, is full of sloth, whose will and thought are weak, that lazy and idle man will never find the way to knowledge.

281.

Watching his speech, well restrained in mind, let

(277.) See v. 255.
(278.) See v. 203.
(279.) 'Dhamma' is here explained, like 'samkhâra,' as the five 'khandha,' *i. e.* as what constitutes a living body.

a man never commit any wrong with his body! Let a man but keep these three roads of action clear, and he will achieve the way which is taught by the wise.

282.

Through zeal knowledge is gotten, through lack of zeal knowledge is lost; let a man who knows this double path of gain and loss thus place himself that knowledge may grow.

283.

Cut down the whole forest of lust, not the tree! From lust springs fear. When you have cut down every tree and every shrub, then, Bhikshus, you will be free!

284.

So long as the love of man towards women, even the smallest, is not destroyed, so long is his mind in bondage, as the calf that drinks milk is to its mother.

285.

Cut out the love of self, like an autumn lotus, with thy hand! Cherish the road of peace. Nirvâṇa has been shown by Sugata (Buddha).

286.

Here I shall dwell in the rain, here in winter and

(282.) 'Bhûri' was rightly translated 'intelligentia' by Dr. Fausböll. Dr. Weber renders it by 'Gedeihen,' but the commentator distinctly explains it as 'vast knowledge,' and in the technical sense the word occurs after 'vidyâ' and before 'midhâ,' in the 'Lalita Vistara,' p. 541.

(283.) A pun, 'vana' meaning both 'lust' and 'forest.'

(286.) 'Antarâya,' according to the commentator, 'givitânta-

summer,' thus meditates the fool, and does not think of his death.

287.

Death comes and carries off that man, surrounded by children and flocks, his mind distracted, as a flood carries off a sleeping village.

288.

Sons are no help, nor a father, nor relations; there is no help from kinsfolk for one whom Death has seized.

289.

A wise and good man who knows the meaning of this, should quickly clear the way that leads to Nirvâna.

---

râya,' *i.e.* interitus, death. In Sanskrit, 'antarita' is used in the sense of 'vanished' or 'perished.'

(287.) See notes to v. 47, and cf. Mahâbh. xii. 9944, 6540.

CHAPTER XXI.

MISCELLANEOUS.

290.

If by leaving a small pleasure one sees a great pleasure, let a wise man leave the small pleasure, and look to the great.

291.

He who, by causing pain to others, wishes to obtain pleasure himself, he, entangled in the bonds of hatred, will never be free from hatred.

292.

What ought to be done is neglected, what ought not to be done is done; the sins of unruly, thoughtless people are always increasing.

293.

But they whose whole watchfulness is always directed to their body, who do not follow what ought not to be done, and who steadfastly do what ought to be done, the sins of such watchful and wise people will come to an end.

294.

A true Brâhmana, though he has killed father and mother, and two valiant kings, though he has destroyed a kingdom with all its subjects, is free from guilt.

295.

A true Brâhmana, though he has killed father and mother, and two holy kings, and even a fifth man, is free from guilt.

296.

The disciples of Gotama (Buddha) are always well awake, and their thoughts day and night are always set on Buddha.

297.

The disciples of Gotama are always well awake, and their thoughts day and night are always set on the Law.

298.

The disciples of Gotama are always well awake, and their thoughts day and night are always set on the Church.

299.

The disciples of Gotama are always well awake, and their thoughts day and night are always set on their body.

(294, 295.) These two verses are either meant to show that a truly holy man who by accident commits all these crimes is guiltless, or they refer to some particular event in Buddha's history. The commentator is so startled that he explains them allegorically. The meaning of 'veyyaggha' I do not understand.

300.

The disciples of Gotama are always well awake, and their mind day and night always delights in compassion.

301.

The disciples of Gotama are always well awake, and their mind day and night always delights in meditation.

302.

The hard parting, the hard living alone, the uninhabitable houses are painful; painful is the company with men who are not our equals; subject to pain are the travelling friars; therefore let no man be a travelling friar, and he will not be subject to pain.

(302.) Unless this verse formed part of a miscellaneous chapter, I should hardly have ventured to translate it as I have. If the verse means anything, it means that parting with one's friends, living in the wilderness, or in wretched hovels, or travelling about from place to place, homeless and dependent on casual charity, is nothing but pain and grief, and, we should say, according to the author's opinion, useless. In other verses, on the contrary, this very life, this parting with all one holds dear, living in solitude, and depending on alms, is represented as the only course that can lead a man to wisdom, peace, and Nirvâna. Such contradictions, strange as they sound, are not uncommon in the literature of the Brahmans. Here, too, works are frequently represented as indispensable to salvation, and yet, in other places, and from a higher point of view, these very works are condemned as useless, nay, even as a hindrance in a man's progress to real perfection. It is possible that the same view found advocates even in the early days of Buddhism, and that, though performing the ordinary duties, and enjoying the ordinary pleasures of life, a man might consider that he was a truer disciple of Buddha than the dreamy inhabitant of a Vihâra, or the mendicant friar who every morning

303.

Whatever place a faithful, virtuous, celebrated, and wealthy man chooses, there he is respected.

304.

Good people shine from afar, like the snowy mountains; bad people are not seen, like arrows shot by night.

305.

He who, without ceasing, practises the duty of eating alone and sleeping alone, he, subduing himself, alone will rejoice in the destruction of all desires, as if living in a forest.

---

called for alms at the layman's door (cf. v. 141-142). The next verse confirms the view which I have taken.

Should it not be 'asamânasamvâso,' *i. e.* living with people who are not one's equals, which was the case in the Buddhist communities, and must have been much against the grain of the Hindus, accustomed, as they were, to live always among themselves, among their own relations, their own profession, their own caste? Living with his superiors is equally disagreeable to a Hindu as living with his inferiors. 'Asamâma,' unequal, might easily be mistaken for 'samâna,' proud.

(305.) I have translated this verse so as to bring it into something like harmony with the preceding verses. 'Vanânte,' according to a pun pointed out before (v. 283), means both 'in the end of a forest,' and 'in the end of desires.'

CHAPTER XXII.

THE DOWNWARD COURSE.

306.

He who says what is not, goes to hell; he also who, having done a thing, says I have not done it. After death both are equal, they are men with evil deeds in the next world.

307.

Many men whose shoulders are covered with the orange gown are ill-conditioned and unrestrained; such evil-doers by their evil deeds go to hell.

308.

Better it would be to swallow a heated iron ball,

(306.) I translate 'niraya' the exit, the downward course, the evil path, by 'hell,' because the meaning assigned to that ancient mythological name by Christian writers comes so near to the Buddhist idea of 'niraya,' that it is difficult not to believe in some actual contact between these two streams of thought. (See also Mahábh. xii. 7176.) 'Abhûtavâdin' is mentioned as a name of Buddha, 'sarvasamskârapratisuddhatvât' (Lal. Vist. p. 555.)

like flaring fire, than that a bad unrestrained fellow should live on the charity of the land.

309.

Four things does a reckless man gain who covets his neighbour's wife,—a bad reputation, an uncomfortable bed, thirdly, punishment, and lastly, hell.

310.

There is bad reputation, and the evil way (to hell) there is the short pleasure of the frightened in the arms of the frightened, and the king imposes heavy punishment; therefore let no man think of his neighbour's wife.

311.

As a grass-blade, if badly grasped, cuts the arm, badly-practised asceticism leads to hell.

312.

An act carelessly performed, a broken vow, and hesitating obedience to discipline, all this brings no great reward.

(308.) The charity of the land, *i.e.* the alms given, from a sense of religious duty, to every mendicant that asks for it.

(309–10.) The four things mentioned in verse 309 seem to be repeated in verse 310. Therefore, 'apuññalâbha,' bad fame, is the same in both: 'gatî pâpikâ' must be 'niraya;' 'danda' must be 'nindâ,' and 'ratî thokikâ' explains the 'anikâmaseyyam.' Buddhagosha takes the same view of the meaning of 'anikâmaseyya,' *i.e.* 'yathâ ikkhati evam seyyam alabhitvâ, anikkhitam parittakam eva kâlam seyyam labhati,' not obtaining the rest as he wishes it, he obtains it, as he does not wish it, *i. e.* for a short time only.

313.

If anything is to be done, let a man do it, let him attack it vigorously! A careless pilgrim only scatters the dust of his passions more widely.

314.

An evil deed is better left undone, for a man repents of it afterwards; a good deed is better done, for having done it, one does not repent.

315.

Like a well-guarded frontier fort, with defences within and without, so let a man guard himself. Not a moment should escape, for they who allow the right moment to pass, suffer pain when they are in hell.

316.

They who are ashamed of what they ought not to be ashamed of, and are not ashamed of what they ought to be ashamed of, such men, embracing false doctrines, enter the evil path.

317.

They who fear when they ought not to fear, and fear not when they ought to fear, such men, embracing false doctrines, enter the evil path.

318.

They who forbid when there is nothing to be forbidden, and forbid not when there is something to be

---

(313.) As to 'raga' meaning 'dust' and 'passion,' see 'Parables,' pp. 65 and 66.

forbidden, such men, embracing false doctrines, enter the evil path.

319.

They who know what is forbidden as forbidden, and what is not forbidden as not forbidden, such men, embracing the true doctrine, enter the good path.

CHAPTER XXIII.

THE ELEPHANT.

320.

Silently shall I endure abuse as the elephant in battle endures the arrow sent from the bow: for the world is ill-natured.

321.

A tamed elephant they lead to battle, the king mounts a tamed elephant; the tamed is the best among men, he who silently endures abuse.

322.

Mules are good, if tamed, and noble Sindhu horses, and elephants with large tusks; but he who tames himself is better still.

(320.) The elephant is with the Buddhists the emblem of endurance and self-restraint. Thus Buddha himself is called 'Nâga,' the Elephant (Lal. Vist. p. 553), or 'Mahânâga,' the great Elephant (Lal. Vist. p. 553), and in one passage (Lal. Vist. p. 554) the reason of this name is given, by stating that Buddha was 'sudânta,' well-tamed, like an elephant.

Cf. Manu, vi. 47, 'ativâdâms titiksheta.'

323.

For with these animals does no man reach the untrodden country (Nirvâna), where a tamed man goes on a tamed animal, viz. on his own well-tamed self.

324.

The elephant called Dhamapâlaka, his temples running with sap, and difficult to hold, does not eat a morsel when bound; the elephant longs for the elephant grove.

325.

If a man becomes fat and a great eater, if he is sleepy and rolls himself about, that fool, like a hog fed on wash, is born again and again.

326.

This mind of mine went formerly wandering about

(323.) I read, as suggested by Dr. Fausböll, 'yath' attanâ sudantena danto dantena ga*kkh*ati.' (Cf. v. 160.) The India Office MS. reads ' na hi etehi *th*ânehi ga*kkh*eya agatam disam, yath' attânam sudantena danto dantena ga*kkh*ati.' As to '*th*ânehi' instead of 'yânehi,' see v. 224.

(326.) 'Yoniso,' *i. e.* 'yonisah,' is rendered by Dr. Fausböll 'sapientiâ,' but the reference which he gives to Hema*k*andra (ed. Boehtlingk and Rieu, p. 281) shows clearly that it meant 'origin,' or 'cause.' 'Yoniso' occurs frequently as a mere adverb, meaning thoroughly, radically (Dhammap. p. 359), and 'yoniso manasikâra' (Dhammap. p. 110) means 'taking to heart' or 'minding thoroughly.' In the Lal. Vist. p. 41, the commentator has clearly mistaken 'yonisah' changing it to 'ye'niso,' and explaining it by 'yamanisam,' whereas M. Foucaux has rightly translated it by 'depuis l'origine.' Professor Weber imagines he has discovered in 'yonisah' a *double-entendre*, but even grammar would show that our author is innocent of it.

as it liked, as it listed, as it pleased; but I shall now hold it in thoroughly, as the rider who holds the hook holds in the furious elephant.

327.

Be not thoughtless, watch your thoughts! Draw yourself out of the evil way, like an elephant sunk in mud.

328.

If a man find a prudent companion who walks with him, is wise, and lives soberly, he may walk with him, overcoming all dangers, happy, but considerate.

329.

If a man find no prudent companion who walks with him, is wise, and lives soberly, let him walk alone, like a king who has left his conquered country behind,—like a lonely elephant.

330.

It is better to live alone, there is no companionship with a fool; let a man walk alone, let him commit no sin, with few wishes, like the lonely elephant.

331.

If an occasion arises, friends are pleasant; enjoyment is pleasant if it is mutual; a good work is pleasant in the hour of death; the giving up of all grief is pleasant.

332.

Pleasant is the state of a mother, pleasant the state

(332.) The commentator throughout takes these words, like

of a father, pleasant the state of a Sramana, pleasant the state of a Brâhmana.

333.

Pleasant is virtue lasting to old age, pleasant is a faith firmly rooted; pleasant is attainment of intelligence, pleasant is avoiding of sins.

'matteyyatâ,' etc., to signify, not the status of a mother, or maternity, but reverence shown to a mother.

CHAPTER XXIV.

THIRST.

334.

The thirst of a thoughtless man grows like a creeper; he runs hither and thither, like a monkey seeking fruit in the forest.

335.

Whom this fierce thirst overcomes, full of poison, in this world, his sufferings increase like the abounding Bîrana grass.

336.

He who overcomes this fierce thirst, difficult to be conquered in this world, sufferings fall off from him, like water-drops from a lotus leaf.

337.

This salutary word I tell you, as many as are here come together: 'Dig up the root of thirst, as he who wants the sweet-scented Usîra root must dig up the Bîrana grass, that Mâra (the tempter) may not

---

(335.) Virana grass is the *Andropogon muricatum*, and the scented root of it is called 'usîra' (cf. v. 337.)

crush you again and again, as the stream crushes the reeds.'

338.

As a tree is firm as long as its root is safe, and grows again even though it has been cut down, thus, unless the yearnings of thirst are destroyed, this pain (of life) will return again and again.

339.

He whose desire for pleasure runs strong in the thirty-six channels, the waves will carry away that misguided man, viz. his desires which are set on passion.

340.

The channels run everywhere, the creeper (of passion) stands sprouting; if you see the creeper springing up, cut its root by means of knowledge.

341.

A creature's pleasures are extravagant and luxurious; sunk in lust and looking for pleasure, men undergo (again and again) birth and decay.

342.

Men, driven on by thirst, run about like a snared

(338.) On 'Anusaya,' *i.e.* 'anusaya,' see Wassiljew, 'Der Buddhismus,' p. 210, *seq.*

(339.) The thirty-six channels, or passions, which are divided by the commentator into eighteen external and eighteen internal, are explained by Burnouf ('Lotus,' p. 649), from a gloss of the '*G*ina-ala*m*kâra:' "L'indication précise des affections dont un Buddha acte indépendant, affections qui sont au nombre de dix-huit, nous est fourni par la glose d'un livre appartenant aux Buddhistes de Ceylan," etc.

'Vâhâ,' which Dr. Fausböll translates by 'equi,' may be 'vahâ,' unda.

hare; held in fetters and bonds, they undergo pain for a long time, again and again.

343.

Men, driven on by thirst, run about like a snared hare; let therefore the mendicant who desires passionlessness for himself, drive out thirst!

344.

He who in a country without forests (*i.e.* after having reached Nirvâ*n*a) gives himself over to forest-life (*i.e.* to lust), and who, when removed from the forest (*i.e.* from lust), runs to the forest (*i.e.* to lust), look at that man! though free, he runs into bondage.

345.

Wise people do not call that a strong fetter which is made of iron, wood, or hemp; far stronger is the care for precious stones and rings, for sons and a wife.

346.

That fetter do wise people call strong which drags down, yields, but is difficult to undo; after having cut this at last, people enter upon their pilgrimage, free from cares, and leaving desires and pleasures behind.

(344.) This verse seems again full of puns, all connected with the twofold meaning of 'vana,' forest and lust. By replacing 'forest' by 'lust,' we may translate: "He who, when free from lust, gives himself up to lust, who, when removed from lust runs into lust, look at that man," etc. 'Nibbana,' though with a short a, may be intended to remind the hearer of Nibbâna.

(345.) 'Apekhâ, apekshâ,' care; see Manu, vi. 41, 49.

(346.) 'Paribba*g*,' *i.e.* 'parivra*g*;' see Manu, vi. 41.

347.

Those who are slaves to passions, run up and down the stream (of desires) as a spider runs up and down the web which he has made himself; when they have cut this, people enter upon their pilgrimage, free from cares, leaving desires and pleasures behind.

348.

Give up what is before, give up what is behind, give up what is in the middle, when thou goest to the other shore of existence; if thy mind is altogether free, thou wilt not again enter into birth and decay.

349.

If a man is tossed about by doubts, full of strong passions, and yearning only for what is delightful, his thirst will grow more and more, and he will indeed make his fetters strong.

350.

If a man delights in quieting doubts, and, always reflecting, dwells on what is not delightful, he certainly will remove, nay, he will cut the fetter of Mâra.

351.

He who has obtained rest, who does not tremble,

(347.) The commentator explains the simile of the spider as follows: "As a spider, after having made its thread-web, sits in the middle or the centre, and after killing with a violent rush a butterfly or a fly which has fallen in its circle, drinks its juice, returns, and sits again in the same place, in the same manner creatures who are given to passions, depraved by hatred, and maddened by wrath, run along the stream of thirst which they have made themselves, and cannot cross it," etc.

who is without thirst and without blemish, he has broken all the thorns of life: this will be his last body.

352.

He who is without thirst and without affection, who understands the words and their interpretation, who knows the order of letters (those which are before and which are after), he has received his last body, he is called the great sage, the great man.

353.

'I have conquered all, I know all, in all conditions of life I am free from taint; I have left all, and through the destruction of thirst I am free; having learnt myself, whom shall I teach?'

354.

The gift of the law exceeds all gifts; the sweetness of the law exceeds all sweetness; the delight in the law exceeds all delights; the extinction of thirst overcomes all pain.

355.

Pleasures destroy the foolish, if they look not for the other shore; the foolish by his thirst for pleasures destroys himself, as if he were his own enemy.

(352.) As to 'Nirutti,' and its technical meaning among the Buddhists, see Burnouf, 'Lotus,' p. 841. Fausböll translates 'niruttis vocabulorum peritus,' which may be right. Could not 'sannipâta' mean 'samhitâ' or 'sannikarsha'? 'Sannipâta' occurs in the Sâkala-prâtisâkhya, but with a different meaning.

(354.) The 'dhammadâna,' or gift of the law, is the technical term for instruction in the Buddhist religion. (See 'Parables,' p. 160, where the story of the 'Sakkadevarâga' is told, and where a free rendering of our verse is given.)

356.

The fields are damaged by weeds, mankind is damaged by passion: therefore a gift bestowed on the passionless brings great reward.

357.

The fields are damaged by weeds; mankind is damaged by hatred: therefore a gift bestowed on those who do not hate brings great reward.

358.

The fields are damaged by weeds, mankind is damaged by vanity: therefore a gift bestowed on those who are free from vanity brings great reward.

359.

The fields are damaged by weeds, mankind is damaged by wishing: therefore a gift bestowed on those who are free from wishes brings great reward.

clvii

CHAPTER XXV.

THE BHIKSHU (MENDICANT).

360.

Restraint in the eye is good, good is restraint in the ear, in the nose restraint is good, good is restraint in the tongue.

361.

In the body restraint is good, good is restraint in speech, in thought restraint is good, good is restraint in all things. A Bhikshu, restrained in all things, is freed from all pain.

362.

He who controls his hand, he who controls his feet,

(362.) 'Agghattarata,' *i. e.* 'adhyâtmarata,' is an expression which we may take in its natural sense, in which case it would simply mean, delighting inwardly. But 'adhyâtmarata' has a technical sense in Sanskrit and with the Brahmans. They use it in the sense of delighting in the Adhyâtman, *i. e.* the Supreme Self, or Brahman. (See 'Manu,' vi. 49, and Kullûka's commentary. As the Buddhists do not recognize a Supreme Self or Brahman, they cannot use the word in its Brahmanical sense, and thus we find that Buddhaghosha explains it as "delighting in meditation on the Kammasthâna, a Buddhist formulary, whether externally or internally." I am not certain of the exact mean-

he who controls his speech, he who is well controlled, he who delights inwardly, who is collected, who is solitary and content, him they call Bhikshu.

363.

The Bhikshu who controls his mouth, who speaks wisely and calmly, who teaches the meaning and the Law, his word is sweet.

364.

He who dwells in the Law, delights in the Law, meditates on the Law, follows the Law, that Bhikshu will never fall away from the true Law.

365.

Let him not despise what he has received, nor ever envy others: a mendicant who envies others does not obtain peace of mind.

366.

A Bhikshu who, though he receives little, does not

---

ing of Buddhaghosha's words, but whatever they mean, it is quite clear that he does not take 'adhyâtmarata' in the Brahmanical sense. The question then arises who used the term first, and who borrowed it, and here it would seem, considering the intelligible growth of the word in the philosophical systems of the Brahmans, that the priority belongs for once to the Brahmans.

(363.) On 'artha' and 'dharma,' see Stanislas Julien, 'Les Avadânas,' i. 217, note: "Les quatre connaissances sont; 1° la connaissance du sens (artha); 2° la connaissance de la Loi (dharma); 3° la connaissance des explications (niroukti); 4° la connaissance de l'intelligence (prátibhâna)."

(364.) The expression 'dhammârâmo,' having his garden or delight (Lustgarten) in the Law, is well matched by the Brahmanic expression 'ekârâma,' *i. e.* 'nirdvandva.' (Mahâbh. xiii. 1930.)

despise what he has received, even the gods will praise him, if his life is pure, and if he is not slothful.

367.

He who never identifies himself with his body and soul, and does not grieve over what is no more, he indeed is called a Bhikshu.

368.

The Bhikshu who acts with kindness, who is calm in the doctrine of Buddha, will reach the quiet place (Nirvâṇa), cessation of natural desires, and happiness.

369.

O Bhikshu, empty this boat! if emptied, it will go quickly; having cut off passion and hatred, thou wilt go to Nirvâṇa.

370.

Cut off the five (senses), leave the five, rise above the five? A Bhikshu, who has escaped from the five fetters, he is called Oghatiṇṇa, "Saved from the flood."

371.

Meditate, O Bhikshu, and be not heedless! Do not direct thy thought to what gives pleasure! that

---

(367.) 'Nâmarûpa' is here used again in its technical sense of body and soul, neither of which is 'âtman,' or self. 'Asat,' what is not, may therefore mean the same as 'nâmarûpa,' or we may take it in the sense of what is no more, as, for instance, the beauty or youth of the body, the vigour of the mind, etc.

(371.) The swallowing of hot iron balls is considered as a punishment in hell; see v. 308. Professor Weber has perceived

thou mayest not for thy heedlessness have to swallow the iron ball (in hell), and that thou mayest not cry out when burning, "This is pain."

372.

Without knowledge there is no meditation, without meditation there is no knowledge: he who has knowledge and meditation is near unto Nirvâna.

373.

A Bhikshu who has entered his empty house, and whose mind is tranquil, feels a more than human delight when he sees the law clearly.

374.

As soon as he has considered the origin and destruction of the elements (khandha) of the body, he finds happiness and joy which belong to those who know the immortal (Nirvâna).

375.

And this is the beginning here for a wise Bhikshu: watchfulness over the senses, contentedness, restraint under the Law; keep noble friends whose life is pure, and who are not slothful.

376.

Let him live in charity, let him be perfect in his duties; then in the fulness of delight he will make an end of suffering.

---

the right meaning of 'bhavassu,' which can only be 'bhâvayasva,' but I doubt whether the rest of his rendering is right, 'Do not swallow by accident an iron ball.'

377.

As the Vassikâ-plant sheds its withered flowers, men should shed passion and hatred, O ye Bhikshus!

378.

The Bhikshu whose body and tongue and mind are quieted, who is collected, and has rejected the baits of the world, he is called Quiet.

379.

Rouse thyself by thyself, examine thyself by thyself, thus self-protected and attentive wilt thou live happily, O Bhikshu!

380.

For self is the lord of self, self is the refuge of self; therefore curb thyself as the merchant curbs a good horse.

381.

The Bhikshu, full of delight, who is calm in the doctrine of Buddha will reach the quiet place (Nirvâna), cessation of natural desires, and happiness.

382.

He who, even as a young Bhikshu, applies himself to the doctrine of Buddha, brightens up this world, like the moon when free from clouds.

(381.) See verse 368.

CHAPTER XXVI.

THE BRÂHMAṆA.

383.

Stop the stream valiantly, drive away the desires, O Brâhmaṇa! When you have understood the destruction of all that was made, you will understand that which was not made.

384.

If the Brâhmaṇa has reached the other shore in both laws (in restraint and contemplation), all bonds vanish from him who has obtained knowledge.

385.

He for whom there is neither this nor that shore, nor both, him, the fearless and unshackled, I call indeed a Brâhmaṇa.

386.

He who is thoughtful, blameless, settled, dutiful,

(385.) The exact meaning of the two shores is not quite clear, and the commentator who takes them in the sense of internal and external organs of sense, can hardly be right. See v. 86.

without passions, and who has attained the highest end, him I call indeed a Brâhmana.

387.

The sun is bright by day, the moon shines by night, the warrior is bright in his armour, the Brâhmana is bright in his meditation; but Buddha, the Awakened, is bright with splendour day and night.

388.

Because a man is rid of evil, therefore he is called Brâhmana; because he walks quietly, therefore he is called Sramana; because he has sent away his own impurities, therefore he is called Pravragita (a pilgrim).

389.

No one should attack a Brâhmana, but no Brâhmana (if attacked) should let himself fly at his aggressor! Woe to him who strikes a Brâhmana, more woe to him who flies at his aggressor!

390.

It advantages a Brâhmana not a little if he holds his mind back from the pleasures of life; when all wish to injure has vanished, pain will cease.

(388.) These would-be etymologies are again interesting as showing the decline of the etymological life of the spoken language of India at the time when such etymologies became possible. In order to derive 'Brâhmana' from 'váh,' it must have been pronounced 'bâhmano; 'váh,' to remove, occurs frequently in the Buddhistical Sanskrit. (Cf. Lal. Vist. p. 551, l. 1; 553, l. 7. See note to verse 265.)

(390.) I am afraid I have taken too much liberty with this verse. Dr. Fausböll translates: 'Non Brâhmanae hoc paulo me-

391.

Him I call indeed a Brâhmana who does not offend by body, word, or thought, and is controlled on these three points.

392.

After a man has once understood the Law as taught by the Well-awakened (Buddha), let him worship it carefully, as the Brâhmana worships the sacrificial fire.

393.

A man does not become a Brâhmana by his platted hair, by his family, or by both; in whom there is truth and righteousness, he is blessed, he is a Brâhmana.

394.

What is the use of platted hair, O fool! what of the raiment of goatskins? Within thee there is ravening, but the outside thou makest clean.

395.

The man who wears dirty raiments, who is emaciated and covered with veins, who lives alone in the forest, and meditates, him I call indeed a Brâhmana.

---

lius, quando retentio fit mentis a jucundis.' In the second verse he translates 'himsamano,' or 'himsamano,' by 'violenta mens;' Dr. Weber by 'der Geist der Schadsucht.' Might it be 'himsyamânah,' injured, and 'nivattati,' he is quiet, patient? 'Ahimsâmanah' would be, with the Buddhists, the spirit of love. (Luke xi. 39.)

(394.) I have not copied the language of the Bible more than I was justified in. The words are 'abbhantaran te gahanam, bâhiram parimaggasi,' interna est abyssus, externum mundas.

(395.) The expression 'Kisan dhamanisanthatam,' is the San-

CHAPTER XXVI.

396.

I do not call a man a Brâhmana because of his origin or of his mother. He may be called "Sir," and may be wealthy: but the poor, who is free from all attachments, him I call indeed a Brâhmana.

397.

He who has cut all fetters, and who never trembles, he who is independent and unshackled, him I call indeed a Brâhmana.

398.

He who has cut the girdle and the strap, the rope with all that pertains to it, he who has burst the bar, and is awakened, him I call indeed a Brâhmana.

399.

He who, though he has committed no offence, endures reproach, bonds, and stripes, him, strong in endurance and powerful, I call indeed a Brâhmana.

400.

He who is free from anger, dutiful, virtuous, without weakness, and subdued, who has received his last body, him I call indeed a Brâhmana.

---

skrit 'krisam dhamanisantatam,' the frequent occurrence of which in the Mahábhárata has been pointed out by Boehtlingk, s. v. dhamani. It looks more like a Brâhmanic than like a Buddhist phrase.

(399.) The exact meaning of 'balânika' is difficult to find. Does it mean, possessed of a strong army, or facing a force, or leading a force? The commentary alone could help us to decide.

401.

He who does not cling to pleasures, like water on a lotus leaf, like a mustard seed on the point of an awl, him I call indeed a Brâhma*n*a.

402.

He who, even here, knows the end of his suffering, has put down his burden, and is unshackled, him I call indeed a Brâhma*n*a.

403.

He whose knowledge is deep, who possesses wisdom, who knows the right way and the wrong, who has attained the highest end, him I call indeed a Brâhma*n*a.

404.

He who keeps aloof both from laymen and from mendicants, goes to no house to beg, and whose desires are small, him I call indeed a Brâhma*n*a.

405.

He who finds no fault with other beings, whether

(401.) 'Anokasâri' is translated by Dr. Fausböll 'sine domicilio grassantem;' by Dr. Weber, 'ohne Heim wandelt.' The commentator seems to support my translation. He says that a man who has no intercourse either with householders or with those who have left their houses, but may still dwell together in retirement from the world, is 'anâlaya*k*ara,' *i.e.* a man who goes to nobody's abode, in order to see, to hear, to talk, or to eat. He then explains 'anokasârin' by the same word, 'anâlaya*k*ârin,' *i.e.* a man who goes to nobody's residence for any purpose,—and in our case, I suppose, principally not for the purpose of begging.

weak or strong, who does not kill nor cause slaughter, him I call indeed a Brâhmaṇa.

406.

He who is tolerant with the intolerant, mild with fault-finders, free from passion among the passionate, him I call indeed a Brâhmaṇa.

407.

He from whom anger and hatred, pride and envy have dropt like a mustard seed from the point of an awl, him I call indeed a Brâhmaṇa.

408.

He who utters true speech, instructive and free from harshness, so that he offend no one, him I call indeed a Brâhmaṇa.

409.

He who takes nothing in the world that is not given him, be it long or short, small or large, good or bad, him I call indeed a Brâhmaṇa.

410.

He who fosters no desires for this world or for the next, has no inclinations, and is unshackled, him I call indeed a Brâhmaṇa.

411.

He who has no interests, and when he has under-

(411.) 'Akathaṃkathî' is explained by Buddhaghosha as meaning, free from doubt or hesitation. He also uses 'kathaṃkathâ'

stood (the truth), does not say How, how?—he who can dive into the Immortal, him I call indeed a Brâhmana.

412.

He who is above good and evil, above the bondage of both, free from grief, from sin, from impurity, him I call indeed a Brâhmana.

413.

He who is bright like the moon, pure, serene, and undisturbed, in whom all gaiety is extinct, him I call indeed a Brâhmana.

414.

He who has traversed this mazy, impervious world and its vanity, who is through, and has reached the other shore, is thoughtful, guileless, free from doubts, free from attachment, and content, him I call indeed a Brâhmana.

415.

He who, leaving all desires, travels about without a

---

in the sense of doubt (verse 414). In the Kâvyâdarsa, iii. 17, the commentator explains 'akatham' by 'kathârahitam, nirvivâdam,' which would mean, without a 'kathâ,' a speech, a story without contradiction, unconditionally. From our passage, however, it seems as if 'kathamkathâ' was a noun derived from 'kathamkathayati,' to say How, how? so that neither the first nor the second element had anything to do with 'kath,' to relate; and in that case 'akatham,' too, ought to be taken in the sense of 'without a Why.'

(412.) See verse 39. The distinction between good and evil vanishes when a man has retired from the world, and has ceased to act, longing only for deliverance.

home, in whom all concupiscence is extinct, him I call indeed a Brâhmana.

416.

He who, leaving all longings, travels about without a home, in whom all covetousness is extinct, him I call indeed a Brâhmana.

417.

He who, after leaving all bondage to men, has risen above all bondage to the gods, who is free from every bondage, him I call indeed a Brâhmana.

418.

He who has left what gives pleasure and what gives pain, is cold, and free from all germs (of renewed life), the hero who has conquered all the worlds, him I call indeed a Brâhmana.

419.

He who knows the destruction and the return of creatures everywhere, who is free from bondage, welfaring (Sugata), and awakened (Buddha), him I call indeed a Brâhmana.

420.

He whose way the gods do not know, nor spirits (Gandharvas), nor men, and whose passions are extinct, him, the venerable, I call indeed a Brâhmana.

421.

He who calls nothing his own, whether it be before, behind, or between, who is poor, and free from the love of the world, him I call indeed a Brâhmana.

422.

The manly, the noble, the hero, the great sage, the conqueror, the guileless, the master, the awakened, him I call indeed a Brâhmana.

423.

He who knows his former abodes, who sees heaven and hell, has reached the end of births, is perfect in knowledge and a sage, he whose perfections are all perfect, him I call indeed a Brâhmana.

PREFACE

(BY CAPTAIN ROGERS)

TO THE

TRANSLATION OF BUDDHAGHOSHA'S PARABLES.

The following translation of the Burmese version of the Parables of Buddhaghosha has been made from a work entitled, the Dhamma-Pada-Vatthu, or 'Stories about the Dhamma Pada.' In the translation I have followed the printed text of Latter's 'Selections from the Vernacular Boodhist Literature of Burmah,' collating it with a palm-leaf manuscript of the same work in the East-India Office library. The collating, however, has been of but little use, for though the two copies are in most parts identical or nearly so, yet in the obscure passages they almost invariably differ considerably, and one is rarely more intelligible than the other. Any sensible variation between the manuscript and the printed text will be found in the foot-notes. I have also marked those few passages which their impenetrable obscurity has compelled me to omit.

The difficulties under which a translator labours, owing to the careless transcribing of the native copyists, is well exemplified in the English translation of 'The Decisions of Princess Thudamasāri,' by the late Col. Sparks; another portion of Latter's 'Selections,' and a very amusing collection of stories, where the numerous emendations of the text, which the translator was compelled to make, are marked in the notes.

Although I have paraphrased as decently as possible many of the expressions employed in the original, yet the Oriental ideas of propriety are so different from those of Western nations that I found myself altogether unable, without completely sacrificing the sense, to do more than slightly tone down some of the passages.

I have to acknowledge the great advantage I have derived from collating my own translation with a close and very accurate translation of the same work by Captain Sheffield Grace, of H.M. 68th Regiment, which Professor Max Müller forwarded to me while I was revising my manuscript for the press.

H. T. R.

BUDDHAGHOSHA'S PARABLES.

I worship the Adorable who is worthy of all homage, who is radiant with the six glories, and the possessor of all wisdom.

CHAPTER I.

STORY OF *K*AKKHUPALA MAHATHERA.

THE most excellent Parā,[1] brilliant in his glory, free from all ignorance, beholding Nibbāna,[2] the end of the migration of the soul, lighted the lamp of the law of the good.

This law he preached during his residence at the *G*etavana monastery in the Sāvatthi country, illustrating it by an account of the Mahāthera[3] *K*akkhupāla.

At a former time there lived in the Sāvatthi country a T*h*ugyuè[4] named Mahâ-sva*nn*a. This T*h*ugyuè went out one day to bathe; on the road he saw a banyan-

---

[1] "The Lord," or "Master," *i.e.* Gotama, the founder of the Buddhist religion.

[2] Nibbāna is the last and unchangeable state of the soul, in which it is never more subject to transmigration,—the heaven of the Burmese Buddhists.

[3] Mahāthera means among the Burmese a Buddhist priest of ten years' standing or more; but here it signifies a distinguished disciple of Gotama.

[4] The wealthy class.

tree; thinking that there must dwell there a Nat[1] of great power, he cleared the space at the foot of the tree, made an offering of a flag,[2] a lighted lamp, flowers and perfumes, and prayed: "My lord Nat, if you will give me a son or a daughter, I will make you large offerings;" then he returned home.

At that very time the T*h*ugyuè's wife became pregnant, and the T*h*ugyuè was delighted. After ten months,[3] a son was born, to whom he gave the name of Mahāpāla, because he had obtained him through his prayers to the Nat. After this another son was born, who received the name of *K*ulla-pāla. These two sons, when they reached years of maturity, both married.

At this time Parā Taken[4] was preaching the law to the assembly in the *G*etavana monastery, and Mahāpāla, after listening to his discourse, became fearful about his future state, and asked Parā Taken for permission to become a Rahan.[5] Parā Taken said, "If there is any one whose leave you should ask, go first and do so." Mahāpāla accordingly sought the leave of his younger brother, *K*ulla-pāla; but *K*ulla-pāla objected, saying, "Our parents are both dead, and I now look on you as my father and mother; do not become a Rahan, but stay at home and make offerings. Mahāpāla, however, would not listen to his brother's objections, but delivered over to him a large amount of property, and then leaving him, went to Parā Taken and became a Rahan.

[1] A being of an order superior to man.
[2] A streamer of cloth, often fastened to a tree as an offering to the Nat supposed to reside there.
[3] Lunar months alone are employed by the Burmese in calculations of time.
[4] The Lord and Master, *i.e.* Gotama.   [5] A Buddhist priest.

After he had become a Pankānga,[1] and had passed five lents[2] with the teacher Upagghāya, he said to Parā Taken, "My lord and master, what are the duties of a priest, according to the divine system?" Parā Taken said, "Mahāpāla, my divine system consists of Gandha-dhūra and Vipassanā-dhūra, these two." Mahāpāla said, "Lord and master, what is Gandha-dhūra? and what is Vipassanā-dhūra?" Parā Taken replied, "Gandha-dhūra means knowing by heart the three books of the Pitaka[3] in the Pāli language;

---

[1] A priest who is proficient in the five qualifications.

[2] The priests in Burmah take rank according to the number of Lents or annual fasts of three months which they have spent in their monasteries; accordingly, a priest of five Lents means a priest of five years' standing or thereabouts. The Burmese priests, if they find the monastic austerities too heavy a burden, are at liberty to become laymen at any time, but if they wish to re-enter the priesthood, they forfeit all advantages of seniority, and must commence afresh in the lowest rank.

[3] The Buddhist scriptures comprise, according to Burmese authorities, three great books, which are again subdivided into fifteen parts, thus:—

1. Sutta	Sutta-silakkha (?)
	Sutta-mahāvā (?)
	Sutta-pādeyavā (?)
2. Vinaya	Parāgika
	Pākitana
	Mahāvagga
	Kūlavagga
	Parivāra
3. Abhidhamma	Dhamma sangani
	Vibhanga
	Dhātukathā
	Puggalapaññatti
	Katbāvatthu
	Yamaka
	Patthāna

Vipassanā-dhūra means, repeating the Kamma*tth*āna[1] and the Bhāvanā."[2] Mahāpāla said, "Lord and master, I have entered the priesthood at too advanced an age to acquire the Gandha-dhūra, give me the Vipassanā-dhūra." Parā Taken gave him the Kamma*tth*āna, which has the power of making a man a Rahanda.[3] Mahāpāla, after performing the Pavāra*n*ā,[4] made his obeisance to Parā Taken, and went away with sixty Rahans to a place distant 120 yo*g*anas[5] from the Sāvatthi country. Depending for subsistence on a neighbouring village, he took up his residence in a forest, where he occupied himself in repeating the Kamma*tth*āna. The people of the village felt kindly towards them, and offered them boiled rice,[6] and Mahāpāla and the sixty Rahans received daily alms of food in the village.[7]

One day, a doctor in the village made a respectful request to them, that if ever they had need of medi-

---

[1] Short sentences for repetition.

[2] The same, but shorter.

[3] An Ariya of the highest order. An Ariya is one who will attain Nibbāna at the close of his present life.

[4] Confession made by one priest to another.

[5] A yo*g*ana is thirteen and a half English miles.

[6] Buddhist priests receive all their food cooked from the pious laity, on whom they are entirely dependent for their subsistence. Nothing is cooked in the monasteries.

[7] It is the custom of the Burmese priests to go out every morning about eight o'clock to collect food for the day. At this hour, in every town or village where there is a monastery, may be seen a long file of priests with their bright yellow clothes and shaven and uncovered heads walking slowly and solemnly along, with their eyes fixed upon the ground, looking neither to right nor left, and keeping rigid silence; each man carrying his t*h*abet, into which the people from their houses as the procession passes come and pour food, principally boiled rice.

cine of any kind they should command him. Some
time after this the Mahāthera Mahāpāla suffered from
a continual effusion from the eyes, just like water
running from a leaky water-pot, and the Rahans
accordingly went to the doctor, and begged of him to
make an offering[1] of some medicine. The doctor gave
them some refined oil. Mahāpāla, because he would
not desist from repeating the Kamma*tth*āna, applied the
medicine to his eyes without moving from his sitting
posture, and then went into the village to collect his rice.
The doctor, as soon as he saw him, asked him if he had
used the medicine, and he said he had. Then he asked
him how his eyes were, and received the reply that
they were as bad as before. "How is this?" said the
doctor; "one application always removes the disease.
Did you apply the medicine sitting or lying down?"
Mahāpāla kept silence. The doctor continued, "Lord
and master, if you only lie down and apply the medicine, you will be cured." Mahāpāla said, "Leave
me, Dārakā;"[2] and the doctor made his obeisance and
went away. Mahāpāla then communed with himself
thus: "O Mahāpāla, you cannot count the number of
times you have been blind in the different states of
existence, of which no commencement can be found;
fix your mind on the religious system of Parā Taken
incessantly, and take no sleep during this Lent for the
whole of the three months; then if blindness come, let
it come." Saying these words, he gave himself up
entirely to the repetition of the Kamma*tth*āna, and on

---

[1] Every gift made by the laity to a priest is regarded as a religious offering to be rewarded in succeeding states of existence.

[2] The title given by priests to those of the laity who support
them.

that very day, exactly at midnight, he became a Rahanda, but he lost the sight of both eyes.

From this time Mahāpāla confined himself to the precincts of the monastery. When the Rahans next morning told him that it was time to go and collect the food; he said to them, "My sight is gone; go by yourselves and collect it." When the Rahans saw his blindness they wept bitterly, and said to him, "My Lord, have no anxiety, we will feed and tend you;" then they went into the village to collect food. When the villagers saw that Mahāpāla was not with them, and on inquiry learned that he was blind, they greatly pitied him and sent him many dainties.

Kakkhupāla[1] continued to instruct the sixty Rahans, and these, giving their whole hearts to his teaching, arrived at the stage of a Rahanda. When Lent was over the Rahans expressed a wish to go and contemplate Parā Taken; Kakkhupāla said to them, "Go, but I am infirm and blind, and must remain behind. When you arrive there tell my younger brother Kullapāla of my condition. If he will conduct me I shall be able to go."

When the Rahans arrived they contemplated Parā Taken and the two chief disciples.[2] On the following day early in the morning the Rahans went to collect food at the house of Kulla-pāla; when he saw them and found his brother was not with them, he asked after him. The Rahans told him how he was blind of both eyes, and how he had said that he could not come

---

[1] Mahāpāla's name is here changed to Kakkhupāla in reference to his blindness, kakkhu meaning eye.

[2] Sāriputta the right-hand disciple, and Moggallāna the left-hand disciple.

unless his brother would conduct him. When Kulla-pāla heard this, he wept aloud, and making his nephew Pālita enter the priesthood, he sent him back with the Rahans. The novice as soon as he reached the residence of Kakkhupāla, presented some food to him, saying, "I have brought this from your younger brother Kulla-pāla." Kakkhupāla asked him who he was, and hearing he was his nephew, said "Very good," and giving him the end of his staff to guide him, set out on his journey.

As they were travelling in a thick forest, the novice Pālita, hearing the voice of a woman who was engaged in collecting fuel, and was singing very prettily over her task, said to Kakkhupāla, "My Lord, wait here for one moment, I will be back with you directly." The novice then went away, and introducing himself to the young woman, spent a considerable time in her society. Kakkhupāla finding the novice did not return, and suddenly recollecting that he had heard a woman singing, came to the conclusion that the novice had failed in his duty.[1]

When the novice returned after his interview with the damsel, he said, "My Lord, let us proceed," and offered to take the end of the staff; but the Rahanda said, "One who has been guilty of a vile action must not touch the end of my staff." The novice trembled and was silent: then assuming the garment of a layman, he again approached him and said, "I have become a layman; it was from no inclination for its duties that I entered the priesthood, but only from fear of the dangers of the journey; now let us proceed. But Kakkhupāla said, "Though you have gone back to

---

[1] The Buddhist priesthood are devoted to celibacy.

the laity, you are not fit to be my companion; I will not go with you." Then Pālita urged, "Do not remain here, my Lord! for there are Bilūs[1] and all sorts of dangers." The Rahanda replied, "I care not for these dangers, if I must die, I must die; but I will not be conducted by you." When Pālita heard this, he was utterly dismayed, and weeping bitterly fled away.

By the power of Kakkhupāla's devotion, the throne of the Sakka King[2] became rigid,[3] and its occupant looking forth observed the Rahanda in his difficulty, and leaving the Nat country descended to earth; then taking care that his footfall should be heard by Kakkhupāla he went along in front of him. Kakkhupāla asked whose footstep it was, and the Nat-King answered that he was a wayfarer, and asked the Rahanda whither he was going; on receiving the reply that he was bound for the Sāvatthi country, he suggested that they should travel together; but the Mahāthera said, "Dārakā, I am very infirm and shall delay you on your journey." The Sakka King rejoined, "Not so, my Lord, I have no need of haste, and by accompanying you I shall obtain one of the ten results of good actions." The Rahanda seeing that this was a pious person, gave him the end of his staff, and they went on together, and in consequence

[1] A kind of Ghoul.
[2] The King of the Nats.
[3] The Throne of the Sakka King is of stone, which is so soft that when he is seated on it in his usual cross-legged position, he sinks into it up to his knees as if it were a cushion; but if any mortal requires his assistance and has sufficient power to invoke his aid, the stone becomes rigid, and the king consequently rises up, and looking about him sees who requires his help.

of the Nat having made a short and easy road, they arrived at the Getavana monastery the same evening; here Kakkhupāla, hearing sounds of Brahminical shells[1] and elephants, asked what it was, when he was astonished to hear that he was in the Sāvatthi country. "Why," said he, "when I came here formerly I was a very long time on the journey."—"Yes," replied the Nat, "but you see I knew a short cut." Then the Rahanda knew that this must be the Nat-King.

The Sakka Nat-King having conducted Kakkhupāla to the monastery where he formerly resided, created for him a numerous company of Rahans to be his associates, and then went to Kulla-pāla to acquaint him with his brother's arrival. Kulla-pāla went at once to the monastery, and when he saw his brother, he fell down, and embraced his feet and wept, saying, "Oh, my Lord, although I could not foresee this misfortune, did I not try to prevent you from becoming a Rahan?" then he made two of his slaves probationers for the priesthood, and ordered them to attend upon him.

Some time after this some village Rahans, who were going to contemplate Parā Taken, and were passing from monastery to monastery, arrived near Kakkhupāla's residence, and were going to contemplate the Rahanda when very heavy rain came on, which compelled them to defer their visit till the morrow. The rain did not cease till midnight, and in the early morning, as Kakkhupāla was walking up and down his verandah, earnestly engaged in his duties, the insects which had come out of the ground, owing to its being damp from the previous rain, were constantly being crushed

---

[1] A sort of trumpet.

by his footsteps. When the Rahans arrived, and saw in the verandah all the dead insects, they asked who had been walking there, and on hearing that it was Kakkhupāla, they reviled him, saying, "When he had his sight he would never walk up and down his verandah, but was always lying down; but now that he is blind he has taken to walking there, and destroys numbers of lives." Not satisfied with abusing him, they went to Parā Taken, and told him how Kakkhupāla destroyed insects by walking in his verandah. Parā Taken asked them if they had seen him killing them, and they said they had not. "Well," said Parā Taken, "you did not see him kill the insects, neither did he see the insects; a Rahanda's heart can never wish for the destruction of life." Then the Rahans said, "Lord and God, how comes it that although he is a Rahanda, he is blind?" Parā Taken replied, "Rahans! Kakkhupāla's blindness is the consequence of sins committed in a previous existence." The Rahans asked what these sins had been, and Parā Taken continued, "Rahans! this Kakkhupāla a long time ago was a doctor in Benares, and was in the habit of wandering through the different towns and villages practising medicine. Seeing one day a woman suffering from blindness, he said to her, 'If I cure your eyes, what will you give to me?' She replied, 'If you really give me back my sight, my sons, my daughters, and myself shall all be your slaves.' The doctor agreed to this, and with one application of his medicine restored her sight. The woman, however, being afraid of being enslaved with her whole family, pretended to be still blind; and when the doctor came and asked her if she was cured, she replied that she could not yet see, and that her eyes were more painful even than before. The doctor, enraged at her deceit, went home to procure some medicine which should make her blind again, and told his wife about it; his wife said nothing, and the doctor applied the medicine and rendered the woman again totally blind. Kakkhupāla Mahāthera was that doctor; his sin followed steadily behind him, just as the cart-wheel follows the draught bullock."

The End of the Story of Kakkhupala Mahathera.

CHAPTER II.

STORY OF MADDHAKUNDALI.

Para Taken, while he was in the Sāvatthi country, preached the law as follows, giving as an illustration of it an account of the T*huthe*'s[1] son, Maddhaku*n*dali.

In the Sāvatthi country there lived a T*huthe* named Adinnapubbaka; he was called by this name because he would never give away anything to any one. This T*huthe* had an only son, whom he loved very dearly, but he was so niggardly that, rather than pay a goldsmith for his work, he made him a pair of earrings[2] with his own hands, and on that account his son received the name of Maddhaku*n*dali.

One day Maddhaku*n*dali became very seriously ill, when his father, fearing the expense of medicine and attendance, shut the boy up in the house, in order that no one should know anything about it; the

---

[1] The same as T*h*ugyuè, one of the wealthy class.

[2] The earrings worn by the Burmese are hollow cylinders of gold, about one and a half inches long and three-quarters of an inch in diameter, thrust into the lobe of the ear; for this purpose the lobe of the ear is pierced in the ordinary manner, and the aperture gradually enlarged by introducing substances constantly but by very slow degrees increasing in size. These earrings are worn by both men and women.

mother, seeing the child so ill, begged him to send for a doctor, but the *Thuthe* cried out, "Woman! would you squander all my wealth?" Then he went himself to a doctor, and, explaining the symptoms of the disease, asked him what remedy should be employed: the doctor, seeing what a hard man he was, told him that the root and bark of the Hū-Hū-Nyā-Nyā tree would be beneficial. The *Thuthe* went home and treated the invalid as he had been directed, but the disease increased in severity, and became beyond all remedy; then, when it was too late, he sent for the doctor. The doctor, the moment he saw the lad, knew at once that there was no hope, so he said, "I am very busy just now, and have no time to attend to this case; you had better send for some one else." The *Thuthe* then, fearing that all his relatives and friends might get a sight of his wealth, had the boy carried into one of the outer rooms of the house.[1]

---

[1] This means that the miser was afraid that if the boy died, the people, who would be sure to come and see the corpse the moment they heard of the death, would, if it were laid out in any of the principal rooms, observe his plate, jewels, etc. These alone constitute the wealth of the Burmese, who rarely, if ever, hoard actual money, but keep all their property in the more portable form of gold and jewels.

His expectation of being inundated with visitors alludes to the way of conducting the funeral ceremonies in Burmah, which bear a very strong resemblance to an Irish wake. The moment that the breath has left the body all the people in the house (but more especially the women) raise the most fearful shrieks; as soon as the first paroxysms of grief have passed away, they send invitations to all their friends and neighbours to attend the ceremonies. These come at once in great numbers, with a band of music and a party of professional mourners hired for the occasion. The nearest relative sits at the head of the corpse, eulogies of the

At daybreak on the following morning when Parā Taken arose with the perfected spirit of charity and love, his first thought was as to whom he should deliver from a state of punishment; on looking around him he beheld the T*hu*th*e*'s son Maddhaku*n*dali, who he at once knew was about to become a Sotāpan[1]; then he considered, "Has this dear lad perfect faith and love in me?" and finding that he had, and seeing that he was about to enjoy the happiness of the Nats in the Tāvatinsa region, he took with him the whole of his attendant priesthood and went into the Sāvatthi country. As soon as he reached the door of the house of the T*hu*th*e* Adinnapubbaka, he despatched his sacred appearance to the T*hu*th*e*'s son,[2] who directly he saw him, with his heart full of faith and love, raised his hands and paid him homage. Parā Taken then left, and the boy dying with his heart full of faith and love passed as it were from sleeping to waking, and found himself in a palace thirty yoganas in extent in the midst of the Tāvatinsa Nat country.

After burning the body of his son, Adinnapubbaka used to go every day to the tomb weeping bitterly for his loss. When Maddhaku*n*dali from his palace in the Nat country saw his father weeping over his tomb, he

---

deceased and lamentations over his departure are uttered in turn by the different relatives, refreshments are handed round among the guests, and within twenty-four hours of the death the procession is formed, and the body taken to be either buried or burnt.

[1] The first state of an Ariya or one who will attain Nibbāna at the close of his present life.

[2] Parā Taken here and in another of these stories is represented as having the power of sending out one or more appearances of himself.

formed the resolution of going to him, to reason with him, and bringing him to a better frame of mind rescue him from his errors. Accordingly, assuming the appearance he had borne among men he descended to earth, and throwing himself down near the tomb where his father was, began to weep with violence; on this, the T*hu*t*h*e said, "Young man, why are you weeping?" "I am weeping," he replied, "because I want the sun and the moon to make a pair of wheels for my cart." "Young man," said the T*hu*t*h*e, "you must be mad: who can make cart-wheels out of the sun and moon!" The son of the Nat rejoined, "You are weeping for a mortal whose transient life has passed away, but I weep for the sun and moon which I continually have before me." The T*hu*t*h*e on hearing this began to recall to his mind the law of the righteous, and took comfort; then he said, "Are you a *K*atu Mahārā*y*a Nat,[1] or are you the Sakka King?" The Nat's son replied, "I was Maddhaku*n*dali, the T*hu*t*h*e's son. Because at the point of death my heart was filled with faith and love towards Parā Taken, I have become a Nat's son and live in the Tāvatinsa country in a palace thirty yo*y*anas in extent." When the T*hu*t*h*e heard this, his heart was filled with joy, and he determined to go that very day and contemplate Parā Taken. The Nat's son after bidding the T*hu*t*h*e go and make an offering in token of homage to Parā Taken and keep steadily the five commandments,[2] returned to the Nat country.

[1] A Nat of the first stage of the world of Nats, of which there are six stages.
[2] 1. Kill not. 2. Steal not. 3. Commit not adultery. 4. Lie not. 5. Take nothing that intoxicates.

The T*hu*the after contemplating with reverence Parā Taken asked him this question, "Can a man without performing any good works at all, by a pure and loving heart alone, obtain the happiness of the Nats?" Parā Taken replied, "Why do you ask me this? Your son Maddhaku*nd*ali told you that because he died with his heart full of love and faith towards me, he was now enjoying the happiness of the Nats." —"When was it," said the T*hu*the, "that he told me this?"—"This very day at the tomb," replied Parā Taken.

Once again Parā Taken related the story of Maddhaku*nd*ali, and seeing that the mind of the T*hu*the Adinnapubbaka (the boy's father) was still full of error, he commanded that Maddhaku*nd*ali with his palace should descend to earth. Maddhaku*nd*ali appeared in his palace, and descending from it made his obeisance to Parā Taken. Parā Taken said to him, "Young Nat, by means of what offerings and other good works did you obtain the happiness of the Nats?" The Nat's son replied, "Without performing one good work, but from dying in faith and love to my Lord and master I obtained the happiness of the Nats." Then Parā Taken said, "It is the heart of love and faith accompanying good actions which spreads as it were a beneficent shade from the world of men to the world of Nats." This divine utterance was like the stamp of a king's seal upon a royal edict.

When Parā Taken had finished his discourse, 84,000 of the congregation were converted. Maddhaku*nd*ali obtained the reward due to Sotāpatti,[1] and Adinnapub-

---

[1] One state or condition of an Ariya, of which there are altogether eight.

baka becoming a Sotāpan,[1] and sedulous in the performance of his duties as such, spent large sums of money in the performance of good works.

END OF THE STORY OF MADDHAKUNDALI.

[1] One who has obtained the state of Sotāpatti.

CHAPTER III.

THE STORY OF TISSA-THERA.

Parā Taken preached the Law as follows, in the Sāvatthi country, reciting as an illustration of it the story of Tissa-thera:—

Tissa-thera was the son of the younger sister of King Suddhodana, the father of Parā Taken. At an advanced age he became a Rahan, and in consequence of living entirely upon the presents which Parā Taken sent him, he became very stout. He used to live in a Zayat[1] in the middle of a monastery, and wore a t*h*ingan[2] of many folds. One day some pilgrim priests arrived at the Zayat on their road to contemplate Parā Taken; seeing Tissa-thera they thought he must be a priest of high rank, and coming before him prepared to offer him the respectful salutations due to his superior degree, but the Rahan took no notice of them. The young priests then said to him, "Lord and master, how many Lents have you passed?" Tissa-thera replied, "I was old when I entered the

[1] A building open on all sides or nearly so, employed for the accommodation of travellers, or for the laity to assemble to hear the priests preach.

[2] A priest's garment, consisting of different folds of cloth of a bright yellow colour in three separate pieces.

priesthood, I do not know how many Lents I have passed;" then the young priests said, "You obstinate old man; at your age not to know how many Lents you have passed, and to be in doubt whether or not the Rahans who visit you are of higher rank and entitled to receive from you the different marks of respect, such as descending to receive them and such like observances!" Saying this they clapped their hands at him and abused him. The passion of Tissa was like that of an enraged king. "Whom," said he, "did you come here to visit?"—"We have come," they replied, "to see Parā Taken."—"Do you know," he said, "what relation I am to Parā Taken; are you desirous of destroying yourselves, and extirpating your whole race?" Then with tears of rage and vexation he rushed into the presence of Parā Taken. The Rahans fearing that he might raise the anger of Parā Taken against them, followed him. Parā Taken, when he saw him, said, "What is it that makes your face so clouded?"—"My Lord and master," said Tissa, "these Rahans have abused me." Parā Taken asked him where he was when they abused him, and he replied that he was in the Zayat in the centre of the monastery. "Did you," said Parā Taken, "on the arrival of the Rahans perform the duty of descending to receive them?"—"I did not," he replied. Parā Taken said, "A Rahan of only a few Lents, who does not perform his duty of receiving with the proper respect the Rahans of a higher number of Lents, has no right to be in the centre of a monastery. Tissa, you are in fault; pay homage to these Rahans." Tissa replied, "I will pay no homage." Three times did Parā Taken ask him to pay homage, and three times received the same reply. Then the Rahans said to Parā Taken, "This Rahan Tissa is excessively obstinate." Parā Taken replied, "Beloved Rahans, this is by no means the first occasion of his obstinacy; in times gone by he was equally deaf to all admonition." The Rahans said, "Lord and master, his present obstinacy we see, but of his contumacy in former times we know nothing; will you favour us by relating the account of it." Parā Taken related the story as follows:—

Rahans! This Tissa, in times long gone by, was the Rishi[1] Devala, who used to reside in the Himavanta Forest. On one occasion, wishing to procure some savoury food, he came to the country of Benares, and took up his residence in the Oden Zayat.[2] At this time the Rishi Nārada, who had come to Benares from the Himavanta Forest for a similar purpose, arrived at the same Zayat; after asking permission of Tissa, who was already settled in the Zayat, he too made it his residence, and the two Rishis passed the day in conversation. When night came, and it was time to sleep, the Rishi Nārada, after carefully noting where the Rishi Devala was going to sleep, the position of the door and so forth, lay down. Devala, wishing to annoy the other Rishi, moved away from his proper sleeping place and lay down across the doorway. Nārada going out through the door, trod on his pigtail;[3] Devala, starting up cried out, 'Who trod on my pigtail?' Nārada

---

[1] A devotee, ascetic.

[2] The potter's Zayat, so called probably in consequence of having been erected by some potter as a pious offering.

[3] The Burmese priests shave the head and face entirely; the story must allude to a Hindu priest, some of whom wear a very

replied, 'Master, it was I, Nārada the Rishi, who accidentally trod on it, bear with me, I do you homage;'[1] saying this he went outside and presently came back. Now, Devala, knowing that the Rishi on his return would pass carefully round by his feet, changed his position, and placed his head where his feet had previously been, so that when Nārada came in and passed as he thought by his feet, he trod right on the other Rishi's neck; whereupon Devala starting up again cried out, 'Who trod on my neck?' to which Nārada replied, 'It was I, Nārada the Rishi, I accidentally trod on your neck; I do you homage.' But Devala cursed him, saying, 'you bad Rishi Nārada, you have trodden on my pigtail, you have trodden on my neck; at sunrise may the head of the Rishi Nārada split into seven pieces!' Nārada replied to this, 'My friend, I am in no way to blame, your curse will not fall on me but on him who is the guilty one; and it is his head which will split into seven pieces.' Now, Nārada was a Rishi of great power and glory, his wisdom could contemplate forty past and forty future grand cycles of time. When by means of this great wisdom he began to consider whose head would split into seven pieces at sunrise, and saw that it would be that of the Rishi Devala, he had compassion upon him, and by means

---

small tuft of hair at the back of the head, plaited into a pigtail a few inches long. The laity in Burmah both men and women wear their hair as long as it will grow.

[1] This doing of homage is the way in which the Burmese ask pardon of each other. The words, "I do you homage," accompanied by a reverential movement with the hands are equivalent to the English "I beg your pardon."

of his great power and glory prevented the sun from rising on the following day.

When the people of the country found that the sun did not rise, and that there was total darkness, they went to the gate of the king's palace, and cried out, "Great King, you who rule over this country, do you not always act in conformity with the ten laws? Make therefore the sun to rise, for this darkness will be the destruction of all your subjects."

The king meditated upon his own state, and, finding that he was free from all guilt, came to the conclusion that the phenomenon must have been caused by some Rishi or Rahan of great power having quarrelled and uttered an invocation; he accordingly inquired of the people of the country, who told him that in the Oden Zayat there were two Rishis whom they had heard quarrelling and cursing. The king immediately had torches lighted, and went off to the Zayat; there, seeing the Rishi Nārada, he respectfully saluted him, and said, "My lord Rishi Nārada, the people of Gambudvīpa[1] have never before known such darkness as now encompasses them; whence does it arise?" Nārada related to the king the whole circumstances of the curse of the Rishi Devala, and when the king asked the nature of the curse, he said, "Although no fault whatever could be imputed to me, Devala cursed me, saying, 'when the sun rises, may your head split into seven pieces!' but I told him that, as I was innocent, the curse would fall not on me, but on whosoever was in fault. Then foreseeing by the power which I have, that at sunrise Devala's head would

---

[1] One of the four great islands surrounding Mount Meru, which is supposed to be the centre of the universe.

split into seven pieces, I felt pity for him, and prevented the sun from rising." The king said to him, "Is there any way by which Devala may escape this calamity?" Nārada replied, "He can escape it by doing homage to me." Then the king approached Devala, and said to him, "My lord Rishi Devala, do homage to the Rishi Nārada;" but Devala answered, "Great King, this deceitful Rishi Nārada trod on my pigtail and on my neck. I will not do homage to him." The king, much concerned about the calamity impending over him, repeated several times his request with great earnestness, but he could get no other reply from Devala than "I will do no homage to him." At last the king, through his pity for the Rishi, took hold of him, and forced his head down to the feet of Nārada. Nārada said, "Rise, Rishi Devala; I forgive you." Then he told the king that as Devala had not paid him homage of his own free will, in order to save him from his terrible fate, he must take him to a tank, make him go into the water up to his neck, and then, after placing a clod of earth on his head, make him do homage. The king, in accordance with these instructions, took Devala to a tank, whither Nārada followed them. When the king had placed Devala up to his neck in water, and fixed the clod of earth on his head, Nārada said, "O Rishi Devala, I am now, by the power which is in me, about to make the sun rise; the moment it rises, duck under water,[1] after which cross to the other side of the tank, and take your own way." When he had said this, the sun immediately rose, Devala ducked down his

---

[1] The ducking the head under water is supposed to answer for bowing the head down in homage.

head, and the clod of earth that was upon it split into seven fragments; and the Rishi, thus escaping his dreadful doom, crossed, as he had been told, to the opposite side of the tank, and fled away.[1]

When the sun rose, and the light again appeared, all the people of the country were greatly rejoiced.

Parā Taken, at the close of the story, said, "Beloved Rahans, the people whom I have mentioned in my story, and who lived long ago, are this day among us. The King is now Ānanda, the Rishi Devala is this Rahan Tissa, the Rishi Nārada is myself the Parā; you see, then, that this is not the first time that this Tissa has been obstinate and deaf to admonition; his obstinacy was quite as great in times that have long gone by." Then he called Tissa to him, and said, "Rahans should never bear a grudge against any man, saying 'this man was angry with me, this one oppressed me, or this one took away my property,' for in this way hatred is fostered; but they should bear no grudge, and should say 'let him do this to me' or 'let him say that to me,' for in this manner all angry feelings die away."

When Parā Taken had finished this discourse, a hundred thousand Rahans obtained the reward of Sotāpatti, and Tissa, so obstinate before, became docile and gentle.

END OF THE STORY OF TISSA-THERA.

---

[1] This story bears a curious resemblance to the "Leech of Folkestone" in the 'Ingoldsby Legends,' where exactly the same expedient is adopted to evade the effects of witchcraft.

CHAPTER IV.

THE STORY OF KULLAKĀLA AND MAHĀKĀLA.

At another time, while Parā Taken was living in the ebony forest near the city of Setavya, he preached a discourse about Kullakāla and Mahākāla. These, Kullakāla and Mahākāla, used to travel about with carts laden with merchandise, and trade in the different places they came to. On one occasion they reached the Sāvatthi country with 500 carts full of goods, and rested midway between the city of Sāvatthi and the Getavana monastery. Mahākāla, seeing the people of the country carrying sweet-scented flowers to the monastery, asked them whither they were going; and on being told that they were on their road to the monastery to hear the law preached, he resolved to accompany them; and, giving over all the property to the care of his younger brother Kullakāla, he provided himself with sweet-scented flowers, and, following the crowd, came into the presence of Parā Taken, and heard his exposition of the law, regarding the vileness of lust and the rewards to be obtained hereafter by Rahans. At the conclusion of the discourse, Mahākāla begged Parā Taken to make him a Rahan. Parā Taken told him that if there was any one whose leave he ought first to ask, he should go and obtain his permission. Accordingly Mahākāla went to his younger brother, and told him that he was about to become a Rahan, and that he gave up to him the whole of their joint property. His brother endeavoured earnestly to dissuade him from his project, but seeing that he was not to be deterred, he at last gave way, and accorded his permission. Mahākāla then returned to Parā Taken, and became a Rahan. Some time afterwards Kullakāla also, in company with his elder brother, practised the duties of a Rahan.

Mahākāla, when he had reached the stage of a Pañkānga, addressed Parā Taken thus: "Lord and master, in your church how many religious duties are there?" Parā Taken replied, "There are two: viz., Gandhadhūra and Vipassanādhūra." Mahākāla said, "Lord and master, I entered the priesthood at too advanced an age to acquire the Gandhadhūra; give me the Vipassanādhūra." Parā Taken, seeing that Mahākāla would become a Rahanda, gave him the duty of Susāna,[1] which has the power of conducting to the state of a Rahanda.

Mahākāla having thoroughly acquired the Susāna duty, when the evening watch was passed, and every one was asleep, went to the burial-place, and remained there engaged in this observance; at daybreak, before any one was stirring, he returned to the monastery. This practice he continued every day.

One day, the woman who watched the cemetery and burned the bodies, seeing the Rahan Mahākāla walk-

---

[1] Susāna means a cemetery, where bodies are either buried or burnt.

ing to and fro repeating the Kamma*tth*āna,¹ began to consider who it could be who came to her place, and accordingly meeting him at the midnight watch, she addressed him thus: "Lord and master, the Rahans who perform Susāna have a preparatory duty to execute." Mahākāla said, "Dārakāma,² what duty is this?"—"Lord and master," replied the woman, "they should ask the permission of the keeper of the burial ground and the owner of the village."—"Why so?" said Mahākāla. "Because thieves, when they have committed a robbery, often flee for refuge to a burial-ground; and the owners of the property pursuing them thither, finding the property sometimes abandoned in the graveyard, if they saw Rahans there, would ill-treat them seriously; but if the burial-ground keepers and the owners of villages were to say that such a Rahan had asked permission of them, he would be known to be guiltless." The Rahan Mahākāla then said to her, "Besides what you have already said, have you anything else to tell me?" She replied, "Lord and master, the Rahans who remain in burial-grounds must abstain from fish, curry stuff, bread, oil, and treacle, and they must never sleep in the daytime. They must employ themselves energetically, and by means of these energetic efforts in the repetition of the Vipassanā, they secure the completion of a Rahan's duties." Mahākāla said to her, "How are the funeral rites performed to the corpses which are brought here?" She replied, "My lord

¹ Forty short sentences.
² Dāraka (masc.) and Dārakāma (fem.) are titles used by the priests when addressing the laity; the meaning is, supporter of the priesthood.

and master, rich people are placed in a coffin, adorned with a red woollen cloth, and then burnt; with regard to poor people, a heap of wood is piled up and set on fire, then they are cut in pieces with the edge of a spade, so as to burn easily, and are so consumed." When Mahākāla heard this, he said to the burial-ground keeper, "Tagāma,[1] let me know when the changing of the form of a human body shall take place, that I may recite a Kamma*tth*āna over it." The woman agreed to do so, and Mahākāla remained engaged in the Rahan's duty of Susāna.

About this time, Mahākāla, the Rahan, having worldly thoughts, began to regret his family, his wife and children. One day, while he was performing his duties in the burial-ground, the parents of a very beautiful girl who had died suddenly brought the body, together with the necessary firewood, to the cemetery, and, delivering it to the burial-ground keeper, gave instructions for her to burn it; then, after giving her the customary fee, they went away. The body-burner, on removing the numerous garments which covered the body, seeing how very beautiful she was, thought that she was worthy of having a Kamma*tth*āna said over her, and accordingly went and told Mahākāla. Mahākāla looked at the corpse on the pyre, and examined it from the soles of the feet to the ends of the hair; then he said a Kamma*tth*āna over the body, which had the beautiful colour of gold, and withdrew, saying to the body-burner, "Let me know when the features are becoming destroyed." The body-burner, as soon as the features were chang-

---

[1] Tāgā (masc.) and Tagāma (fem.) are used in the same way as Daraka, and mean a man or woman of the laity.

ing, went and told him, and he returned and said another Kamma*tth*āna over the body. The body, now losing its appearance, looked like a speckled cow,—the feet fell down, the hands, bent and warped, were raised up, from the forehead downwards the body was divested of its skin and flesh. Mahākāla-thera, seeing this, said, "This young girl only just now had the appearance of gold, but now she has come to utter destruction." Then, after again repeating the Kamma*tth*āna, he exclaimed, "This is the law of mutability! there is nothing permanent!" On this, he redoubled his exertions in repeating the Vipassanā law, and reached the state of a Rahanda.

At that time, Parā Taken, surrounded by his Rahans, and accompanied by Mahākāla-thera, arriving in the Setavya country, entered the ebony forest. The wives of *K*ullakāla, on the arrival of Parā Taken, plotting to get back their husband, invited Parā Taken to take rice. Parā Taken accordingly went to the house of *K*ullakāla's wives, accompanied by all his Rahans, and ordered Mahākāla-thera to have a place prepared for him before he arrived. Mahākāla-thera directed his younger brother, the Rahan *K*ullakāla, to go before, and have a place prepared; and *K*ullakāla, going quickly to the house of his wives, began to prepare for the reception of Parā Taken. His wives thereupon said to him, "Who appointed you a preparer of places of reception? Who gave you leave to become a Rahan? Why did you become a Rahan?" Then they stripped off his priest's garments, fastened a layman's waistcloth round him, bound a turban on his head, adorned him with flowers, and saying to him, "Now go, and meet Parā Taken on the road, and conduct him here," they sent him off with some slaves to receive Parā Taken. Kullakāla, not at all ashamed of having re-entered the laity before keeping his first Lent, went as a layman to receive Parā Taken. Parā Taken, after eating his rice, preached the law, and then took his departure. Kullakāla's wives took their husband, now a layman, home with them.

Mahākāla's wives hearing of this, said to themselves, "Kullakāla's wives have got their husband back; we will recover ours in the same way." Accordingly, they invited Parā Taken to come and take rice, thinking that their husband Mahākāla would come to prepare for his reception; but Parā Taken sent another Rahan for this purpose. The wives being so far foiled in their plot, after entertaining Parā Taken with rice, addressed him thus: "Lord and master, when you take your departure, leave Mahākāla-thera with us, to preach to us the benefits resulting from offerings of rice." Parā Taken then turned to leave, but when he reached the door, the Rahans said to him, "Parā Taken, if you leave Mahākāla-thera behind, his wives will drag him off; only recently Kullakāla, in consequence of being sent to prepare for your reception, was pulled away by his wives, and has become a layman; hence it is really not fitting that Mahākāla-thera should be left behind by himself. Parā Taken replied, "Rahans, my dear sons, do you think that Mahākāla resembles Kullakāla? Kullakāla is like a [drift] tree that has reached the shore, but Mahākāla-thera is like a mountain of solid rock, which nothing can shake."

Mahākāla-thera's wives, surrounding him, said, "Whose permission did you ask, when you became a

Rahan? Who told you to become a Rahan? Now become a layman again." Saying this, they dragged him along, and tried to strip off his priest's clothes, but Mahākāla-thera, knowing what his wives were about, by means of his miraculous power, rose from the ground, and, flying away over the roofs of the houses through the steeples and spires to the place where Parā Taken was, descended to the ground, made his obeisance to him, and remained in his company.

At the conclusion of this discourse, the Rahans obtained the reward of Sotāpatti.

END OF THE STORY OF *K*ULLAKALA AND MAHAKALA.

CHAPTER V.

THE STORY OF QUEEN SAMAVATI, QUEEN MAGANDIYA, AND THE SLAVE KHU*GG*UTTARA.

On another occasion, Parā Taken, when he was in the Kosambī country, and residing in the Ghositārāma monastery, preached a discourse upon the subject of Queen Sāmavatī and Queen Māgandiyā.

A long time ago, two kings, King Allakappa and King Ve*th*adīpaka, between whom there had existed a friendship of long standing, dating from their earliest childhood, were learning together the different sciences. On the death of their parents, they both entered on their governments. After performing the functions of kings for a very long time, tired of the world and impressed with the law of fear, they both abandoned their countries, and, becoming Hermit-Rahans, took up their residence in the Himavanta forest.

These two hermits having built a monastery each, on a separate hill, resided in it, and at every quarter of the moon they used to observe the day (as a sabbath), and lighting a lamp as a signal, thus communicated to each other intelligence of their existence. One day, the Rishi Ve*th*adīpaka died, and became a Nat of great glory. When the day of the quarter of the moon came round, Allakappa, seeing no light in his friend's monastery, knew that he was dead.

Now the Nat's son, Ve*ṭh*adīpaka, the moment that he became a Nat, entering upon all the enjoyments of that condition, began to consider by what good deed he had obtained this happiness, and saw that he owed it to having abandoned his country and lived as a hermit in the forest. Assuming the guise of a traveller, he went to his old friend Allakappa, and after making obeisance to him, stood before him. Allakappa, the Rishi, said to him, "Dārakā, whence come you?"[1] "Lord and master," he replied, "I am Ve*ṭh*adīpaka; on my death, I became a Nat of great glory; I have come to contemplate my lord and master." After this he resumed, "Lord and master, have you any difficulties or troubles here?" Allakappa replied, "In this place the elephants with their footsteps make great holes in the ground and dirty the precincts of the monastery, and I have great trouble in keeping the place clean and filling up again the holes with earth." The Nat's son said, "Do you wish to keep the elephants away?" He replied, "Yes; all I want is to prevent them coming here."—"Very good, then," he said, and he gave him the charm called "Hatthi-kanta," which has the power of driving away or bringing elephants, and shewing him a three-stringed lute, he taught him the threefold spell, saying, "If you strike this string and repeat this charm, the elephants will run away; strike this one and repeat this charm, and they will come to you, and, bending down, will carry you." After giving these instructions, he

[1] This is the ordinary salutation of the Burmese, answering to the "How do you do?" of Europeans.

went away. Allakappa, sounding the note which would drive away elephants, kept them away from his vicinity.

At this time, in the Kosambī country, King Parantapa one day was with his queen outside a Pyathat;[1] the queen was in the family way, and the king had made her put on a large scarlet cloak, and had placed on her finger a ring of the value of a hundred thousand (ghazikas); just then a Hatthilinga, a monster bird, flew down from the sky and taking the queen for a piece of flesh, fluttered his wings with a tremendous noise; the king hearing the sound went inside the Pyathat;[1] but the queen, owing to her condition, being unable to escape was swept off by the bird, for the Hatthilinga has the strength of five elephants. The queen fearing for her life kept perfectly quiet, thinking that if she made any noise the bird would let her fall. The Hatthilinga, arriving at the Himavanta Forest, dropped her in the fork of a banyan-tree in order to devour her. When he began to fly around the place where he intended to perch, to examine all around the vicinity as it is the nature of birds to do, the queen seized the opportunity, and clapping her hands, shouted lustily, and the bird startled at the unexpected noise, flew away.

At this time the sun went down, and from the effect of past sins committed by the queen, the wind began to blow and violent rain came on, and she passed a sleepless and miserable night. At dawn, the rain ceased, and when the sun rose the queen

---

[1] A Pyathat is a building ornamented with a number of roofs rising one above the other; the word is a corruption of the Sanskrit Prāsāda " a palace."

gave birth to a son. To this son she gave the name of Udena, because at his birth he had experienced the three seasons, the cold season, the hot season, and the rainy season. Now, the banyan-tree was at no great distance from the residence of the Rishi Allakappa. It was the Rishi's habit to collect and eat the bones of the fish and meat which the birds dropped from this tree; accordingly, going as usual to the banyan-tree he was surprised to hear the crying of a child among the branches, and looking up he saw the queen. "Who are you?" he cried. The queen replied, "A woman."—"How did you get into the banyan-tree?" said he. "The monster bird," she replied, "brought me and left me here."—"Then come down," he said; but the queen answered, "I am afraid of losing my caste."—"Of what race are you?" he asked. "A king's wife," she replied. The Rishi rejoined, "I also am a king."—"If so," said the queen, "repeat the mystic formula of kings." The Rishi, who had abandoned a great kingdom to become a hermit, repeated the formula. "Now," said the queen, "come up here and take down my son." The Rishi then placing a ladder against the tree, took the child from the queen, without touching her, and brought it down. The queen also descended, and the Rishi conducted her to his monastery, where he lived with her without failing in his duty of chastity. He supplied her, for her food, with honey and rice. After some time the queen began to reflect thus: "I do not know the road by which I came; I do not know what road I should have to take; if this Rishi should leave me here, my son and I would perish in the forest;" so she formed the design of making the Rishi break his vows. Keeping constantly as near him as possible, she endeavoured by wearing her garments indecorously and by various other feminine wiles, to overcome his chastity. At length she succeeded, and they began to live together as man and wife. One day Allakappa when he was looking at the stars observed that the star of Parantapa had faded; he immediately went to the queen and said, "Queen, King Parantapa in the country of Kosambī is dead."—"How does my Lord the Rishi know this?" she asked. "I know it," he replied, "because I saw his star had faded." Then the queen began to weep. The Rishi said, "Queen, why do you weep?"—"That King Parantapa is my husband," she replied. "Queen, weep not," said the Rishi, "among men there is not one who has not to die, all is mutability." The queen said, "I know the law of mutability, but I weep for the misfortunes of my son who, were he in the Kosambī country would now be king over his father's dominions." The Rishi replied, "Have no fear for him; I will render your son such assistance as will secure his being made the king;" saying this, he gave to the young boy Udena the lute which the elephants loved, and taught him the spell to attract them.

Prince Udena sounded the lute, and immediately more than a thousand elephants came to the foot of the banyan-tree. The Rishi gave him minute instructions as to the different duties and observances of kings, and when he had completed them, he made the prince one day climb into the fork of the banyan-tree and sound the lute. No sooner was the sound of the magic Hatthikanta lute heard than a huge elephant bringing with him more than a thousand other elephants came close up to where the prince was, as much as to say, "Mount on my back." Then the Rishi made him mount the elephant, and calling to the queen, said to her, "Acquaint the prince with all his circumstances, and he will not fail to be king." The queen accordingly told him: "My dear child, you are the son of King Parantapa, in the Kosambi country; a monster bird carried me off in this scarlet cloak, and dropped me in this banyan-tree where I gave birth to you. When you arrive in that country if the nobles and ministers do not believe your story, show them this ruby ring and the scarlet cloak with which your father covered me;" so saying, she gave him the ring and the cloak. The prince then made his obeisance to his mother and the Rishi, mounted the huge elephant, and surrounded by over a thousand more of these animals started on his journey, carrying in his bosom the Hatthikanta lute. When he came to the villages on the outskirts of the country, he called out, "Those who wish to receive my favour, let them follow me;" and he took great numbers with him.

As soon as he reached the Kosambi country he erected a stockade with the branches of trees; then he sent to the inhabitants, saying, "Will you fight, or will you give me up the country?" They returned for answer, "We will neither fight nor give up the country; we know nothing about this story of our monarch's queen having been carried away with an unborn child by a monster bird; we do not know whether there is a queen or not." Then he went to the ministers and nobles and said to them, "I am the son of the queen," and told them his name; but no one would believe his story. At last he showed them the cloak and the ring which had belonged to his father; then the ministers and all the inhabitants said, "This is really the son of our king," and they made him monarch over their country.

One day King Udena opening the door of his summer palace, and looking out, saw the young girl Sāmavatī, and asked whose daughter she was. Now, this Sāmavatī was the daughter of the T*hu*ṭ*he* Bhaddavatī, of the Bhaddavatī country; at a time when that country was ravaged by famine and pestilence she came to the Kosambī country of which Udena was king, and had been adopted by the T*hu*ṭ*he* Ghosita[1] as his daughter. Shortly after this, Sāmavatī, after being very handsomely dressed, was conducted to the king, who, the moment he saw her fell violently in love with her, and immediately had the inaugural ceremony of pouring water performed, and raised her to the rank of his queen; and Sāmavatī became a great queen, surrounded by 500 female attendants.

In another country called U*gg*enī there reigned a king named Ka*nd*apa*gg*ota; he had a daughter called Vāsuladattā. This king, one day while he was walking about his garden, observing the magnificence of his army, asked his nobles, "Is there any other king who possesses an army like mine or such elephants and horses?" The nobles replied, "Your Majesty, the army and elephants and horses of King Udena in the Kosambī country are exceedingly numerous." King Ka*nd*apa*gg*ota said, "If this be so, I will take prisoner King Udena." The nobles said, "Your Majesty will not be able to take King Udena."— "How so?" he asked. They replied, "Because he possesses the Hatthikanta charm; by repeating this

---

[1] Text has Ghosaka, and manuscript Ghosa.

spell he can make elephants and horses take to flight; he has also a charm to make them come to him." When King *Kaṇḍapajjota* heard what the nobles said, he said, "I will contrive to take him, and gain possession of his charm."

He had an elephant very well made of wood and carefully painted; then he had machinery fixed inside to be worked with ropes, and enclosing sixty men to pull the ropes started it off across the boundary of King Udena's territory, and made it walk up and down near a tank, and moreover, had a quantity of elephants' dung scattered all round the edge of the tank. A hunter happening to see it went and told King Udena, who immediately started off with all his forces. King *Kaṇḍapajjota* as soon as he heard that King Udena had set off, brought out a large army and posted them in ambuscade on either side of the road which King Udena would take; the latter not knowing that the other king was coming, set off in pursuit of the elephant; the men inside pulling hard at the ropes sent it off at great speed. King Udena struck the lute and uttered the spell, but the elephant being a wooden one paid no attention to it, and made off faster than ever, with King Udena in pursuit. The king seeing that he could not gain on it, descended from his elephant and mounted his horse; his army unable to keep up with him were soon left behind. After he had gone some considerable distance he came on the army of King *Kaṇḍapajjota*, who seized him and carried him off to their king.

When the army of King Udena knew that he was captured, they halted, and built a fortification with branches of trees. King *Kaṇḍapajjota* placed King

Udena in prison, and set a guard over him; then he gave a great feast to his army which lasted for three days. On the third day King Udena said to those who were guarding him, "What is your king doing with his army that they make so much noise?" They replied, "He is giving a great feast to his army because he has conquered his enemy."—"Your king," said Udena, "is acting like a woman; after conquering a hostile king he should either kill him or let him go; why does he inflict all this misery upon me?" When the guards told King Kandapaggota what Udena had said, he came to the prison and asked him if he had really said so. King Udena at once acknowledged that he had said so. "Very well," said the other king, "if you wish to be released, give me the charm that you know, and I will give you your liberty." King Udena replied, "If you will pay homage to me I will give it to you." The other king said, "I will pay no homage to you." Udena persisted, "If you will not pay homage to me you shall not have it." King Kandapaggota said, "If you do not give it me I will have you executed." Udena rejoined, "Do what you like with me; you have power over my body, but none over my mind."

The king on hearing the bold words of Udena began to think that only by craft he could succeed in obtaining the charm from him, and came to the conclusion that the only plan would be to make his daughter procure the charm from him, and then learn it from her, as it would not do for others to have the knowledge of it. Accordingly he went to Udena and said to him, "Would you give up the charm to any one else who would pay homage to you?" He replied,

"I will give it to the person who pays homage to me."—"If that be so," said the other, "there is in my house a hunchback; I will put her inside a curtain, and you remaining outside of it, repeat the charm to her." After firmly impressing upon him that his daughter was a hunchback, he went to his daughter and said to her, "There is a leper here who will teach you a charm that is worth a hundred thousand golden pieces, but you must do obeisance to him from the inside of a curtain, the leper remaining outside will repeat to you the charm, and you must learn it very carefully." Now, the reason of the king making Udena think his daughter was a hunchback, and his daughter think that Udena was a leper was, that he thought that otherwise they might contract an improper intimacy with each other.

When all the arrangements were made, the Princess Vāsuladattā, from the inside of the curtain, bowed down in homage, and King Udena, on the outside, recited the charm to her. After repeating the charm several times, when the princess had not succeeded in learning it, Udena became very angry, and cried out to the princess, "Oh, you hunchback! you have got very thick lips, rub them with a potsherd." The princess, very indignant, retorted, "You leper! do you dare call a princess like me a hunchback?" On this, Udena opened the curtains, and, looking in, saw the princess: "Why, I thought you were a hunchback; your father told me so, and he has told you I was a leper. I am King Udena."—"If this be so," said the princess, "come under the curtain." Udena then went inside the curtain, and the result the king had feared took place. After some time, King Kan-

*d*apa*gg*ota cried out, "Have you learned it?" and the princess replied, "I do not know it yet; I am still learning it."

One day, King Udena said to the princess, "If ever a woman follows the wishes of a husband, neither brothers nor sisters have any power to oppose her; if you wish me to save my life, follow implicitly my wishes: I will then raise you to the rank of my queen, and give you a retinue of 500 female attendants." The princess, after making him engage by a solemn promise to keep his word, went to her father, and, with a woman's deceit, said to him, "My father, your Majesty, in order that I may succeed in learning the charm, it will be necessary for me to repeat the spell by night, after noting a certain position of the stars, and then procure a certain medicinal root; therefore place an elephant at my disposal, and have one of the doors left open." The king said, "Daughter, take any elephant you like, and have one of the doors left open."

Now, King *K*anda*pagg*ota was possessed of the five swift conveyances:—the female elephant called Bhaddavatī, which would travel fifty yo*g*anas[1] in one day; a slave named Kāka,[2] who could travel sixty yo*g*anas in a day; a horse called *K*elakan*th*i, who could travel twenty yo*g*anas in a day; a horse called the Muñ*g*akesi; an elephant called Nālāgiri, who could travel one hundred yo*g*anas in a day. The circumstances under which he became the owner of these five kinds of swift conveyance were as follows:—

[1] The Burmese yūzanā is 13½ English miles according to Judson, but the Sanskrit yōgana is stated by Wilson to be 9 miles, or according to some computations only 4½ miles.

[2] Text and manuscript have Kāla.

King Kandapaggota, in a former state of existence, was a slave. One day, while accompanying his master on a journey, they fell in with a Pakkekabuddha.[1] His master said, "Lord and master, have you had rice?"—"Tagā," he replied, "I have not yet had any." Then the master of the slave, who was the embryo King Kandapaggota, sent him back home to procure some rice. The slave quickly returned with the rice, and presented it to the Pakkekabuddha, and his master said to him, "Because you have used such diligence in bringing the rice, I make over to you half of the future rewards to be acquired by the offering." Then the slave made this invocation: "As the reward of my having so quickly procured and presented this offering of rice, may I hereafter be the possessor of the five swift conveyances." In consequence of this invocation, the slave afterwards became King Kandapaggota.

One day, King Kandapaggota went out to amuse himself in the garden. King Udena, thinking this a good opportunity to escape, filled a leather bag with a large quantity of gold and silver, and placing the Princess Vāsuladattā on a swift female elephant, fled away. When the palace guards acquainted the king with the flight of Udena and the princess, he sent off his people at once in pursuit. Udena, seeing that he was pursued, immediately began to scatter the gold and silver along the road and into every bush he passed. His pursuers, delaying to pick up the treasure, dropped behind, and Udena reached in safety the fortification which his army had built of branches

[1] A semi-Buddha, who occasionally appears in the intervals between real Buddhas.

of trees, while the hostile party, giving up the pursuit, returned home. Udena, after returning with his army to his own country, raised the Princess Vāsuladattā to the rank of his queen, and gave her 500 female attendants.

This is the account of how King Udena obtained possession of the Princess Vāsuladattā.

In the Kururaṭṭha country there lived a Brahmin named Māgandiya. He had a daughter whom he had named Māgandiyā, and his wife's name, moreover, was Māgandiyā, and he had an uncle whose name was Kullamāgandiya. This Brahmin's daughter Māgandiyā was very lovely; she was as beautiful as a Nat's daughter. Princes and sons of Thuthes sent to demand her hand, but her father the Brahmin daunted them all with the reply that they were not worthy of her. At this time Parā Taken, one morning at daybreak looking about to see who deserved to be released,[1] saw that the Brahmin Māgandiya and his wife would attain to Anāgāmi;[2] then he went into the vicinity of their village. Māgandiya the Brahmin, who at this time was going about in search of a husband suitable for his daughter, met Parā Taken on the road. At once, from his appearance, he saw that he was a fit husband for his daughter, and approaching him, said, "My lord Rahan, my daughter is worthy of you, she is as lovely as a Nat's daughter. She will tend upon my lord Rahan; my lord Rahan, look upon my daughter as your wife. I will send for her. Remain here." Then he made haste back to his house, and said to his wife, "Brahminī, I have found a husband suitable

---

[1] From sin and its punishment.
[2] The third state of an Ariya.

to our daughter. Adorn her quickly." When his wife had completed the adornment of her daughter as quickly as possible, they all three started off to Parā Taken, and the people followed them, shouting noisily as they went along, "Look here, the Brahmin and his wife are going to give their daughter a husband." At this moment Parā Taken, marking with his sacred footstep the site of a *K*etiya[1] on the spot where the Brahmin had told him to remain, went and stood at another place close by. The sacred footsteps of Parā Takens are only apparent upon the spots which they command to be hereafter relics. When they do not so command, their footsteps are always invisible. Moreover, only those people for whom they have earnestly prayed can see those footsteps. Such appointed footstep no elephant or any animal that exists, not the heaviest rain, not the most violent wind, can obliterate. At this time, the Brahmin's wife said to him, "Where is this young man?" and he replied, "I told him to be in this place." Then looking about, he saw the *K*etiya footstep, and said, "This must be his footstep." The Brahmin's wife, who was thoroughly versed in the book of outward signs and in the three Vedas, on examining the different signs of the footstep, exclaimed, "O Brahmin, this footstep does not belong to any one who is subject to the five passions.[2] This footstep is that of a Parā Taken, free from every evil disposition."

[1] A pagoda, enshrining the relic of a Buddha.
[2] The Brahmini here recites in poetry the signs of the footmark of the lustful, the angry, and the ignorant man. The printed text and the manuscript differ greatly here, and neither are intelligible.

The Brahmin said to his wife, "You see signs, like seeing an alligator in a cup of water, or thieves in the midst of a house. Hold your tongue and say nothing, or people will hear you;" then, after looking about, he descried Parā Taken. "Here is the young man," said he, showing him to his wife, and he went up to Parā Taken, and presenting his daughter Māgandiyā, said, "My lord Rahan, I give you my daughter." Parā Taken said, "I will tell you something; listen to me. From the sacred forest to the foot of the Aya-pāla banyan-tree the Mān-nat King fought with me, but unable to overcome me, took to flight; that king's daughter, with amorous wiles, and all the beauty and witchery of the Nats, sought to beguile me, but she failed to raise any feeling of passion. How should I desire your daughter, who is subject to the vilest necessities of humanity? I would not have her touch even the sole of my foot." Then he recited some verses, at the conclusion of which the Brahmin and his wife received the reward of the state of Anāgāmi. The Brahmin's daughter Māgandiyā was greatly incensed against Parā Taken. She said, "This Rahan not only says that he does not want me, but that, subject as I am to the vilest necessities of humanity, he would not have me touch the sole of his foot. When I have married a husband of family, wealth, and influence, I will do what ought to be done to the Rahan Gotama." And she bore a grudge against him. The question will arise, "Was Parā Taken aware of Māgandiyā's anger?"—He was not ignorant of it; he knew it. Again, "If he knew it, why did he recite the verses?"—Because, although the daughter had resentful feelings, he wished to profit the other two Brahmins, her parents. Parās take no account of anger, but preach the law to those who are deserving of the reward of the right way. The Brahmin and his wife, after receiving the reward of Anāgāmi, gave their daughter into the charge of her uncle, and becoming Rahans, reached the state of Rahandas.

The uncle, determined to give his niece to none but a king of high family, took her away with him, and presented her to King Udena. The king, falling violently in love with her the moment that he saw her, had the ceremony of pouring water performed, gave her a retinue of 500 female attendants, and raised her to the rank of his queen. Thus, King Udena had three queens, residing in three palaces, with 1500 female attendants, or 500 for each queen. The king used to give to Queen Sāmavatī every day eight kahāpanas to buy flowers to adorn herself with. A female slave of Queen Sāmavatī, named Khugguttarā, used to go every day, and buy the flowers from the flower-woman, Sumanā, but she never bought more than four kahāpanas' worth, keeping the other four for herself. One day, this Sumanā, the flower-woman, resolved to go and make an offering of rice to Parā Taken, and when Khugguttarā came as usual to her to buy flowers, she said to her, "Wait a little, Khugguttarā, I have no time now, for I am just going to offer some rice to Parā Taken."—"If that be so," said Khugguttarā, "let us go together and hear the law." The flower-woman agreeing to this, they went together. Sumanā made an offering of rice to Parā Taken and his attendant Rahans. When Parā Taken had eaten the rice, he preached the law, and Khu*gg*uttarā after hearing it, received the reward of Sotāpatti.[1] On this occasion, Khu*gg*uttarā, who had been in the habit of keeping four kahāpa*n*as every day for herself, expended the whole of the eight kahāpa*n*as in flowers, owing to her having become a Sotāpan in consequence of listening to the law of Parā Taken.

The queen, when she saw so many more flowers than usual, exclaimed, "Khu*gg*uttarā, what a number of flowers there are! Has the king given to-day more than the ordinary flower-money?" Khu*gg*uttarā replied, "Lady, every day I have been in the habit of spending four kahāpa*n*as on the flowers, keeping the other four for myself, but to-day I went with Sumanā who was making an offering of rice to Parā Taken, and after listening to his preaching of the law have obtained the reward of Sotāpatti, and therefore I do not steal." The queen, instead of being angry with her, merely said, "Was it right for you to take my property in this way every day?" and told her to preach to her the law she had just heard. Khu*gg*uttarā said, "Very good, I will preach the law to you, but you must bathe me." The queen accordingly had her bathed with sixteen pots of perfumed water, and presented her with two cloths. One of these cloths Khu*gg*uttarā put on, and one she threw over her; then, taking up her position in a place of honour, she preached the sacred law precisely as Parā Taken had preached it. Queen Sāmavatī and her 500 female attendants, joining their hands in an attitude of devotion, listened to the law, and when it was finished, the whole of them became Sotāpans; and the queen, paying hom-

[1] The first state of an Ariya.

age to Khu*gg*uttarā, said, "Khu*gg*uttarā, from this day I shall never call you a slave, henceforth you must do no work; from this time I regard you as my mother and my teacher, and you must go and hear Parā Taken preach the law, and come and repeat it to me."

In obedience to the queen's commands, Khu*gg*uttarā went regularly to hear Parā Taken preach the law, and repeated it to the queen and her 500 attendants. In consequence of Khu*gg*uttarā knowing the three books of the Pi*t*aka,[1] Parā Taken said to the Rahans, "Beloved Rahans, Khu*gg*uttarā is most excellent in the preaching of the law;" and he placed her in a position of superiority.

One day, Queen Sāmavatī said, "Khu*gg*uttarā, I wish to contemplate Parā Taken. Invite him to come here." Khu*gg*uttarā replied, "Lady, kings' houses are very difficult of access, and your Majesty would not dare to go outside."—"Very well, then," said the queen, "when Parā Taken comes to receive rice, you must point out to me which is Parā Taken, and which is Sāriputta and Moggalāna."—"Very good," said Khu*gg*uttarā; "my lady must make holes through the walls of her apartment, and then, looking through them, do homage." Queen Sāmavatī accordingly, with her 500 female attendants, made holes in the walls of their apartment, and when Parā Taken came to receive rice, they made obeisance and worshipped him.

One day Queen Māgandiyā going to the Pyat*h*at, and seeing the holes in the wall, asked what they were made for; Queen Sāmavatī not knowing that Māgandiyā had a grudge against Parā Taken, replied that they were made for the purpose of worshipping Gotama

[1] The Buddhist scriptures.

Parā Taken. Queen Māgandiyā then thought to herself, "I will do what I ought to do to the Rahan Gotama, and I will destroy Queen Sāmavatī." With this design she went to King Udena and said to him, "The inclination of Sāmavatī is not towards you, but towards another; in a day or two she will kill you." King Udena, convinced that Sāmavatī could not do such a thing, would not believe her. Māgandiyā said, "If your Majesty does not believe me go and examine her apartment." The king went to Sāmavatī's apartment, and on inquiring why holes had been made in the wall, was told by Sāmavatī that when Parā Taken came to receive rice, she had worshipped him. When the king heard this, he was not at all angry, but he had the holes filled up and windows made in their place; and it was in King Udena's reign that for the first time windows were made in the upper apartment of a palace.

Māgandiyā, unable to do anything against Sāmavatī, formed the design of compelling the Rahan Gotama, who had so shamed her, to leave the neighbourhood; to carry it out, she gave a large quantity of gold and silver to the people of the country, and told them when Parā Taken came to receive rice, to hoot him and insult him, so as to make him go to some other place. Accordingly, those who were heretics and who did not respect the three jewels,[1] when they saw Parā Taken approaching to receive rice, shouted at him, "O you bad priest, are you not a rascally thief? You stupid priest, you are like a bullock, like the brute beasts suffering for former sins." When the people thus insulted him my lord Ananda[2] said, "Lord and

---

[1] Gotama, the law, and the priesthood.
[2] Younger brother of Gotama.

master, these people have insulted us, it is better that we should go elsewhere to collect rice." Parā Taken replied, "Ananda, if there also you should meet with insult where would you go? Who has insulted you?" Ananda said, "Lord and master, people engaged in labour as slaves have insulted us." Then Parā Taken said, "I am like an elephant who has just reached the battle-field, whose duty it is to sustain the flights of arrows which attack him from every side. My duty is to bear all the insults which the heretics launch against me. Ananda, be under no anxiety; these people will have finished insulting us after seven days; on the seventh day they will be silent. The distress of Parā Taken cannot last for more than seven days.

Māgandiyā, failing in her attempt to make Parā Taken leave the neighbourhood by having him insulted, began to consider, "This Sāmavatī with her 500 attendants supports this Rahan Gotama, so I will contrive to ruin her." Accordingly, she told her uncle the Brahmin to procure eight live fowls and eight dead ones, and that she would wait on the steps of the palace till he came and told her they had been obtained. As soon as they were procured, the Brahmin came and told Māgandiyā. Māgandiyā directed the slaves who brought the fowls to put down the eight dead fowls, and to follow her with the eight live fowls; these she took to King Udena in the place where he drank spirits, and presented them to him. When the king saw the live fowls thus presented to him, he asked who understood how to cook them well. Māgandiyā said, "Your Majesty, Sāmavatī knows how to cook them very nicely." Udena said, "Very good, then let her cook them," and he told the slaves to take them to Sāmavatī, and to tell her to cook them herself, without letting any one else touch them. These directions the slaves gave to Sāmavatī. Sāmavatī and her 500 attendants said, "We do not take life." This the slaves reported to the king. When Māgandiyā heard it, she cried, "Do you hear that, your Majesty? This Sāmavatī will not as much as prepare your Majesty's food, and uses rebellious words. You can soon know whether she will take life or not. Let her have them to cook for the Rahan Gotama." The king, according to Māgandiyā's suggestion, sent a message to Sāmavatī to cook the fowls and send them to Gotama. Then Māgandiyā bribed the king's messengers with gold and silver, and made them put down the live fowls and take the dead ones to Sāmavatī, with the King's request that she should cook them and send them to Gotama. When Sāmavatī saw the dead fowls she said, "Very good," and took them. The people who had taken the fowls, on being asked by the king what Sāmavatī had said, told him that as soon as she heard that the fowls were for the Rahan Gotama, she was greatly delighted, and taking them, said she would cook them. Then Māgandiyā exclaimed: "There, your Majesty, do you see this? This Sāmavatī when she was told that it was for your Majesty, said, 'We do not take life;' but when she was told to cook them, and present them to the Rahan Gotama, —mark this, your Majesty,—she cooks them with the greatest delight." Though King Udena heard all this, he would not believe it, but bearing it patiently, kept silence.

When Māgandiyā found that the king would not

believe her, she began to consider what other plan she should have recourse to. It was the custom of the king to spend seven days at a time in each of the three queens' Pyat/ats. Māgandiyā, knowing that on the following day the king would go to Sāmavatī's Pyat/at, sent word to her uncle the Brahmin to procure a cobra, and after breaking its fangs, to bring it to her. The Brahmin, according to her directions, brought her the cobra with its teeth broken. Now, it was the habit of King Udena to take a lute with him to whichever Pyat/at he went, so Māgandiyā put the cobra into the cavity of the lute, and fastened it up with a bunch of flowers; and the cobra remained inside the lute for two or three whole days. Then Māgandiyā said to the king, "Which Pyat/at does your Majesty go to to-day?" The king replied, "I am going to Sāmavatī's Pyat/at." Māgandiyā said, "Your Majesty, I had a dream last night which has much disturbed me, it is not right that you should go to Sāmavatī's Pyat/at;" but the king would not listen to her, and went off to the Pyat/at. Māgandiyā, unable to prevent him from going, followed him. The king on arriving at the Pyat/at laid his lute on the bed, and said to Māgandiyā, "You may retire;" but Māgandiyā would not go away, and commenced walking up and down by the side of the bed. The king, after adorning himself with the different garments, flowers, and perfumes presented to him by Sāmavatī and her 500 attendants, put his lute at the head of the bed, and lay down. Māgandiyā pretending to be only walking about close to the bed, took the bunch of flowers out of the hollow of the lute, and threw it away. The cobra coming out expanded its hood, and Māgandiyā as soon as she saw it cried out, "O your Majesty! how foolish you are. Here is my dream fulfilled; look at the snake." Then she began to scream out abuse at both the king and Sāmavatī, and reviled the latter, saying, "You put the snake in the lute to kill the king; do you think that if the king died you would live?" When the king saw the snake, he started and exclaimed, "Infamous as Sāmavatī is, I gave no credence to Māgandiyā when she accused her. Before this, she made holes in the wall of her palace; again, she would not dress the fowls for me, and now she lets loose a snake in my bed." Saying these words he became furiously enraged. Sāmavatī seeing the king's anger exhorted her 500 attendants not to give way to anger against either the king or Māgandiyā, but to meditate only on the Sara*n*agamana,[1] which has the power of preventing all evil emotions.

The king, exasperated with Sāmavatī, took a bow made of goats' horns, which required a thousand soldiers to string, and fixing a poisoned arrow, he had Sāmavatī placed in front with her 500 attendants in a row behind her; then he let fly the arrow at the centre of her bosom; but owing to her loving disposition the arrow returned, and made as if it would enter the king's breast. The king reflecting, "The arrow that I shot would have gone through a stone slab; yet it came back and made as if it would pierce my breast," trembled and said, "Even this lifeless arrow recognised the merit of Sāmavatī, while I, a man, could not see it." Then he threw away the arrow, and falling at her feet raised his hands in adoration, and ad-

[1] A formula of worship, viz. I worship Parā, I worship the Law, I worship the priesthood.

dressed her as follows, in poetry: "Sāmavatī, I am utterly lost, everything is confusion; save me and be to me an object of worship." Saying this he made the humble gesture of apology. Queen Sāmavatī, the disciple of Parā Taken, far from allowing the king to worship her, replied, "Do not worship me; I worship Parā Taken; do you also worship him. It is you, great king, who should rather be an object of worship to me." The king said, "Let him then be my object of worship," and listening to the advice of Sāmavatī, he went for seven days in succession to Parā Taken, made offerings of rice to him, and heard the law. He also offered to Queen Sāmavatī a magnificent present, but she said to him, "Your Majesty, I have no wish for gold or silver, give permission that Parā Taken and his Rahans may visit continually my Pyathat." The king accordingly invited Parā Taken to visit continually the queen's Pyathat, but Parā Taken replied, "It is not fitting that a Parā Taken should go continually to one palace only, for many people long to contemplate him."—"If this be so," said the king, "Lord and master, depute one of your disciples," and Parā Taken replied, "I depute my lord Ananda." The lord Ananda accompanied by 500 Rahans then visited Sāmavatī's Pyathat, and ate their rice there; and the queen with her 500 female attendants, after listening to the law, presented to Ananda 500 garments, and each priest's garment was worth 500 (pieces of gold).

Māgandiyā, foiled in her designs, planned another stratagem. One day King Udena was amusing himself in the garden, and Māgandiyā, blind to the state (of soul) in which she was, thought that this was a good opportunity to complete her evil designs. She sent for her uncle the Brahmin, and told him to get a quantity of cloths, saturate them with oil, wrap them round Sāmavatī's Pyathat, and then set fire to them. The Brahmin accordingly procured a number of coarse cloths, washed them, and saturated them with oil; then he took them to Sāmavatī's Pyathat, and after wrapping them round all the door-posts and the leaves of the doors, he closed all the entrances. Sāmavatī said to him, "Brother Brahmin, why are you wrapping these cloths round the doors?" and he replied, "The king has given me strict orders to do so, but why I do not know." Then he set fire to them and went away.

Sāmavatī exhorted all her attendants, saying, "In the countless existences that have had no beginning, it would be impossible to reckon the number of times that we have perished by fire; let us keep this in mind." When the walls of the palace were wrapped in flames and they began to suffer acutely, she repeated the Kammathāna,[1] and several of her attendants obtained the reward of Anāgāmi.[2] The assembly of Rahans said to Parā Taken, "Lord and master, while King Udena is engaged in his garden, Sāmavatī's palace is in flames, and the queen with her 500 attendants is being burned to death; what will be the future state of these handmaidens?" Parā Taken replied, "Some are settled in the reward of Sotāpatti,[3] some in that of Sakadāgāmi,[4] and others in that of

---

[1] Forty sentences for repetition.
[2] The third state of an Ariya.
[3] The first state of an Ariya.
[4] The second state of an Ariya.

Anāgāmi.[1] These attendants do not die without future reward, the whole of them have received the right course. All people who are subject to the influence of their former deeds are constantly experiencing both happiness and misery."

The intelligence of Sāmavatī's Pyat*h*at being on fire was quickly carried to the king. Unable to reach it before it was burnt down, he remained surrounded by his nobles overwhelmed with grief. He thought of all the good qualities of Sāmavatī, and came to the conclusion that it was the work of Māgandiyā. Knowing that he could not extort a confession from her by threats, he had recourse to artifice, and said to his nobles, "From this day forth I shall be in comfort; many a time did Sāmavatī plot my destruction; unsuccessful in her attempts she has now met her death; from this day forth my mind will be at rest, and I shall be able to sleep in peace. Whoever compassed the death of Sāmavatī I call my friend." Māgandiyā, who was near the king when he said this, directly she heard it, exclaimed, "Your Majesty, could any one else have contrived this? It was I who managed the plot, and my uncle the Brahmin carried it into effect." When the king heard this he pretended to be greatly delighted, and said to her, "You are indeed a friend to me; I will reward you for this; send for the whole of your relations;" saying this he dismissed her.

When Māgandiyā had brought all her relations, the king, in order that none of them might be forgotten, made them all very handsome presents. Seeing this, those who were only most distantly connected with Māgandiyā came forward and claimed relationship. The

[1] The third state of an Ariya.

king, having thus caught all Māgandiyā's relations, had a hole dug in front of him as deep as a man's waist; he then had all of them placed in it, and the hole filled up with fine earth. Above the hole he then had scattered a quantity of straw and rubbish which he caused to be set on fire. After all their hair and skin was burnt off, he had their bodies cut into pieces by passing iron harrows over them. With regard to Māgandiyā herself, strips of flesh were cut off with an excessively sharp knife from every part of her body, which, after being fried in oil, she was compelled to eat, and thus underwent the most horrible torture.

Such is the history of Māgandiyā.

One day the assembly of Rahans said to Parā Taken, "Lord and master, the death of Sāmavatī and her 500 attendants who were all full of faith and love was by no means right."—"Beloved Rahans," replied Parā Taken, "this Sāmavatī and her 500 attendants, a long time ago, when Brahmadatta was king of the Benares country, were the concubines of that king. One day when the king was playing in the river with his concubines, these finding themselves very cold, and wishing to warm themselves at a fire, began to search here and there for fuel or rubbish to make a fire with. Finding on the bank of the river a bush of dry reeds, and thinking it was only rubbish, they set fire to it and warmed themselves at it. Now, in this bush was a Pakkekabuddha practising the Nirodhasamāpatti.[1] When the concubines saw the Pakkekabuddha in the flames, they cried out, "We have burned the Pakkekabuddha, the king's teacher; if this come to the king's ears we

[1] Some supernatural attainment; a kind of ecstasy or trance.

THE STORY OF QUEEN SAMAVATI. 59

shall all be executed; let us go and get some firewood and burn him up altogether." So saying they brought a log each, and making a large heap, set fire to it; then thinking that the body would be entirely consumed and leave no trace, they went away. Although these concubines had no intention to take life, still their sin followed them in due course; for a thousand years they suffered in hell, and now at last their house has been set on fire, and they themselves have been burnt to death. Such is the account of the former sin of Sāmavatī. As to the Pakkekabuddha, if a thousand cart-loads of fuel had been burnt around him while he was in the state of Sammāpāta, they would not have made him feel hot; on the seventh day he arose from the state of Nirodhasamāpatti, and went his way in comfort."

Again the Rahans said to Parā Taken, "On account of what evil deeds was Khugguttarā a slave? And owing to what good deeds did she become so learned and acquire the three books of the Pitaka; from what good deeds is it that she is now settled in the reward of Sotāpatti?" Parā Taken replied, "Beloved Rahans, in a former existence of Khugguttarā there was a Pakkekabuddha in the country of Benares, who was rather hump-backed. Khugguttarā when she saw him, laughed at his deformity; and for this sin she became hump-backed herself. But when this same Pakkekabuddha came to the king's palace to receive alms of food, and the king poured an offering of cow's milk into his thabet, which completely filled it, Khugguttarā, seeing the Pakkekabuddha shifting the thabet from hand to hand on account of the great heat of the milk, immediately took off her arm eight ivory bracelets which she was wearing, and making a stand for the pot with them, presented them as an offering. It was for this good deed that she has acquired such great wisdom, and is conversant with all the three books of the Pi*t*aka. Those ivory bracelets are extant to this day in the Nandamūla mountain cave. It was in consequence of her having formerly made offerings of rice to that Pa*kk*ekabuddha that she is established in the reward of Sotāpatti. Such is the account of the results of the good and bad actions performed by Khu*gg*uttarā before I became a Parā.

"In the time of the Parā Kassapa this Khu*gg*uttarā was the daughter of a T*hu/he* at Benares. One day when she was very handsomely attired, a Rahan who was on his way to contemplate the Parā, came to her house, and she said to him, 'Just reach me that little basket which is there.' For this she became a slave."

END OF THE STORY OF SAMAVATI AND KHU*G*GUTTARA.

CHAPTER VI.

STORY OF KULLA-PANTHAKA.

The most excellent Parā, when he was residing in the Veluvana monastery, preached the following discourse on the subject of Kulla-Panthaka.

Formerly there lived in the Rāgagaha country the daughter of a Thuthe named Dhanasethi. When she reached the age of maturity, her parents placed her in a Pyathat with seven stages of roofs, and there, being a girl of strong passions, she committed herself with one of the slaves; then fearing that any one should know of it, they ran away to another village, and lived there together. She soon became in the family-way, and when her time was nearly come, she said to the young man, "My time is very near; I shall go to my parents' village to be confined." The young man, afraid that if he went there they would kill him, would not accompany her, so the Thuthe's daughter, thinking what unalloyed affection parents have for their children, set out without her husband; but he, as soon as he found that she had gone, followed her.

On the road the Thuthe's daughter gave birth to a son, whereupon she returned home without visiting her parents' village. In consequence of the boy having been born on the road, they gave him the name of Panthaka.

Shortly afterwards, the Thuthe's daughter became again pregnant; and when her time was approaching, in the same way as before she started for her parents' village, and was a second time confined on the road. On this occasion also she gave birth to a son, whom she called Kulla-Panthaka, distinguishing her firstborn by the name of Mahā-Panthaka.

When Mahā-Panthaka grew up, he said one day to his mother, "I hear others calling people their grandfather, or grandmother, or uncle; but we have no grandfather or grandmother, or any relations at all." His mother replied, "My dear son, your grandfather and grandmother, and all your relations live in the Rāgagaha country; your grandfather is the Thuthe Dhanasēthi. In that Rāgagaha country my relations are very numerous."—"Then why, mother," said he, do you not go to the Rāgagaha country?" The Thuthe's daughter remained silent; at last, when he persisted in asking the question, she replied, "My son, your father was a slave in your grandfather's house, so I ran away from home and came to live here."—"If that be so," said the lad, "take my younger brother and me to the place where our grandfather and grandmother live."

The Thuthe's daughter took her two sons to the Rāgagaha country, and when she reached the city, she went with them into the Zayat[1] at the gate and stopped there. When the Thuthe's neighbours saw her, they went to him and said, "My lord Thuthe's

[1] A building for the accommodation of travellers.

daughter with her two sons is staying in the Zayat." The *Thuthe*, thinking that if they were to remain in the Zayat, people would speak ill of him, took away his two grandchildren, and gave them gold and silver, food and clothes; but having no affection for his daughter, he sent her away, telling her to go and live where she had been always living: so she went away and lived with her slave-husband in the same place as before.

When the two lads had grown up under their grandfather's care, Mahā-Panthaka went with his grandfather to hear Parā Taken preach the law. The discourse was upon the future reward of the life of a Rahan, and Mahā-Panthaka, after listening to it, became desirous of entering the priesthood. He accordingly obtained his grandfather's permission, and became one of the Rahans of Parā Taken.

Performing the duties of a Rahan, Mahā-Panthaka acquired the sacred Pāli[1] of Parā Taken, and becoming a Pañkānga[2] at the age of twenty, after employing himself in the repetition of the Kamma*tthā*na[3], he reached the state of a Rahanda.[4]

When Mahā-Panthaka had become a Rahanda, he made his brother Kulla-Panthaka a Rahan, and kept him steadily employed in the religious duties enjoined by Parā Taken.

Now Kulla-Panthaka, being wanting in ability

---

[1] The sacred language of the Burmese, a modification of Sanskrit.
[2] A priest who is a proficient in the five duties, *i.e.* an ordained Rahan.
[3] Forty sentences for repetition.
[4] An Ariya of the highest order.

could not learn a verse although he studied it for the whole four months of the rainy season. The reason of this was that in the time of the Parā Kassapa, Kulla-Panthaka, who was then a Rahan, derided another Rahan for his want of ability in reciting Pāli; in consequence of which, the Rahan was so ashamed that he altogether gave up the study of the sacred language. On account of this evil deed, Kulla-Panthaka when he subsequently became a Rahan in the time of the present Parā was so stupid that he forgot everything he learned.

At last Mahā-Panthaka said to Kulla-Panthaka, "Oh, Kulla-Panthaka, you are a being who is unworthy to obtain his deliverance[1] in this church. You cannot learn a single verse in four months, therefore you are unfit for the duties of a Rahan;" so saying, he turned him out of the monastery.

At this time Mahā-Panthaka performed the duty of distributing the rice. One day the physician Gīvaka came to him and said, "My lord Mahā-Panthaka, I wish to present rice to-morrow to Parā Taken: how many priests are there?" Mahā-Panthaka replied, "Kulla-Panthaka is stupid and unworthy of deliverance; besides him, there are 500 Rahans." The physician then said, "Invite and bring with you to-morrow Parā Taken and the 500 of his assembly." Kulla-Panthaka thought within himself, "My elder brother, Mahā-Panthaka, has accepted the invitation for all the Rahans, but has excluded me. My brother's love for me is lost. I will no longer be a Rahan, but will re-enter the laity;" and he determined to quit the monastery the next morning.

[1] *I. e.* Salvation, proximate or ultimate.

At daybreak on the following day, as Parā Taken was looking to see who was worthy of deliverance, he perceived Kulla-Panthaka. Then going to the arched entrance through which he would pass, he began to walk up and down. On his arrival, Parā Taken stood still: Kulla-Panthaka made obeisance to him. Parā Taken said to him, "Kulla-Panthaka, where are you going at this early hour of the morning?" He replied, "Lord and master, my brother has expelled me from the monastery; I am now going away to re-enter the laity."—"Kulla-Panthaka," said Parā Taken, "when your brother expelled you, why did you not come to me? When you become a layman again, what will you do? Remain with me." So saying, he stroked his head, and made him come with him to the monastery. When they arrived there, he placed him at the gate of the Gandhakuṭi[1] building, with his face to the east, and said to him, "Take this coarse cloth, and, rubbing it, repeat the words, Ragoharanam Ragoharanam,[2] and do not move from here." Parā Taken, after thus issuing his authoritative commands, gave him a coarse cloth of spotless white, and then went to the house of the physician Gīvaka to receive the alms of rice, accompanied by all his assembly.

Kulla-Panthaka, looking at the rising sun and rubbing the coarse cloth, continued to repeat "Ragoharanam, Ragoharanam." While repeating these words, the cloth as he was rubbing it lost its spotless white colour, and became soiled and dirty. Seeing this, he became impressed with the law of Samvega,[3] and exclaimed, "This cloth only now so pure and white is

---

[1] The abode of fragrance.   [2] Removal of dirt.
[3] Fear of the future consequences of sin.

soiled and dirty. This is my own state, soiled (by sin). Again, this is the law of mutability; nothing is permanent." Saying this he devoted himself earnestly to the repetition of the Vipassanā, and succeeded in acquiring it.

Parā Taken even while he was at the house of the physician *G*īvaka, knowing that *K*ulla-Panthaka had acquired the Vipassanā, dispatched an appearance[1] of himself to him, and preached to him the verses of the *K*amma*tth*āna, "O *K*ulla-Panthaka! Your body is full of minute atoms of dust which are lust, and the other evil passions. These minute atoms of dust you must get rid of." In this way he preached to him the law just as if he had actually been present; and he continued, "My dear son, *K*ulla-Panthaka, lust you must call Ra*g*a,[2] atoms of dust you must not call Ra*g*a. Ra*g*a means lust. When you have got rid of the atoms of dust which are lust, you are fit to be a member of the Church of Parā Taken. The same is to be said regarding anger and ignorance." At the close of the discourse upon these verses *K*ulla-Panthaka arrived at the state of a Rahanda possessed of intuitive knowledge, and Parā Taken knew that he had become a Rahanda.

At this time the physician *G*īvaka, before presenting rice to Parā Taken, was offering him water to wash his hands. Parā Taken said, "Dārakā, there is still in the monastery a Rahanda," and he remained with

---

[1] Gotama is said to have had the power of appearing in more than one place at once. The expression always used is that found in the text here, viz. "To send off his appearance."

[2] This word is Pāli, of which Parā Taken is teaching the meaning. "Ra*g*as" in Sanskrit means both "dust" and "passion."

his T*h*abet[1] closed. On this Mahā-Panthaka said that there were no Rahans left in the monastery; but G*i*vaka sent a slave to see whether any Rahans had been left there or not. At this moment Kulla-Panthaka saying to himself, "My brother says there are no Rahans in the monastery," created a thousand Rahans and filled with them the whole of the buildings, and the mango garden, some putting on their garments, others engaged in repeating the scriptures, and all exactly like himself.

When the messengers arrived at the monastery they found all the buildings and the mango garden completely filled with Rahans. As soon as the messengers had returned with this intelligence to Parā Taken, he said to them, "Go and invite the Rahan Kulla-Panthaka to come here." They went back and called out, "My Lord Kulla-Panthaka, Parā Taken has sent for you." The whole of the thousand Rahans replied, "I am Kulla-Panthaka." The messengers returned to Parā Taken and said, "Lord and master, the whole thousand Rahans say that they are Kulla-Panthaka, so we cannot find him out." Parā Taken said, "Go and call him again, and seize the hand of the Rahan who first answers, then all the rest will disappear." The messengers accordingly went again to invite Kulla-Panthaka, and laid hold of the hand of the Rahan who first of the whole thousand answered the summons; immediately all the other Rahans vanished. Kulla-Panthaka accompanied the messengers to the house of the physician G*i*vaka, and received his portion of rice in presence of Parā Taken.

[1] The vessel which the priests carry suspended round their necks, and held under the left arm, to receive the alms of food.

When the repast was finished Parā Taken said to Gīvaka, "Take off Kulla-Panthaka's Thabet, for he is going to preach the law." Gīvaka took off the Thabet, and Kulla-Panthaka, seeing that such was Parā Taken's wish, began in a voice like that of the Lion-King to preach the law of Anumodana,[1] reciting it from the three books of the Pitaka.

After Parā Taken had returned to the monastery in the cool of the evening, the Rahans of the assembly were saying to each other, "Masters! Mahā-Panthaka, not conversant with the mind of Kulla-Panthaka, and unable in four months to teach him a single verse, drove him from the monastery. A Parā Taken being an unrivalled master of the law, has the power of conducting a man in a single morning to the state of a Rahanda possessed of intuitive knowledge, and of rendering him acquainted with the three books of the Pitaka. "Wonderful indeed are the Parās!"

Parā Taken said to them, "This is not the first time that I have afforded assistance to Kulla-Panthaka," and he proceeded to relate as follows the events of times long gone by:—"This Kulla-Panthaka a long time ago was a young man of Benares: while engaged in the acquisition of learning and science in the Takkasilā country, he attended on and supplied food to the teacher Disāpamokkha, and received instruction from him for three months. Through his excessive stupidity, however, he failed to learn anything at all. His master, grateful for the care and attention which his pupil bestowed on him in serving him and supplying all his wants, redoubled his efforts, but all to no effect. At last, the youth, seeing that he could learn nothing,

[1] Joy.

asked his teacher's permission to leave. The master thinking himself much indebted to his pupil for his kindness to him, took him away into a forest to present him with a charm, and instructed him as follows:—" Gha/esi Gha/esi kim kāra*n*a? tava karmam aham *g*ānāmi.[1] Repeat this charm constantly so as never to forget it. It will always provide you with a living. Wherever you may happen to be, you have only to utter the charm."

On the young man's return to Benares, he went to live with his parents.

About this time the king of Benares, disguising himself, went out one night to discover whether the actions of his subjects were good or evil. Coming to the house of the young man who had learned the charm, he placed himself close up against the wall and began to listen. It happened that some thieves having dug a mine in the space between this house and the next, were just about to rob the house. At this moment the young man who had returned from the Takkasilā country awoke and began to recite the charm, "Gha/esi Gha/esi kim kāra*n*a? tava karmam aham *g*ānāmi." The thieves as soon as they heard the charm, said, "This young man has found us out," and ran away. The king seeing the thieves running away, and knowing that this was in consequence of their hearing the charm, carefully noted the position of the young man's house, and returned home.

When daylight came, the king called some of his people, and told them to go to such a place and find out the young man who had returned from the Takkasilā country, and bring him to him. When they had

[1] Why are you busy? Why are you busy? I know your design.

brought the young man before him, he said, "Young man, give me the charm you were repeating last night."—"Take it, your Majesty," he replied, and he recited it to the king, who repeated it till he knew it. After learning it the king gave him a present worth a thousand (pieces of gold), as a teacher's fee.

At this time the prime minister, having formed the design of taking the king's life, went to his Majesty's barber and said to him, "When you shave the king's beard, take a very sharp razor and cut his throat. When I am king I will give you the post of prime minister." He made the barber a present worth a thousand [pieces of gold], and the man agreed to do it. Accordingly, after he had soaked the king's beard with perfumed water before shaving it, he took the razor and was just going to cut his throat when at that moment, the king thinking of the charm, began to recite, "Gha*t*esi, Gha*t*esi kim kāra*n*a? tava karmam aham *j*ānāmi." The barber no sooner heard this than he said, "The king has discovered my intention;" then he dropped the razor and fell trembling at the king's feet. The king exclaimed, "Oh, you barber! do you not know I am the king?"—"Your Majesty," said the barber, "it was no plot of mine; the prime minister gave me a present worth a thousand [pieces of gold] to cut your Majesty's throat while I was shaving you; it was he who induced me to attempt it." The king said to himself, "It is owing to this young man who taught me the charm, that my life has been saved." Then he sent for the prime minister and banished him from the country, saying, "Since you have plotted against my life, you can no longer live within my territory." After this, he called the young man who had given him the charm, and making him a very handsome present as an acknowledgment of his services, conferred on him the post of prime minister.

That young man is now Kulla-Panthaka, and the teacher Disāpamokkha is now I the Parā.

When he had finished preaching the law, the whole of the assembly who listened to it were settled in the reward of Sotāpatti.

END OF THE STORY OF KULLA-PANTHAKA.

CHAPTER VII.

STORY OF THE PROBATIONER TISSA.

On another occasion Parā Taken, while residing in the Getavana monastery, preached a discourse with reference to the probationer Tissa.

In the country of Rā*g*agaha there lived a Brahmin named Mahāsena, who was a friend of the Brahmin Vanga, the father of Sāriputta.

Sāriputta, taking pity on the Brahmin Mahāsena, came and stood at the door of his house with the intention of assisting him. Mahāsena said to himself, "Here is Sāriputta, the son of my friend Vanga, who is evidently waiting to receive rice,[1] and I have nothing of which I can make him an offering." And he went and hid himself.

One day, Mahāsena went to a T*hulh*e's house and received a cloth and a cup of cow's milk.[2] Then he thought he would make an offering to Sāriputta.

---

[1] The word rice used in the text here and elsewhere means any kind of food offered to a priest, though its literal meaning is cooked rice.

[2] The printed text and manuscript vary greatly here: the former says, "after presenting grass he received a cloth," etc.; the latter says, "Going to a T*hulh*e's house to obtain alms of food for the day, he received," etc.

STORY OF THE PROBATIONER TISSA.

Sāriputta at that very moment, rising from the performance of Samāpatti, was looking to see whom he should deliver, and knowing that Mahāsena, having an offering to make, wished to come to him, he went to the Brahmin's house and stood at the door. As soon as the Brahmin saw him, he invited him to come up into his house and poured into his thabet some rice cooked in milk. Sāriputta, after taking half of the rice, closed his thabet. The Brahmin said, "Lord and master, save me in my life to come; give me no help in this life;" saying this, he poured the rest of the rice into the thabet. Sāriputta then ate the rice; when he had finished, Mahāsena made him an offering of a coarse cloth with this invocation, " Lord and master, the law which you know may I also know." Sāriputta, after having preached the law, took his departure.

The Brahmin Mahāsena dying in natural course, became an embryo in the womb of one of the congregation of Sāriputta in the Sāvatthi country. The young girl, from the day that she became pregnant, was very desirous to supply food to Sāriputta and all his priests, and to wear herself the thingan,[1] and to drink milk prepared as for priests, out of a golden cup. Now the girl wishing to wear the thingan from the time that she was in the family-way, was the sign that the child in her womb would become a Rahan in the church. The girl's parents, thinking that if their daughter wished to be a Rahan, it was in accordance with the sacred law, supplied Sāriputta and his priests with cow's milk, and dressing the girl in a thingan, placed her after all the priests, and gave

[1] Priest's garment.

her her share of the offering of milk in a golden cup.

At the end of ten months she gave birth to a son. After the boy was washed, he was laid upon a coverlet worth a hundred thousand (gold pieces). Sāriputta was also invited, and had food presented to him. The child, lying on the coverlet and contemplating Sāriputta, thought to himself, "This priest is my old teacher; it is to him that I owe all this luxury. I must make him an offering."

At this moment the parents, wishing to name the child, took him up from the coverlet; but the child, wrapping his little finger in it, lifted it up with him. The parents tried to disengage his finger, but the child, retaining his hold of it, began to cry; so they took him up, coverlet and all, and laid him at the feet of my lord Sāriputta; the child, dragging the coverlet with his finger, placed it at Sāriputta's feet. When the child's parents saw this, they said to Sāriputta, "Lord and master, deign to accept the coverlet which the child offers you." He accepted it. Then the parents said, "Give a name to your disciple;" and he called the child 'Tissa.'

On every occasion of their performing ceremonies for the child, the parents regularly invited Sāriputta, and supplied him with food. When the child was seven years old, his parents delivered him to Sāriputta, to be made a Rahan. Sāriputta, after teaching the little boy to repeat the Kamma*tth*āna, made him a Rahan. For seven days the child's parents made offerings of food to Sāriputta, and the whole of his priests; after which they retired to their home.

On the seventh day, the probationer Tissa accompanied the Rahans to the Sāvatthi country, to collect alms. As soon as they arrived there, the inhabitants came out to meet the young probationer, and made him an offering of five hundred Putzos[1] and five hundred rice-bowls.

One day, going to the monastery where the probationer resided, they made an offering of five hundred more putzos and five hundred more rice-bowls, so that when he was only seven years old he had a thousand putzos and a thousand rice-bowls; these he presented to the Rahans of the assembly. His acquiring all these things was the result of his having given a single coarse cloth and a cup of milk to Sāriputta at the time that he was the Brahmin Mahāsena. From that day the probationer was always called Pindapātika[2] Tissa.

One night, when it was very cold, the probationer, going to the monastery to perform his duties, saw the Rahans warming themselves at a fire. "My masters," said he, "why do you warm yourselves at a fire?" —"Probationer," they replied, "we are warming ourselves because it is so cold."[3]—"If you are cold," said he, "wrap yourselves in coverlets." The Rahans rejoined, "Probationer, you alone have power and can procure these things. Where can we get coverlets from?"—"If this be so," replied the probationer, "those of my masters who wish for coverlets, follow me." Hearing this, because they wanted to wrap themselves in coverlets, a thousand Rahans followed behind a probationer who was only seven years old.

[1] A waist-cloth of about 4 yards long and 1½ wide, of silk or cotton. The national dress of the Burmese.
[2] He who lives on alms. See Burnouf, Introduction, p. 306.
[3] Fires are not properly allowed within monasteries in Burmah.

The probationer, taking with him the thousand Rahans, went outside of the city, and as he visited house after house, the inhabitants as soon as they saw him, feeling the strongest affection for him, presented him with 500 coverlets. When he returned within the city, a wealthy T*hu/he* was selling coverlets in the bazaar. The slave who watched the shop went to his master and said, "Here is a probationer coming with 500 coverlets; hide yours, master." The T*hu/he* said, "Does the probationer take them when they are given to him, or does he take them without their being given to him?"—"He takes them when they are given," replied the slave.—"Very good, then," said the T*hu/he*, "if so, do not hide them; let them be." The novice, with the thousand Rahans, arrived at the place where the coverlets were spread out. The T*hu/he* who owned them no sooner saw the novice than he loved him as his own son, and made him an offering of 500 of the coverlets, making this invocation, "Lord and master, the law which you know may I also know!" The novice preached to him the law of Anumodana.[1]

Thus, this young probationer, obtaining in a single day a thousand coverlets, presented them to the thousand Rahans. From this time, they gave the novice the name of Kambalāra Tissa.[2] It was in consequence of his having made an offering of a coverlet to my lord Sāriputta on the occasion of his giving him the name of Tissa, on the seventh day after his birth, that when he was seven years old he received a thousand coverlets.

Therefore Parā Taken preached, "Beloved Rahans,

---

[1] Joy. [2] Who procures coverlets.

offerings made to the priesthood, though they be but small, are rewarded as if they were large. Large offerings receive still more excellent rewards."

The probationer, after learning the Kammatthāna from Parā Taken, went away and resided in a temporary monastery at a distance of 120 yoganas. There, during the whole three months of the Lent, he practised the repetition of the Kammatthāna, and reached the stage of a Rahanda.

END OF THE STORY OF THE PROBATIONER TISSA.

CHAPTER VIII.

STORY OF MAHĀKAPPINA-THERA.

On another occasion, Parā Taken, residing in the *G*etavana monastery, preached the following discourse on the subject of the priest Mahākappina:—

At a place not far from Benares there lived a thousand weavers. At that time a thousand Pa*kk*eka-Buddhas,[1] who had been residing for eight months at Himavanta, came to the weavers' village. When the head man of the weavers' village saw the Pa*kk*eka-Buddhas, he invited them to come on the following day to receive offerings of rice. The Pa*kk*eka-Buddhas accepted the invitation. The head-weaver then went round the village saying that he had invited the Pa*kk*eka-Buddhas, and that every house was to entertain one priest each. The villagers did as they had been directed, and the Pa*kk*eka-Buddhas, after receiving their rice, preached the law to them. The weavers then invited them to reside with them during the whole of the three months' Lent, and, the invitation being accepted, every weaver built one monastery apiece for the whole thousand, and each supplied one of them with food and all he required.

[1] A semi-Buddha.

When Lent was over, the weavers made an offering to them of a thousand putzos[1] for t*h*ingans.[2] After making this pious offering, when they died, they became inhabitants of the Tāvatinsa Nat-country; having enjoyed all the luxury of the Nats, they appeared in the time of the Parā Taken Kassapa among the T*h*ugyuès[3] of Benares. The head-weaver was the son of the head T*h*ugyuè; the other weavers were all sons of T*h*ugyuès, and their wives daughters of T*h*ugyuès, and they were all married to one another.

One day, when Parā Taken Kassapa was preaching the law, the T*h*ugyuès went into the enclosure of the monastery to hear him. While they were there, it began to rain heavily. Many people who were relations of the teacher were inside the building, but the T*h*uygues, not being his relations, got wet through. They were very much ashamed, and deliberating among themselves, resolved to erect an extensive monastery. The head-weaver put down a thousand (pieces of gold), and the others five hundred each. Then they erected a large and splendid monastery with a thousand spires. This they presented as a grand offering to Kassapa Parā Taken and all his Rahans. At the same time the wife of the head-weaver presented as an offering to the Parā Taken a putzo worth a hundred thousand (pieces of gold), which she had placed on a bouquet of Létsarue-blossoms making this invocation: "Lord and master, in my future states of existence, may I resemble the blossom of

---

[1] Waist-cloth of the laity.
[2] Priests' garments.
[3] Same as T*h*ut*h*e, the wealthy class.

the Létsarue![1] and may I be called Anoṇā!" Kassapa Parā Taken said, "Dārakāma, it shall be fulfilled according to your prayer."

When the T*h*ugyuès, leaving that state of existence, died, they appeared in the Nat country. In the time of the Parā Taken Gotama, after dying and leaving the Nat country, they appeared in the country of Kukkuvatī. The head-weaver became King Mahākappi*na*, his wife was the daughter of the great king of the Sāketa[2] country; owing to her resemblance to the blossom of Létsarue, she was called the Princess Anoṇā. When she grew up she became the wife of King Mahākappina. The other weavers were all sons and daughters of great nobles; and when they were old enough, they became the husbands and wives of each other.

King Mahākappina, enjoying all the luxury of royalty, began to say to himself, "I am a king, but I can neither see nor hear of the three jewels."[3] Having a great longing for them, he sent off one day four of his nobles on horseback from the four sides of his city, telling them to go two or three yoṇanas and see if they could gather any tidings of Parā, the law, and the priesthood. The nobles, however, came back without having procured any intelligence.

One day, while the king, mounted on horseback, was amusing himself in the garden attended by a thousand nobles, there came by five hundred merchants from the country of Sāvatthi. The king asked whence they came, and when he was told they came from Sāvatthi,

[1] A species of nettle.
[2] The city of Ayodhyā, or ancient Oude.
[3] Buddha, the law, and the priests.

he inquired if there was any news in their country. The merchants replied, "Your Majesty, the jewel is there, the Parā. The king, whose heart on hearing this was filled with faith and love, said to them, "I will present you with a hundred thousand (gold pieces). Is there any further news?"—"The jewel, the law, is there," they replied. The king, moved with love and joy at this intelligence, added a present of another hundred thousand, and asked them if they had any more intelligence. They said, "There is the jewel, the priesthood." The king, on hearing this, again increased his present by a hundred thousand more. Then he said to his nobles, "I will go to the place where are to be found the jewel, the Parā; the jewel, the law; and the jewel, the priesthood. I shall not return to my city, but shall go and become a Rahan in the society of Parā Taken." The nobles said, "Your Majesty, we will all go with you and become Rahans." Then the king wrote on a leaf of gold and gave it to the merchants; the writing was this: "To the queen, from King Mahākappina. I am going to become a Rahan with Parā Taken in the Sāvatthi country. My queen, remain here and enjoy all the happiness and luxury of the royal power." He also sent this message to her: "I have offered as an acknowledgment to these merchants three hundred thousand (pieces of gold); give it to them." The king, with his thousand nobles, then set off on their journey.

Parā Taken, on that day at daybreak, was looking out to see who was worthy of deliverance. Seeing that King Mahākappina and his thousand nobles would become Rahandas, he went out to meet him like the

Kakravarti king going to meet the kings owning the subordinate villages. After travelling twenty yoganas, he stopped at the foot of a banyan-tree on the bank of the Kandapa river, emitting from his person six dazzling rays of glory.

King Mahākappina, continuing his journey, came to a river. "What river is this?" he asked. "Your Majesty, this is the Avarakkha river," they replied. "What is the depth and width of it?" he asked. They told him: "One gavyūti[1] deep, and two gavyūtis wide."—"Are there any boats on this river?" he asked. They said, "There are none." Then the king said, "Nobles! our existence is but birth, old age, and death: we have come on account of Parā Taken, let the water bear us firmly." Then, fixing their minds steadily on the virtues of Parā Taken, they went on to the water on their horses and began to cross. The surface of the water became like a stone slab, not even the hoofs of their horses were wetted.

After King Mahākappina with his thousand nobles had reached the opposite shore, they came to another river. "What river is this?" asked the king. The nobles answered, "This is the Nīlavāha river."— "What is the width and depth of this river?" he asked. "Half a yogana wide, and as much deep," they replied. "Are there any boats on this river?" he asked. They replied, "There are none." The king said, "If that be so, our existence is but birth, old age, and death; reflecting on the virtues of the Law, let the water bear us firmly." Then fixing their minds steadily on the virtues of the Law, the king and his thousand nobles stepped on to the water on their horses. The surface

---

[1] A little more than three miles.

of the water became like a stone slab, and not even the hoofs of their horses were wetted.

After reaching the opposite shore they proceeded onwards and came to another river. "What river is this?" asked the king. The nobles replied, "This is the Kandapa river."—"What is the width and depth of it?" he asked. The nobles answered, "A yogana both in width and depth."—"Are there any boats on this river," he asked. They replied, "There are none." The king said, "If this be so, nobles, our existence is but birth, old age, and death; reflecting on the virtues of the priesthood, let the water bear us firmly." Fixing their minds steadily on the virtues of the priesthood, they stepped on to the water on their horses. The surface of the water became like a stone slab; not even the hoofs of their horses were wetted.[1]

The king after crossing the Kandapa river proceeded on his journey, and came near a banyan-tree. Seeing that the branches and leaves were shining like gold, the king said to himself, "This brilliancy is not that of the sun or moon; it must be the glory of Parā Taken." So saying he got off his horse, and advancing with his eyes fixed on the sacred rays, he beheld Parā Taken at the foot of the banyan-tree; when he saw him, he did homage to him and remained at a respectful distance. Parā Taken preached the law to King Mahākappina, and established him in the reward of Sotāpatti.

The king and his thousand nobles having become Sotāpans asked permission to enter the priesthood.

---

[1] The above is a good specimen of the tedious reiteration often found in works of this kind.

Parā Taken began to look, saying to himself, "These[1] people are possessed of great power and glory, will they become wearers of the T*h*abet and T*h*ingan?" Then he saw that King Mahākappina had formerly, when he was a weaver, made an offering of a T*h*ingan to a thousand Pa*kk*ekabuddhas, and that in the time of the Parā Kassapa he had made an offering of twenty thousand T*h*ingans to twenty thousand Rahans. Extending both his sacred hands, he called to them, "Come, Rahans! in order to terminate all suffering, be earnest in performing good deeds." Becoming Rahandas with the eight priestly utensils, they flew up into the sky, and alighting at the sacred feet of Parā Taken, remained in adoration.

The merchants entering the city of Kukkuvatī presented themselves before Queen Ano*g*ā, and said to her, "King Mahākappina and his thousand nobles have gone away to become Rahans with Parā Taken; he directs your Majesty to remain in the enjoyment of the royal power, and has instructed us to ask from your Majesty a present of three hundred thousand." Queen Ano*g*ā said, "Brothers, why did King Mahākappina give my brothers three hundred thousand?" The merchants replied, "Hearing that there was the jewel, the Parā, he gave us a hundred thousand; hearing that there was the jewel, the law, he gave us a hundred thousand; and hearing that there was the jewel, the priesthood, he gave us a hundred thousand." The queen, saying, "The Parā, the law, and the priesthood are indeed the three jewels," made the merchants a present of nine hundred thousand (pieces of gold).

[1] The manuscript has "will these people become wearers of the powerful and glorious T*h*abet and T*h*ingan?"

The queen said to the wives of the thousand nobles, "King Mahākappina has gone away to become a Rahan with Parā Taken, I shall therefore likewise go and become a Rahan with Parā Taken." The wives of the nobles said, "We also will go with you and become Rahans with Parā Taken."

Queen Anogā with the thousand wives of the nobles riding in carriages, started off on their journey. When they came to the three rivers, thinking steadily upon, and fixing their faith in the virtues of the Parā, the law, and the priesthood successively, they went on to the water in their carriages; the surface of the water became like a stone slab, and not even the edges of the wheels were wetted. After crossing the three rivers they came to the banyan-tree; when they saw Parā Taken they did homage to him, and remaining at a respectful distance, said to him, "Lord and master, the great King Mahākappina and his thousand nobles have gone away to become Rahans with my lord the Parā, where are they now?" Parā Taken replied, "You will see them directly, stay here one moment." Then he preached the law to Queen Anogā and her companions. The queen and the nobles' wives all became Sotāpans. The queen asked permission to become a Rahan. Parā Taken preached the law which extends (the truth). The queen and the thousand nobles' wives became Rahans. Then Parā Taken showed them the priest Mahākappina and his companions; and the queen and her attendants when they saw them, did homage to them, saying, "My lords, you have reached the state of Rahandas, let us also become Rahandamas."[1] Paying homage

[1] Female Rahanda.

to Parā Taken they begged him to confer on them the condition of Rahandas. Parā Taken gave them into the charge of the Rahandama Uppalavaṇṇā, who employed them in their duties as Rahans, and they all became Rahandamas.

End of the Story of Mahakappina-thera.

CHAPTER IX.

STORY OF THE PROBATIONER PANDITA.

On one occasion Parā Taken while residing in the Getavana monastery preached the following discourse on the subject of the novice Pandita:—

In former times, when the Parā Taken Kassapa attended by twenty thousand Rahans came to Benares, the people of the country entertained them hospitably and provided for their wants. The Parā Taken preached as follows: "In this country some people make offerings of their own goods, but they do not incite others to do so; these, in whatever state they may hereafter be, have abundance of wealth, but they lack relations and attendants. Some people incite others, but make no offerings themselves; these, in whatever state they may hereafter be, have numerous relations and attendants, but they lack wealth. Some people make offerings of their own goods and also incite others; these, in whatever state they may hereafter be, have abundance of wealth and numerous relations and slaves."

A Dārakā,[1] after listening to this discourse invited Parā Taken to receive an offering of a repast on the

[1] Supporter of the priesthood.

following day. Having first laid down his own money he incited the others, saying, "O townsmen, to-morrow I am going to provide Parā Taken with food. Let each of you submit a written statement mentioning how many of the Rahans of Parā Taken you can supply with food." Accordingly, the inhabitants submitted written statements separately, one engaging to supply with food a hundred, another fifty, another ten, another five. Among them was a very poor day-labourer named Mahādūta, who, when he was urged to contribute, submitted his written engagement to supply one priest. On his return home he said to his wife, "Mother![1] the inhabitants of the city are going to make offerings of food to-morrow to the Parā Taken Kassapa and the twenty thousand priests, and have sent in lists to the Rahans." His wife said, "Very good, it is because we have never made any offerings that we are so poor."

The husband and wife then went out to work for hire. The man went to a Thuthe's house and split firewood, singing very pleasantly all the time he was at work. The Thuthe, pleased at the quantity of firewood he had split, said to him, "Ho! you Mahādūta, you have split a great deal of firewood; what makes you sing so happily over your work?" He replied, "My lord Thuthe, I am happy because I have sent in a written engagement to supply food to one Rahan to-morrow from my day's wages." The Thuthe, pleased with him, gave him eight Kunsās[2] of Namathale[3] rice. Mahādūta's wife also went to a Thuthe's wife to work

---

[1] An interjection of astonishment or distress.
[2] A small measure, about enough for one meal.
[3] One kind of rice.

STORY OF THE PROBATIONER PANDITA.

for hire, and when the lady gave her rice to pound, she exerted herself diligently, singing all the while over her task. The Thuthe's wife said to her, "Why do you sing so pleasantly while you pound the rice?" She replied, "My lady Thuthema, I am rejoicing because to-morrow I am going to provide food for a holy Rahan." The Thuthema, pleased with her, gave her a Kunsā of Namathale rice, a ladle-full of butter, a cup of curdled milk, and a suitable quantity of chilis and onions. The husband and wife arose early on the following morning, and Mahādūta went to collect herbs. A fisherman, hearing him singing pleasantly as he was gathering the herbs, said to him, "What makes you sing so pleasantly as you gather the herbs?" He replied, "I sing while I gather them, because my heart is so full of love since I am going to present food to a Rahan." The fisherman was so pleased with him that he brought out four Ngagyings[1] which he had buried in the sand, and gave them to him.

In the morning, at daybreak, Parā Taken, looking to see who was worthy of deliverance, observed Mahādūta. Then he went into the Gandhakuṭi building.

Mahādūta took the fish home and cooked them very carefully.

The Sakka king, inspired by affection for Mahādūta, and knowing that Parā Taken was going to Mahādūta's house to receive an offering of food from him, disguised himself as a traveller, and, going to his house, said to him, "O Mahādūta! let me join with you in

---

[1] Name of a fish—a species of carp.
[2] The king of the Nats.

the offering, and share its reward." Mahādūta agreed to share it, saying, "Join with me." Then the Sakka king laid out the rice and all the other provisions, and imparted to them the exquisite flavour of the Nats; after this, he said, "Mahādūta, go and invite the Rahan who has been appointed to you according to your written agreement." Mahādūta went and said to the registrar, "Give me the Rahan appointed to me according to my written agreement." The registrar said, "I forgot to put you in the list, and all the Rahans are now provided for." Mahādūta, in great distress, burst into tears. Then the registrar said to him, "Parā Taken has just gone in at the door of the Gandhaku*t*i building, follow him, and give him an invitation." The king, the ministers, chiefs, T*hut*hes, and others, thinking Mahādūta a beggar, said to him, "Oh, you Mahādūta, he has not yet taken his repast, how can any offering of alms be made to you now? Go away." Mahādūta said, "I am going in to do homage to Parā Taken;" then laying his head on the sill of the door of the Gandhaku*t*i building, and doing homage to Parā Taken, he said, "Lord and master, in this country there is no one so miserable as I; have pity on me and help me." Parā Taken, opening the door of the Gandhaku*t*i building, gave his sacred t*h*abet to Mahādūta, who, carrying it on his shoulder, went out just as if he had obtained all the wealth and power of the *K*akravarti king. The king, the heir-apparent, the ministers, and all the others, said to Mahādūta, "O Mahādūta, take a thousand (pieces of gold), and give me the t*h*abet; you are a poor man, take the money." So saying, they all earnestly entreated him, offering him five hundred each, and a thousand each. But Mahādūta, saying, "What shall I do with money?" would not give up the t/abet, and took it away with him. Though the king himself endeavoured to persuade him, he would not give up the t/abet, but carried it off. Neither the king nor any one else dared to take by force the sacred t/abet which Parā Taken had given with his own sacred hand. The king, saying to himself, "Mahādūta is a poor man, where can he get proper rice or provisions for an offering; so, when he has nothing to offer, I will take the t/abet and give Parā Taken an invitation." With this design he followed Parā Taken to Mahādūta's house, where the Sakka king, after arranging the rice and the other provisions, had prepared a place for the Parā Taken.

Mahādūta, when Parā Taken, accepting his invitation, arrived at his house, told him to enter. Mahādūta's house was so low that no one could go into it without stooping. Now Parā Takens never bow their heads to enter a house. Accordingly, as Parā Taken entered the house, the earth sank down and he went in. The roof of the house also rose up. Such is the power of Parās. On taking their departure, the ground and the house become as before. Parā Taken, therefore, entering Mahādūta's house erect, went to the place prepared for him. The king also entered the house, and, occupying a suitable place, said to Mahādūta, "Mahādūta, when I asked you for the sacred t/abet you would not give it to me. Now, where are the rice and other provisions to offer to Parā Taken? Show them to me." The Sakka king uncovered the vessels containing the rice, cow's milk, and other provisions; and the fragrance they exhaled was so intense that it perfumed the whole country. The king, seeing the rice, milk, butter, and other provisions, exclaimed, "Never before have I seen food so full of fragrance!" Then, thinking that his presence would displease Mahādūta, and be a constraint upon him, he made obeisance to Parā Taken, and took his departure.

The Sakka king presented the provisions to Parā Taken. Parā Taken, when he had finished his repast, preached the Anumodana law and went away; and Mahādūta accompanied him with the sacred t/abet on his shoulder. The Sakka king, after going part of the way with them, returned to Mahādūta's house, and as he stood outside at the door and looked up to the sky, there fell a rain of the seven jewels: Mahādūta's house was so filled with gold and silver that there was not even room for any one to go into it; all the water-pots, baskets, and utensils of every description were filled with it. Mahādūta's wife, unable to get into the house for the gold and silver, had to remain outside with her little boy.

Mahādūta, after taking back the sacred t/abet, returned home. On his arrival, seeing his wife and little boy on the outer platform[1] of the house, said, "Mother, why do you stay on the outer platform; the sun is very hot." His wife replied, "Mahādūta, the whole house is so filled with gold and silver and jewels that we cannot stop there with any comfort, so we are staying outside." Mahādūta, seeing that this was the result of the offering he had made that day, went to the king and said to him, "Your Majesty, my house is filled with gold and silver and jewels;

[1] This is an uncovered platform, forming the entrance to a Burmese house.

deign to accept them." The king thought to himself, "The offering made only to day to Parā Taken has already terminated in its result. I must see this gold and silver and jewels." Then he despatched a thousand carts for the treasure, and had it all piled up before him; the heap was as high as the top of a palmyra-tree. The king said to the inhabitants, "Is there such a treasure as this in the country?" and they replied, "There is not." Then the king gave Mahādūta all the treasure, together with the insignia of a Thuthe.

Mahādūta, after attaining the rank of a Thuthe, asked the king to give him some land to build a house on, and the king made over to him the site of the house of a former Thuthe. Mahādūta, after having a quantity of wood and bamboos cut and stored ready for building his house, had the site cleared, digging up all the bushes and levelling the inequalities. In the course of this work they came upon a large number of pots of gold, all with their brims touching each other, so numerous that the whole of his land was full of them. The king, when he heard of this, said to him, "Mahādūta, this is owing to your great glory; you alone take them." Mahādūta, when he had finished building his house, during seven whole days supplied Parā Taken and all his Rahans with provisions, and made them magnificent offerings. After performing numerous good works he died, and his next existence was in the country of the Nats.

During the whole interval between two Parās, Mahādūta lived in the enjoyment of all the luxuries of the Nats. Leaving the Nat country on his death, in the time of this most excellent Parā Gotama, he became an embryo of the family of Sāriputta in the Sāvatthi country.

The T*h*u*th*e's daughter, from the day that she became pregnant,[1] had a great longing to eat Ngagying fish and rice. The reason of her having this longing was that she was desirous of making an offering of some Ngagying fish and rice to Sāriputta and the Rahans. She also wished to wear a putzo dyed in phanyī,[2] and, remaining in the lowest position among all the Rahans, to eat of the Ngagying fish and rice. Her parents accordingly made an offering of Ngagying fish to Sāriputta; and, dressing her in a putzo dyed with phanyi supplied her with a portion of the priests' rice and Ngagying fish in a golden cup. After having eaten in this way, she felt contented. The reason of her thus desiring to wear the t*h*ingan and partake of the priests' food was that her unborn child was destined to become a Rahan of the holy church.

After the lapse of ten months the young girl gave birth to a boy. She invited Sāriputta to come and name the child; and, after regaling him with rice, she said to him, "My lord Sāriputta, deign to bestow a name on your disciple." My lord Sāriputta named the child Pa*n*dita. When the child Pa*n*dita was seven years old, he became a Rahan with Sāriputta; and his parents, on the occasion of his entering on his probation, made offerings of rice for seven whole days. On the eighth day, when my lord Sāriputta took the probationer Pa*n*dita into the village with him, the boy, on the road (seeing) a labourer digging a ditch, an arrow-maker straightening his arrows over a fire, a car-

---

[1] With the former Mahādūta.
[2] Some kind of dye, probably of a yellow colour.

penter cutting wood with an adze, acquired the Kamma-ṭṭhāna.[1] Then he asked Sāriputta to let him go back to the monastery; when Sāriputta told him he might go back if he wished, he said, "Lord and master, if you bring me any offerings of food bring me some Ngagying fish." My lord Sāriputta said, "Probationer, where is any Ngagying fish to be procured?" The probationer replied, "Though it cannot be procured through the glory of my lord and master, it can be obtained through my glory." The probationer then went to my lord Sāriputta's monastery, and concentrating the wisdom that was in him, and meditating on his own condition, employed himself in repeating the law of the Rahans.[2] The Sakka king made the Katulokapāla Nats keep watch. They kept at a distance all the discordant sounds of birds and beasts. The Nat of the moon and the Nat of the sun kept the sun and moon waiting; the Sakka king himself kept guard at the door of the building. The probationer Pandita, in the morning, before he had taken food, meditating on his state, obtained the reward of Anāgāmi. When Sāriputta came to the house of his relations, they made him stay inside the house, and gave him Ngagying fish to eat; and after washing the thabet, filled it again with similar provisions. Sāriputta, thinking the probationer must be hungry, made haste to go to him.

At this time Parā Taken, after finishing his morning repast, looking to see whether the probationer

---

[1] This passage is obscure, both in the printed text and manuscript, which differ from each other here.

[2] This passage is also obscure, text and manuscript differing widely.

Pandita would become a Rahanda before taking food, and seeing that he would, conceived this project: "Sāriputta is hastening with food to the probationer; before he arrives I will go and post myself at the door, and will ask Sāriputta the questions; the probationer Pandita, hearing them from within, will become a Rahanda." Parā Taken accordingly was standing at the door of the building when Sāriputta arrived. He asked him, "What have you brought?"—"Lord and master," replied Sāriputta, "I have brought food."—"To what does food conduct?" he continued. "To the sensation of happiness," he replied. "To what does the sensation of happiness conduct?"—"An object of sense," he answered. "To what does the object of sense conduct?" he asked. "The act of feeling," he replied.[1]

The meaning of these questions is this: when a hungry man eats, as soon as he is full, a feeling of happiness is produced, and his person is beautified.

When Parā Taken had asked these four questions, and the probationer from within the building had heard the law as revealed in the replies given to them by Sāriputta, he reached the stage of a Rahanda possessed of intuitive knowledge. Then Parā Taken said, "Sāriputta, let the probationer eat." Sāriputta went up to the door of the building and made a noise. The probationer came to the door, and taking the thabet, put it down, and began to fan Sāriputta. Sāriputta said, "Probationer, eat your rice;" then he ate the rice and Ngagying fish.

In this way a probationer for the priesthood, only seven years of age, became a Rahanda.

[1] Almost all this is omitted in the manuscript.

The Sakka King dismissed again on their course the Nat of the sun and the Nat of the moon, and relieved from their watch the four Katulokapāla Nats.

On the completion of this discourse the whole assembly was established in the reward of Sotāpatti.

END OF THE STORY OF THE PROBATIONER PANDITA.

CHAPTER X.

THE STORY OF KISĀGOTAMI.

Para Taken, while he was staying in the *G*etavana monastery in the Sāvatthi country, preached the following discourse on the subject of Kisāgotamī:—

In the Sāvatthi country there was a T*huthe* who was worth four hundred millions. One day all the wealth in his house turned into charcoal. The T*huthe*, seeing this, was so wretched that he refused food and took to his bed. A friend of his, paying him a visit, seeing the miserable expression of his face, asked him why he was so wretched, and he told him that he was miserable because all his wealth had been changed into charcoal. His friend, who was also a T*huthe*, seeing that this had happened to him because he was not worthy of his wealth, said to him, "My friend T*huthe*, have no anxiety about this; I know a plan; will you do as I direct?" The T*huthe* said, "I will."—"Then," said his friend, "spread some mats in the bazaar, and pile up upon them all your wealth that has turned into charcoal, and pretend to be trafficking in it. People seeing the heap will say to you, 'O you T*huthe*, every one else sells clothes, tobacco,[1] oil, honey, and treacle; why do you sell charcoal?' Then you reply to them, 'I am selling my goods.' If any one say to you, 'Why do you sell so much gold and silver?' say to them, 'Bring it to me;' then take what they bring in their hand, and in your hand it will become gold and silver. If the person be a woman, marry her to your son; and making over to her the four hundred millions of your property make use of whatever she shall give you. If it be a man, marry your daughter to him, and making over the property to him, make use of what he shall give you."

The T*huthe*, following his friend's instructions, spread some mats in the bazaar, and piling upon them a large heap of his property which was turned into charcoal, pretended to be selling it. Some people, seeing it, said, "Why does he sell charcoal?" Just at this time a young girl named Kisāgotamī, who was worthy to be the owner of the property, and who having lost both her parents was in a wretched condition, happened to come to the bazaar on some business. When she saw the heap, she said, "My lord T*huthe*, all the people sell clothes, tobacco, oil, honey, and treacle; how is it that you pile up gold and silver for sale?" The T*huthe* said, "Madam, give me that gold and silver." Kisāgotamī, taking up a handful of it, brought it to him; what the young girl had in her hand no sooner touched the T*huthe*'s hand than it became gold and silver. The T*huthe* married the girl to his son, and having delivered over to her the whole

---

[1] The Burmese word rendered here "tobacco" means also "drugs" or "pigments" of any kind.

of the four hundred millions of his property, made use daily of the gold and silver which she gave him.

Some time after this, Kisāgotamī became in the family way, and when the ten months were completed, gave birth to a son. When the boy was able to walk by himself, he died. The young girl, in her love for it, carried the dead child clasped to her bosom, and went about from house to house asking if any one would give her some medicine for it. When the neighbours saw this, they said, "Is the young girl mad that she carries about on her breast the dead body of her son!" But a wise man thinking to himself, "Alas! this Kisāgotamī does not understand the law of death, I must comfort her," said to her, "My good girl, I cannot myself give medicine for it, but I know of a doctor who can attend to it." The young girl said, "If so, tell me who it is." The wise man continued, "Parā Taken can give medicine, you must go to him."

Kisāgotamī went to Parā Taken, and doing homage to him, said, "Lord and master, do you know any medicine that will be good for my boy?" Parā Taken replied, "I know of some." She asked, "What medicine do you require?" He said, "I want a handful of mustard seed." The girl promised to procure it for him, but Parā Taken continued, "I require some mustard seed taken from a house where no son, husband, parent, or slave has died." The girl said, "Very good," and went to ask for some at the different houses, carrying the dead body of her son astride on her hip.[1] The people said,

---

[1] The ordinary way of carrying children in Burmah and India.

"Here is some mustard seed, take it." Then she asked, "In my friend's house has there died a son, a husband, a parent, or a slave?" They replied, "Lady, what is this that you say! The living are few, but the dead are many." Then she went to other houses, but one said, "I have lost a son;" another, "I have lost my parents;" another, "I have lost my slave." At last, not being able to find a single house where no one had died, from which to procure the mustard seed, she began to think, "This is a heavy task that I am engaged in. I am not the only one whose son is dead. In the whole of the Sāvatthi country, every where children are dying, parents are dying." Thinking thus, she acquired the law of fear, and putting away her affection for her child, she summoned up resolution, and left the dead body in a forest; then she went to Parā Taken and paid him homage. He said to her, "Have you procured the handful of mustard seed?"—"I have not," she replied; "the people of the village told me, 'the living are few, but the dead are many.'" Parā Taken said to her, "You thought that you alone had lost a son; the law of death is that among all living creatures there is no permanence." When Parā Taken had finished preaching the law, Kisāgotami was established in the reward of Sotāpatti; and all the assembly who heard the law were also established in the reward of Sotāpatti.

Some time afterwards, when Kisāgotami was one day engaged in the performance of her religious duties, she observed the lights (in the houses) now shining, now extinguished, and began to reflect, "My state is like these lamps." Parā Taken, who was then in the Gandhakuṭi building, sent his sacred appearance to her, which said to her, just as if he himself were preaching, "All living beings resemble the flame of these lamps, one moment lighted, the next extinguished; those only who have arrived at Nibbāna are at rest." Kisāgotamī, on hearing this, reached the stage of a Rahanda possessed of intuitive knowledge.

END OF THE STORY OF KISĀGOTAMI.

CHAPTER XI.

STORY OF THE GIRL AND THE HEN.

A FISHERMAN, an inhabitant of the village of Pan*d*apura, close to the city of Sāvatthi, who was going to the city, found on his road, on the bank of the A*k*iravatī river, some turtles' eggs. He took these to the house of a friend in the city of Sāvatthi, cooked them and ate them all but one, which he gave to his friend's daughter to eat. From that time the girl would not eat any other kind of food, but lived on hens' eggs which her mother used to cook for her. Afterwards, actuated by her greediness, the girl took to cooking them with her own hands and eating them every day.

The hen, seeing the girl eating the egg which she laid daily, bore a grudge against her, and prayed that in her existence hereafter, she might become a ghoul and eat up the girl's offspring.

When the hen died she became a cat in the same house, and the girl on her death became a hen in her mother's house. Whenever the hen laid eggs, the cat, who bore a grudge against her and was her enemy, ate them up. After this had happened several times, the hen prayed that in her future existence she might devour the cat and all her progeny. The girl dying, and leaving her condition of a hen, became a leopard, and the cat, when she died, became a deer. The deer gave birth to a fawn, and the leopard, who bore her a grudge, ate them both up. In this way, during the whole course of five hundred existences, each of them devoured the other in turn.

In their last existence of all, one became a Bilūma;[1] and the other, a young girl in the Sāvatthi country. Parā Taken, who was residing in that country in the *G*etavana monastery, preached to them: "No one must bear a grudge against another, saying, he has injured me, he has beaten me, he has robbed me, he has conquered me; for if he does this, hatred will be repeated successively in future existences; but if no grudge be borne, enmity subsides." At the end of the discourse, the Bilūma, repeating the Sara*n*agamana,[2] and observing the five[3] commandments, was released from her hatred, and the girl was established in the reward of Sotāpatti.

END OF THE STORY OF THE GIRL AND THE HEN.

---

[1] A female Bilū, a sort of ghoul.
[2] The formula, "I worship Parā, the law, and the priesthood."
[3] Against murder, theft, adultery, falsehood, intoxication.

CHAPTER XII.

STORY OF THE HEN AND THE LITTLE SOW.

At another time, Parā Taken, when he was in the Getavana monastery, preached a discourse about a little sow.

Parā Taken, one day, as he was entering the Rāgagaha city to collect food, seeing a little sow at the gate of the city, smiled. My lord Ānanda asked him why he smiled. " Ānanda," he replied, " I am smiling at this little sow." Ānanda asked him what there was about the sow to make him smile, and he said:

" Ānanda, this little sow, in the time of the Parā Kakusandha was a hen; hearing a Rahan in a forest-monastery repeating the Vipassanā Kamma*tth*āna, and knowing that it was the Law, she listened to it; from the influence of this good deed, when she died, she became the princess Upari. The princess, going one day to a certain place, saw there a heap of maggots; repeating the Puluvakasañā, she obtained the first state of Dhyāna. After her death she was born again in the Brahma[1] country. Now this princess, from an inhabitant of the Brahma country, has, by transition to another existence, been changed into a little sow; it was this that made me smile. When, upon her death, she leaves the condition of a sow, she will become the wife of the prime minister."

[1] The highest order of beings, superior to the Nats.

When the Rahans heard Parā Taken say this, they acquired the law of Samvega.[1]

After the little sow died, and had become the wife of the prime minister residing in the village of Mahāpunna, the Rahans, on their way to collect food, seeing her standing at the door of her house, said, "My masters, the little sow has become the prime minister's wife." The prime minister's wife no sooner heard this than she trembled, and becoming impressed with the law of Samvega, and acquiring the Gātisāra knowledge, which enables the possessor to see his past existences, she saw that in the time of the Parā Kakusandha she was a hen; dying from the condition of a hen, she became in the time of the Parā Gotama the princess Upari; dying from the condition of the princess Upari, she existed again in the Brahma country; dying out of the Brahma country, she became a little sow; dying out of the condition of the little sow, she became the wife of the prime minister.

The moment that she saw all this, she asked her husband's permission, and became a Rahan under the priest Pañkapathaka, and directly after listening to the Satipatthāna law in the Tissamahāvihāra monastery, she was established in the reward of Sotāpatti. After becoming a Sotāpan, and while she was living in the village of Gandhā, to which she had gone and where her relatives resided, she listened to the law of Āsivisut in the Kamlakamahāvihāra monastery, and immediately afterwards became a Rahanda.

END OF THE STORY OF THE HEN AND THE LITTLE SOW.

---

[1] Fear.

CHAPTER XIII.

STORY OF THE PROBATIONER KULLA-SUMANA.

Parā Taken, while he was residing in the Pubbārāma monastery, preached a discourse on the subject of Anuruddha-thera.[1]

Anuruddha-thera, at the time a country lad, having heard that the Parā Taken Padumuttara had advanced one of the laity to the condition of Devakakkhu, made offerings of rice for seven days to Parā Taken, and then made this prayer: "Lord and master, may I also in the time of the future Lord have the superior condition of Devakakkhu!" The Parā Taken Padumuttara, looking through a hundred thousand future cycles, saw that his prayer would be fulfilled, and prophesied, "From the present cycle a hundred thousand cycles hence, in the time of the Parā Taken Gotama, you will be Anurudha-thera, having the faculty of Devakakkhu. The lad, on hearing the prophecy, held it in his mind just as if its fulfilment were to take place the very next day.

The Parā Taken Padumuttara having obtained

---

[1] The affix 'thera' to a name signifies priest or Rahan among the Burmese, but here means one of the disciples of Gotama.

Paranibbāna,[1] the Rahans to whom he had given the Kasina,[2] by which is acquired the Deva*k*akkhu wisdom, remained engaged in the practice of it; the laity having made an offering of a golden pagoda seven yo*g*anas in extent, provided with a thousand lamp-pillars, prayed for the rewards of their good works.

When the lad died, he had his next existence in the country of the Nats. After experiencing the vicissitudes of a hundred thousand cycles in the land of men, and in the land of the Nats, he was born among the poor at Benares in the present cycle. He became the slave of the T*hu*t*h*e Sumana, and used to have to cut grass every day; he was named Annabhāra.

On one occasion as the Pa*kk*ekabuddha Upadi*tt*a arose from the practice of the Nirodha-samāpatti,[3] and was looking to see whom he should deliver, this Annabhāra was coming from the forest after cutting grass there. The Pa*kk*ekabuddha, by means of his glory, flew through the sky and alighted beside him. When Annabhāra saw the Pa*kk*ekabuddha, he said to him, "Lord and master, have you obtained any rice?" —"Not yet," he replied. "Wait here, lord and master," said the boy; and throwing down his bundle of grass, he ran home and returned as fast as possible with the rice which he had provided for his own food. Putting this into the Pa*kk*ekabuddha's t*h*abet, he prayed, "May I never again experience such poverty; never again hear the words 'there is none!'" The Pa*kk*ekabuddha said, "It shall be fulfilled according to your wish," and after preaching the law, went away.

---

[1] Same as Nibbāna; literally, the highest Nibbāna.
[2] One kind of Kamma*tth*āna, in Sanskrit, K*r*itsna.
[3] A kind of trance or ecstasy.

STORY OF THE PROBATIONER KULLA-SUMANA. 109

Just at this time the Nat's daughter, who was guardian of the umbrella[1] of the T*hu*t*he* Sumana, called out three times, "Sādhu.[2]" The T*hu*t*he* said, "Daughter of the Nats, why do you cry 'Sādhu'?" She replied, "Annabhāra, full of love for the Pa*kk*ekabuddha, is making an offering of rice to him; that is why I cry 'Sādhu.'" The T*hu*t*he* asked Annabhāra whether he had made any offering that day, and he told him that he had offered his allowance of rice to the Pa*kk*ekabuddha Upadi*tt*ha. Then the T*hu*t*he* said to him, "Take these thousand (pieces of gold), and divide with me the value of your offering." Annabhāra replied, "My lord, let me first ask the Pa*kk*ekabuddha." Approaching the Pa*kk*ekabuddha, he said to him, "The T*hu*t*he* Sumana has asked me to share with him the offering I made to you of my allowance of rice; is it right that I should divide it with him?" My lord the Pa*kk*ekabuddha answered Annabhāra with this parable: "Dāraka, in a village of a hundred houses a single lamp is lighted; one comes from another house and lights his wick from it, and so from house to house the light is communicated, till it spreads through the village, and the brightness increasing illuminates it all. Dāraka, so also may this offering be diffused; divide it."

Annabhāra returned to the T*hu*t*he*'s house and said to him, "My lord T*hu*t*he*, I present you with a share of my offering; deign to accept it." The T*hu*t*he* accepted it and offered him a thousand (pieces of gold), but Annabhāra said, "If I receive money it will seem

---

[1] The umbrella is one of the chief insignia of rank among the Burmese.

[2] An expression answering to "good!" "bravo!"

as if I sold the offering; I cannot take it, receive simply your share of the offering." Then the T*hu*t*he* said, "Brother Annabhāra, from this day forth, do no more work, but live in comfort and receive this present as a token of my respect." So saying, he presented him with a great number of articles of comfort and luxury, clothing and food. Annabhāra knew that this was the result of the offering he had made that very day to the Pa*kk*ekabuddha as he arose from the Nirodha-samāpatti.

The king, sending for Annabhāra, procured from him a share of his offering, and conferring upon him immense wealth, raised him to the rank of a T*hu*t*he*.

The T*hu*t*he* Annabhāra lived for the rest of his life in great friendship with the T*hu*t*he* Sumana, and on his death appeared in the country of the Nats.

After passing many existences in this way, some in the land of men, and some in the land of the Nats; in the time of the Parā Taken Gotama he became the son of the Sākiya King, in the Kapilavatthu country, younger brother of the father of Parā Taken; he was called Prince Anuruddha, and was possessed of great power and glory.

One day this Prince Anuruddha was gambling with some children for cake; having lost, he sent some slaves to his mother to procure some, and his mother sent him a golden basket full of it. Continuing to lose, he sent several times again to his mother for more cake. At last his mother sent word that there was no more. The slaves told him that there was no more, but the prince not comprehending this, sent the slaves back to get some. His mother, thinking that her son did not understand that there was no more, in order to make him aware of it, washed the golden basket quite clean, put the cover on, and sent it back to him empty. In consequence of the great glory of Prince Anuruddha, the Nats filled the golden basket with cake impregnated with the delicious flavour of the Nats. When the slaves brought the basket to the prince, it was no sooner opened than the whole country was perfumed with the Nats' cake. The Nats, knowing that Prince Anuruddha, when he was the slave Annabhāra, had made an offering of rice to the Pakkekabuddha Upaditha, and had at the time prayed that he might not hear the words, "there is none," had not the power to remain idle, but filled the golden basket for him with cake. The delicious flavour of the cake was such that if the tip of the tongue only touched it, a thousand nerves tingled with delightful sensations. Prince Anuruddha said to himself, "My mother, dearly as she loves me, did not give me every day the 'there-is-none' cake; it is is only to-day that I have had the 'there-is-none' cake to eat."

The prince's mother said to the slaves who took the golden basket, "Did you find any cake in the golden basket after you had conveyed it?" They replied, "Lady, the basket was quite full; we never before saw an empty basket become full of cake." When she heard this, she thought, "Owing to some former good deed and prayer of my son, the Nats must have put the cake in the basket."

Prince Anuruddha said to his mother, "My honoured mother, you never before gave me any cake like this; henceforth only give me the 'there-is-none' cake." His mother accordingly from that day, whenever he asked for cake, used to cover up the empty basket and give it him; and the guardian-Nats of the kingdom never failed to fill it with cake. In this way Prince Anuruddha, living at home and never understanding the words "there is none," used to eat nothing but Nat's cake.

Soon after this, Prince Anuruddha, Prince Bhaddiya, and Prince Kimbila were talking together about the place where rice was produced. Prince Anuruddha, who had never seen the cultivation in the fields, or the pounding of the grain in the mortar, said that the rice was produced in the pot. Prince Kimbila, who had seen the grain put into the granary, said it was produced in the granary. Prince Bhaddiya, who had noticed that the rice-pots were put on the fireplace, said that it was produced in the fireplace.

Prince Anuruddha's elder brothers instructed him upon the duty of marriage, but the prince said, "I have no desire to marry;" and he went to his mother and, having asked her permission, became a Rahan under Parā Taken. He was called Anuruddha-thera, and having acquired the Deva*k*akkhu wisdom, he could see and comprehend a thousand worlds just as though he were looking at a Shishā fruit in his hand. He began to consider what good work it could be through which he had acquired the Deva*k*akkhu wisdom; then, looking with the eyes of a Nat, he saw his prayer to the Parā Taken Padumuttara; looking again at his different existences, he saw his former offering to the Pa*kk*ekabuddha Upadi*th*a at the time when he was the slave called Annabhāra of the T*hu*l*he* Sumana, in the Benares country, and used to cut grass. Hereupon he began to think, "Where is now my friend the T*huthe* Sumana, with whom I shared the offering I made to the Pa*kk*ekabuddha Upadi*tth*a when I was Annabhāra, and who made me such a handsome acknowledgment?" Taking a survey by means of his Deva*k*akkhu power, he saw that he was now *K*ulla-Sumana, the son of Mahāmunda, in the village of Munda; then looking to see whether his friend would derive any advantage from his going to see him, and finding that he would become a Rahanda, he flew up into the sky, and alighted at Mahāmunda's door.

Mahāmunda, as soon as he saw Anuruddha, in consequence of having been his friend in a former existence, asked him to come into his house, and, after setting rice before him, said, "Lord and master, remain here during the three months of Lent." Anuruddha agreed to do so. Mahāmunda made offerings to him during the whole of Lent, of butter, treacle, and other food of pleasant flavour. Anuruddha said to him, "Dārakā, I have no young disciple to attend upon me."—"Lord and master," replied Mahāmunda, "make my son *K*ulla-Sumana a Rahan, and let him attend upon you." My lord Anuruddha said, "Very good, Dārakā;" and the very moment he laid the razor on *K*ulla-Sumana's head to make him a Rahan,[1] the boy became a Rahanda.

When Lent was over, Anuruddha, wishing to contemplate Parā Taken, took *K*ulla-Sumana with him and flew across the sky. Alighting at the Ku*t*i monastery in the Himavanta forest, he walked up and down during the evening and midnight watches, when he was suddenly seized with colic. The probationer, seeing from his face that he was suffering, said to

[1] All priests in Burmah shave the head and face completely.

I

him, "Lord and master, you look ill. What ails you?"—"Probationer," replied my lord Anuruddha, "I am suffering from colic."—"What medicine," asked the boy, "will cure it?"—"Probationer," he replied, "if I can drink some water from the Anavatatta lake, I shall be cured."—"If that be so," he said, "I will go and procure some for you." Then Anuruddha told him, "If you draw water from the Anavatatta lake, the dragon Pannaga there is very haughty; tell him you come from me." The young probationer, after making obeisance to Anuruddha, flew away into the sky, and arrived at the Anavatatta lake, which was five hundred yoganas distant. The dragon Pannaga was sporting with the she-dragons in the water; when the dragon saw the young probationer, he exclaimed, "This son of Munda has let fall on my head the dirt from his feet;" then in a rage he spread out his hood, and covered with it the whole Anavatatta lake, which was fifty yoganas in extent, in order that he should not draw any water from it. The probationer said to him, "O king of the dragons, my teacher Anuruddha is ill with colic, I wish to draw a pot of water for medicine." Then he continued in poetry, "My lord dragon, possessed of great glory, endowed with great power, listen to my words, and give me one pot of water; I come for medicine." The dragon-king, when he heard this, replied in poetry, "Probationer, in the eastern quarter there is a river called the Ganges, which flows into the sea; take some of the water of that river." On this, the probationer began to reflect, "This dragon, of his own will, will not give me any;" then, thinking he would say something to overcome the dragon, and that he could then draw the water, he said, "My lord dragon, my master Anuruddha sent me to draw some of the Anavatatta water and no other, therefore, I am here to draw it." The dragon-king replied, "Probationer, you are more capable than other young men; I like your speech. As for me, I will not give you any; if you can draw it, do so." The probationer said to himself, "I will display the power of the church of Parā Taken and draw the water, and moreover, will make the Nats and Brahmas see how a combat is carried on with me." With this thought he ascended to the six stages of the Nat country, and the sixteen stages of the Brahma country. The Nats and Brahmas, when they saw the young probationer, paid homage to him, and said, "My lord probationer, what occasion brings you here?" He said to them, "Come and see my combat with the dragon Pannaga in the Anavatatta lake." So saying, he descended with all the Nats and Brahmas, and fluttering in the sky over the Anavatatta lake, he said three times to the dragon, "My lord dragon, I am going to draw some water for medicine." The dragon replied, "For my part, I will not give you any; if you can draw it, do so." Saying these words, he remained with his hood expanded, covering up the Anavatatta lake. The Nats and Brahmas from the six stages of the Nat country and the sixteen stages of the Brahma country, completely occupying the whole of the sky, were looking on. A comparison is this: they were like mustard seed in a mortar. They extended over all the Anavatatta lake, and the sky was entirely filled up with them; there was no space left. At this moment the probationer, assuming the appearance of the chief Brahma, descended from a height of twelve yoganas in the sky, and trod right upon the head of the dragon; a column of water as thick as a Palmyra tree rose up; the probationer, remaining up in the sky, filled a water-pot from it, and carried it away.

The Nats and Brahmas extolled this exceedingly, crying out "Sādhu!" and the dragon-king Pannaga, thus put to shame before all the Nats and Brahmas, was violently enraged and set off in pursuit of the probationer, crying out that he would tear open his breast, and taking him by the legs, throw him to the other side of the Ganges.

The probationer presented the Anavatatta water to my lord Anuruddha. The dragon came and said, "Lord and master, the probationer has taken water which I never gave him; do not use it." The probationer said, "Lord and master, I did what was in my power to take it, because the dragon-king told me to take it if I could; therefore make use of it." My lord Anuruddha, reflecting that the probationer, who was a Rahanda, could not tell a falsehood, drank the Anavatatta water, and was immediately cured of his complaint. Then the dragon Pannaga said to him, "Lord and master, the probationer has put me to shame before all the Nats and Brahmas; I shall therefore tear open his breast, and dragging him by the legs, hurl him to the other side of the Ganges." My lord Anuruddha replied, "Dragon-king, the probationer is possessed of great glory; if he fights with you, you, a dragon, can do nothing. Make an apology to him." The dragon-king, seeing the power and glory of the probationer, and having only spoken these words from a sense of shame, did as Anuruddha told him; making the obeisance of apology, he said, "My lord probationer, henceforth, whenever you want any Anavatatta water, deign to say, 'there is my disciple, the dragon Pannaga.' I will convey the water to you." So saying, he paid homage and left.

Anuruddha and the probationer went together to Parā Taken. Parā Taken, seeing Anuruddha coming, sent some Rahans to relieve him of his thabet and other utensils.

When the probationer reached the Getavana monastery, the Pañkāngas[1] and the probationers who were Puthuggana[2] began to stroke his head, ears, nose, and so forth, and pulling him about by the arms, asked him if he did not long for his father and mother. Parā Taken seeing them behaving in this way, in order to let them know the glory of Kulla-Sumana, called to Ānanda, and said to him, "Ānanda, I wish to wash my feet with some Anavatatta water; send for all the Pañkāngas and probationers, and let any one of them who is able to draw the water go and procure some." Ānanda sent for the five hundred Puthuggana-probationers, and telling them that Parā Taken wished to wash his feet with Anavatatta water, ordered them to go and procure it. Out of the whole five hundred probationers, he could not induce a single one to go. Some said "We cannot do it;" others said, "This is not our duty;" even the probationers who were Rahandas said, "We do not know how to draw it;" the Puthuggana-Rahans also declared their inability for the task. Then my lord Ānanda said to Kulla-Sumana, "Probationer, Parā Taken wishes for some Anavatatta water to wash

[1] Proficient in the five qualifications.
[2] One who has not attained the state of an Ariya.

his feet; go and draw some." The probationer, making obeisance to Parā Taken, said, "Do you require me to draw some Anavatatta water for you?"—"Probationer, draw me some," replied Parā Taken. My lord Ananda gave the probationer the golden vessel which was the offering of Visākhā, and which held sixty measures.[1] The probationer took it in his hand and flew straight through the sky to Himavanta. On his reaching the Anavatatta lake, the dragon Pannaga directly he saw him, came forward to meet him. "My lord probationer," said he, "when you have such a disciple as I am, why should you come here yourself?" With these words he took the golden vessel from him, and after filling it with Anavatatta water, he put it on his own shoulder, and saying "Proceed, my lord probationer," followed him as his attendant. After allowing himself to be followed thus for a short time, the probationer said, "Dragon-king, remain behind;" and taking from him the golden vessel, and carrying it by the ornamental rim, he flew through the sky to his destination.

Parā Taken, when he saw the young probationer approaching, said to the assembly of Rahans, "Look at the beautiful appearance of the youthful novice." Kulla-Sumana, putting down the golden vessel in front of Parā Taken, made obeisance to him. Parā Taken said to him, "Probationer, what age are you?"—"Lord and master," he replied, "I am seven years old." Parā Taken said, "Probationer, from this day forth be a Pañkānga," and he conferred upon him the degree of a Pañkānga by inheritance. The degree of a

[1] One of these measures of water would be quite as much as an ordinary man could lift.

Pañkānga by inheritance is this: when Parā Taken says with his own mouth "Receive this inheritance from me," the state of a Pañkānga is obtained without repeating the Kammavākya.[1] In Parā Taken's church, the probationers Kulla-Sumana and Subhāga, these two, obtained the degree of a Pañkānga when they were only seven years of age.

The Rahans in the assembly began to talk about the young probationer Sumana becoming a Pañkānga at the age of only seven years. Parā Taken, overhearing them, said, "Rahans, my dear sons, whoever in my church, young though he be, may have performed good works, shall become celebrated." Then he continued in poetry, "Rahans, whatever young Rahan shall really and truly exert himself in my church, the church of the Parā, this Rahan, like the moon emerging through a gap in the thick clouds, shall illumine this world with his splendour."

At the conclusion of this discourse all the assembly who listened to it were established in the reward of Sotāpatti.

END OF THE STORY OF THE PROBATIONER KULLA-SUMANA.

---

[1] Ordination service.

CHAPTER XIV.

STORY OF THE NAT-KING NĀGADATTA.

At the time when Parā Taken was staying at the Getavana monastery, my lord Sīvali, with five hundred Rahans, went on a journey to Himavanta. When they arrived at the Gandhamādana mountain, the Nat-King Nāgadatta, seeing my lord Sīvali approaching, was greatly delighted, knowing that his coming would be for his good hereafter. From the day of his arrival up to the seventh day he supplied them with food; on the first day, rice cooked in milk; on the second day, curdled milk; on the third day, roots; on the fourth day, the five preparations of milk; on the fifth day, Katumadhu;[1] on the sixth day, a variety of different kinds of food; on the seventh day he supplied food to which had been imparted the delicious flavour of the Nats. The Rahans, observing the endless amount of food offered by the Nat-King, said, "We see no milch cows belonging to the Nat-King; we see no store of milk or curds, no rice cooking on the fire; how is it that such endless offerings of all kinds of preparations of milk are made?"

[1] This word means the food which a priest may eat after noon, which comprises oil, honey, treacle, and butter.

Then they asked this question, in poetry, saying, "King of the Nats, all kinds of milk-food are here in abundance; how are all these kinds of milk-food obtained? What kind of good work did the Nat-King perform in a previous state of existence? Tell us, King of the Nats; we will listen." In reply to the question thus put to him by the Rahans, the Nat-King answered in poetry, "My lords, in the time of the Parā Kassapa I made offerings of milk to the assembly of Rahans. The reward of the offerings I made in those days is now being fulfilled." Then the Nat-King Nāgadatta proceeded to relate to the Rahans his offering in a former state of existence: "In the time of the Parā Kassapa I was a fellow-man. When I had reached the span of that existence, I died, and became Nāgadatta, living on the Gandhamādana mountain, in a golden palace with a thousand daughters of the Nats surrounding me, and possessed of great power and glory. On account of the offerings of milk which I made to the assembly of Rahans, I have been in possession of endless wealth and luxury from the time of the Parā Taken Kassapa to the time of the Parā Taken Gotama." Then he continued in poetry, "The whole surface of the earth, with its mountains and its seas, I can make overflow with milk. Whatever kind and whatever quantity of milk-food I wish, I find to my hand. Whatever I may wish to give away, and in whatever quantity, I am in the same way abundantly supplied with."

My lord Sīvali, after causing the Nat-King Nāgadatta to perform good works for the whole of seven days, left the Gandhamādana mountain and returned to the *Getavana* monastery. After making obeisance to Parā Taken, he gave him an account of King Nāgadatta. Parā Taken preached to the assembly who were listening to the Law the Nāgadatta-vatthu,[1] as follows:—

"At the time when the Parā Kassapa appeared in the cycle when men's lives reached the span of twenty thousand years, and was preaching the Law, King Nāgadatta, listening to the Law, made offerings for the whole of twenty thousand years to the assembly of the Rahans, of milk, butter, and so forth. On his death he became the Nat-King of great power and glory, living in a golden palace on the Gandhamādana mountain, in Himavanta, and surrounded by a thousand daughters of the Nats. King Nāgadatta, when he has come to the end of his span of life on the Gandhamādana mountain, will exist again in all the stages of the Nat country from *K*atumahārā*g* to Paranimmitavasavati.[2] In that Paranimmitavasavati he will develope the first state of Dhyāna,[3] and on his death will reach the Mahā-Brahma abode, and have the brilliancy of glittering gold or the ruby. After completing there countless cycles, and developing the second state of Dhyāna, he will reach the Ābhassara abode. Completing there eight cycles, and developing the third state of Dhyāna, he will reach the Subhakritsna abode.

[1] Each of these stories is called in Pali a Vatthu, or in Burmese, Wutthu, supposed to be the Sanskrit vritta, "an event," v*r*ittānta, "a story." The Sanskrit vastu, the subject of a poem, etc., however, is the only word that could in Pali assume the form of vatthu or vat*t*hu.

[2] There are altogether six stages of the Nat country, as mentioned above.

[3] A certain attainment or state of mind of which there are five degrees.

Completing there sixty-four cycles, and developing the fourth state of Dhyāna, he will exist again in Brihatphala, and the other abodes of the fourth state of Dhyāna. Developing there Vipassanā,[1] he will attain to the reward of Anāgāmi, and will exist again in the Avriha abode. Completing his span of life in the Avriha abode, he will reach in succession, by means of the state of Uddhamsota, the five Sudassana abodes. After this, he will be established in the Akani*th*a abode. When his life there is ended, he will become a Rahanda, and reach Paranibbāna. There will be six other persons who will exist in the same way as the Nat-King Nāgadatta, viz.: Mahāra*th*a, *K*ullara*th*a, Anegava*nn*a, Sakka, Visākha, and Sudatta; these, with the Nat-King Nāgadatta, make in all seven persons. These seven persons all take delight in good works. They take delight in them in all states of existence. Commencing from their present existence, in the order of their future existences, reaching in succession the countries of the Nats and the Brahmas, they will finally attain Paranibbāna in the Akani*th*a abode.

"Whoever shall do nothing but good works will receive nothing but excellent future rewards."

Parā Taken preached as follows, in poetry, to those persons who, like the Nat-King Nāgadatta, had in former existences made excellent offerings to the Rahans:—

"Whatever layman shall really and truly repeatedly perform many good works, the most excellent happiness shall be his; you should therefore make offerings

[1] A kind of wisdom, enabling the possessor to make extraordinary discoveries. (Judson.)

because it is most excellent. Those who make offerings with gentle hearts to the priests, who are the field where are to be sown the seeds of good works full of long suffering, shall have all their desires fulfilled. Even like the Nat-King Nāgadatta their desires shall be fulfilled."

End of the Story of the Nat-King Nagadatta.

CHAPTER XV.

STORY OF THE FOUR T*HUTHE*'S SONS.

It was said that the Nat-King Nāgadatta, after performing many good works, enjoyed a life which extended from the time of Kassapa Parā to the time of Gotama Parā; they who did evil deeds, when they suffered for them, did their lives also extend from the time of the most excellent Parā Kassapa to that of the most excellent Parā Gotama? It was in reference to this that Parā Taken, when he was in the *G*etavana monastery, related the story of King Pasenadikosala as follows:—

"King Pasenadikosala one day, superbly adorned and mounted on his elephant Pūrika, attended by his retinue, made a tour round his city, keeping it on his right hand. While he was making his circuit, a man's wife, who was in a Pyat*h*at with seven roofs, opened a window and looked out. When the king saw her, she seemed like the moon entering an opening in a thick bank of clouds, and he was so inflamed with desire that he very nearly fell off the back of his elephant.

"On returning to his palace, after completing the circuit of his city, the king asked one of the nobles, who was his intimate friend, whether in such-and-such a place he had seen a Pyat*h*at, and he replied that he had seen it. 'Whom did you see there?' the king asked. 'I saw a woman in the Pyat*h*at,' he replied. Then the king sent him to inquire whether the woman had a husband or not. The nobleman went and made inquiries, and returning told the king that there was a husband. Hearing this the king told him to go and bring the husband. The nobleman accordingly went to the man and said, 'The king has sent for you.' The young man thought to himself, 'I shall be destroyed on account of my wife;' but not daring to oppose the king's commands, he went to the palace. When the king saw him, he said, 'Remain always in close attendance upon me.' The man said, 'Let me make an offering of tribute only.' The king said, 'I do not want your tribute; from this day forth remain constantly in close attendance upon me.' So saying he gave him a dā[1] for a weapon. The king's design was to kill the young man as soon as he should be guilty of any offence, and then take his wife; but the young man, in fear for his life, was most unremitting in his attendance.

"When the king found that the young man was free from all fault, he called him and said, 'Here! young man! at a distance of a yo*g*ana from here there is a river; procure from thence a Kamuttarā water-lily and some Aru*n*avatī earth, and bring them here in the cool of the evening; if you fail to do so, I shall punish you." The young man being a slave among many, and therefore unable to refuse, agreed

---

[1] The national and characteristic appendage of the Burmese; a knife varying in size and weight according to the purpose for which it is required.

to do it. The Kamuttarā water-lily and the Aruṇavatī earth were only to be obtained in the country of the dragons. The young man thought, 'What shall I do to procure the lily and the earth?' In fear of his life he ran home as fast as he could, and asked his wife if the rice were cooked; his wife said that it was then being boiled; not able to wait till it was ready, he took the dripping rice out with a ladle and put it into a cup together with some meat; then he started off in all haste on his journey of a yo*g*ana. As he flew along, the rice was steamed.

"When the young man arrived at the bank of the river, he first laid aside the top part of the rice and then began eating. Just at this time he saw a man who wanted something to eat, and he gave him the top part of the rice which he had laid aside, and made him eat it. The young man, after finishing his repast, threw the remains of the rice into the river to feed the fish, and then cried out with a loud voice, 'May the Nāga-Galon[1] Nat-King, who watches this river, help me; the king wanting to fix a fault upon me has sent me to procure a Kamuttarā water-lily and some Aruṇavatī earth. I have made an offering of rice to him who wanted it; the thousand rewards of this offering, as well as the hundred successive rewards of the offering I made to the fish and all the other creatures in the river, I divide with the Nat-King. Procure for me a Kamuttarā lily and some Aruṇavatī earth.' The dragon who guarded the river hearing this, assumed the guise of an old man, and approaching the young man, begged a share of the offering from him; the young man said, 'I share it with you.'

---

[1] A flying dragon.

Then he gave him one of the Kamuttarā water-lilies, and some of the Aruṇavatī earth, which were in the dragons' country.

"At this time the king was thinking to himself, 'Some people possess a charm; they have some kind of wisdom and ability so that I cannot fix a fault upon them.' Reflecting thus, he closed the door, although it was only morning. The young man arrived at the king's bathing-time; 'Open the door,' he cried, 'I come by the king's order.' But the door, by the king's command, remained closed. The young man finding they would not open the door, thought to himself, 'It is a difficult thing for me to save my life.' Then he placed the Aruṇavatī earth upon the door-post, and hung the Kamuttarā lily upon it, and shouted with a loud voice, 'Take notice all, that I have returned from executing the king's commission. The king wanting to kill me, though guilty of no fault, sent me on this errand.' After this, he thought, 'Where shall I go now? The Rahans have gentle hearts; I will go and sleep in the monastery. People when they are happy feel no love for the Rahans; but when their hearts are heavy, they like to take refuge in a monastery; I too can find no other asylum.' With these reflections he went to the monastery and slept there.

"King Pasenadikosala could not sleep; the whole night he was thinking of the woman, and devising how he could kill the young man and get possession of her.

"The people in hell who have been immersed in the copper pot of sixty yoganas in extent, boiling and bubbling like the rice grains in a cooking-pot, after thirty thousand years reach the bottom of the pot; and, according to what one of the scriptures says, after another thirty thousand years they rise again to the edge; these people in hell then put up their heads and endeavour to repeat some sacred verses; but they are only able to utter a syllable at a time, and sink down again into the hell-pot.

At this time the king, unable to sleep, overheard during the daybreak watch the sounds of the hell-people; he trembled and started up. 'Is my life in danger, or my queen's, or does some calamity threaten my country?' Thus exclaiming, he got up at sunrise, after a sleepless night, and sending for the chief priest, he said to him, 'Brahmin, my teacher, in the daybreak watch I heard a great noise like that of a huge drum; is it my country, my queen, or myself that is in danger of some calamity?' The Brahmin said, 'My lord, your Majesty, what sounds were they that you heard?'—'Teacher Brahmin,' replied the king, 'I heard the word "du," the word "sa," the word "na," and the word "so;" these four words I heard.' The Brahmin, like a man going into the dark, seeing nothing at all, said, 'I cannot tell what it means;' then reflecting that he would go without any presents and offerings, he said, 'Your Majesty, I will be responsible; have no anxiety; I know the three Vedas.' The king said, 'What ought to be done?' The Brahmin replied, 'It will be well if you make a sacrifice of every kind of living creature.'—'How shall this be done'? asked the king. He said, 'Procure a hundred elephants, a hundred horses, a hundred bulls, a hundred goats, a hundred camels, a hundred fowls, a hundred pigs, a hundred boys, a hundred girls, a hundred of every living creature.' In order that it should not be found out that he said this merely in order to obtain different kinds of meat to eat, he inserted among the number, elephants, horses, and human beings.

The king, imagining that he was saving his life, ordered every kind of living animal to be procured. The royal slaves, saying, 'The king is going to sacrifice,' took 500 bulls, and as many of every other living creature. The inhabitants, with sorrowful countenances, weeping for their children and grandchildren, raised loud cries of lamentation. Queen Mallikā, hearing the noise of their weeping, went to the king and said to him, 'Why have you taken them?' He replied, 'Queen, do you not know that a poisonous cobra has gone into my ear?' The queen said, 'What cobra?' The king replied, 'When I heard this noise in the night, I asked the Brahmin about it; he told me that a calamity was impending over me, and that in order to avert it I must sacrifice a hundred of every living creature. It is because this sacrifice will avert the calamity, that I have taken them.' The queen said to him, 'How stupid you are! Did your Majesty ever know of a man being killed, and then by means of his death another man's life being saved? You are making numbers of people miserable all through listening to stupid Brahmins. There is Parā Taken, who is superior to the three orders of beings,[1] and can see through the past and the future. Go and inquire of this Parā Taken, and take his advice."

The king, riding in his carriage and accompanied by Queen Mallikā, went to Parā Taken. Overcome

[1] Men, Nats, Brahmas.

with terror for his life, the king was unable to speak a word, but remained motionless before Parā Taken in an attitude of adoration. Parā Taken said, "Great king, what brings you here?" The king kept silence. Then Queen Mallikā addressed Parā Taken, "Lord and master, the king, during the daybreak watch, heard the words 'du,' 'sa,' 'na,' and 'so,' repeated. Hearing these words he was unable to sleep, and went and asked the Brahmin. The Brahmin told him that a calamity was impending, and that in order to avert it, he must sacrifice a hundred of every living creature; that their life-blood would free him from the threatened danger. In consequence of his having a large number of creatures taken for the sacrifice, I have brought him into your sacred presence." Parā Taken said, "Great king, is what the queen says true?"—"It is true, my lord," replied the king. "What sounds did you hear?" asked Parā Taken. The king said, "I heard the word 'du.'" Directly he said this, Parā Taken understood it, and instructed him as follows: "Have no anxiety; no calamity awaits your Majesty. The hell-people, unable to bear their sufferings, made this sound." The king said to Parā Taken, "What did the hell-people do?" Then Parā Taken related the evil deeds of those people as follows:—

"Great king, a long time ago, at a time when people used to live for twenty thousand years, the Parā Taken Kassapa appeared. On the occasion of Parā Taken Kassapa journeying to Benares, surrounded by twenty thousand Rahandas, the people of the city presented the offerings of hospitality. At this time there were in the city of Benares four *Thuthes*, each worth four hundred millions of property, who were great friends with each other. They debated among themselves as to what they should do with the property in their houses. One of the four proposed that they should make offerings to the Parā Taken who had journeyed thither, and attend to their religious duties; this proposition met with no favour from the others. Another suggested that they should procure the very best kinds of meat and intoxicating liquors, and enjoy themselves in eating and drinking. A third said, "We will eat the most delicate and delicious dainties." The last of the T*huthe*'s sons proposed that they should spend their money in procuring other people's wives. This proposal met the unanimous approval of all the T*huthe*'s sons, and they spent their money in procuring handsome women. In this way for twenty thousand years the four T*huthe*'s sons used to commit adultery with other men's wives. When they died they found themselves in the lowest hell, where they were boiled during the whole interval between the appearing of two consecutive Parās. On leaving the lowest hell they appeared again in the Lohakumbha hell-pot sixty yo*g*anas in extent; they reached the bottom of this in thirty thousand years. In another thirty thousand years they came up to the brim again; then these four hell-people endeavoured to repeat one or other of the sacred verses, but they could not say one whole verse; all they could do was to utter one syllable or another at intervals; then they sank down again into the hell-pot."

Parā Taken recited as follows in full the verse which these hell-people were endeavouring to say, " Fellowmen, we have led a bad life; conspicuous in wealth and power, yet we made no offerings. The good works that would have tended to our own profit, that would have taken us to the land of the Nats, we neglected to perform."

Parā Taken, having thus explained the first, and desiring to show the meaning of the second verse, asked the king what next he heard. The king replied, "I heard the word 'sa.'" Then Parā Taken recited the complete verse as follows:

"All of us boiling in the hell-pot, have completed sixty thousand years. When will there be an end to this hell?"

Having thus explained the meaning of the second verse in full, and desirous of conveying the explanation of the third verse, Parā Taken said to the king, "What next did you hear?"—"The word 'na,'" replied the king. Then the most excellent Parā thus recited the third verse "na."

"Fellow-men, hell has no end. When will be the end of hell? In the same way, in the country of men we, and you also, performed evil deeds; we did not see the end of evil deeds."

Parā Taken, having thus explained the meaning of the third verse, and wishing to explain the fourth, said to the king, "What next did you hear?" The king replied "so." The most excellent Parā then recited the fourth verse as follows:

"If we ever return from this hell-country to the country of men, we will perform numerous good works and reverence the three jewels."

Parā Taken thus explained in succession the meaning of the four verses to King Pasenadikosala. He then continued, "The four *Thuthe's* sons in hell, unable to recite the whole of the four verses, but uttering only one syllable of each, sank down again into the Lohakumbha copper-pot." Thus Parā Taken completed his narration.

The king, on hearing the words of Parā Taken, trembled, and impressed with the law of fear, he exclaimed, "To transgress against the wives of others and commit adultery is a grievous thing. To boil in the lowest hell during the whole interval between one Parā and another, then leaving that hell to be boiled again for the whole of sixty thousand years in the Lohakumbha hell-pot of sixty yoganas, with no time of deliverance appearing! Yet I have passed a sleepless night in planning adultery. From this day forth, never will I transgress regarding the wife of another." Then he said to Parā Taken, "This day I know how long a night is." The woman's husband also said, "I too know this day how long a yogana is." Parā Taken, in reference to the words of both, recited this poetry, "Great king, to him who cannot sleep, the night is long; to him who is weary, a yogana's journey is long; to the foolish who know not the law of the righteous, the life to come is long."[1]

After Parā Taken had preached as related, the young man was established in the reward of Sotāpatti, and the assembly who had heard the law were also established in the reward of Sotāpatti. King Pasenadikosala paid homage to Parā Taken and went away. All the creatures who were about to die were released from their bonds. The husband and wife, knowing that they owed their lives to Queen Mallikā, expressed the gratitude they owed her.

[1] See 'Dhammapada,' verse 60.

The four T*huthe*'s sons who have suffered in hell ever since they lived for twenty thousand years in the time of the Parā Kassapa, these hell-creatures when they repeated the four syllables " du," " sa," " na," "so," were up on the surface; since it takes thirty thousand years to go from top to bottom, they have not yet reached the bottom, but are now only in the middle. Such is the story of the four T*huthe*'s sons, who, after committing adultery with the wives of others, had to suffer in hell.

END OF THE STORY OF THE FOUR T*HUTHE*'S SONS.

CHAPTER XVI.

STORY OF THE MODEST GIRL.

When Parā Taken was in the Vesālī country, among the Devadhamma verses[1] he recited the Hiri law,[2] illustrating it by an account of a young village-girl, who by possessing the virtue of modesty, had reached the rank of a queen; and he also related how in a former time she had given birth to a jewel-son, the embryo Kakravarti king.

At one time in the Vesālī country, when Parā Taken was residing there, there was a king named Likkhavi, who was excessively handsome. One day he made offerings of food to Parā Taken and his assembly of Rahans, and, in company with his queen, listened to the law. When Parā Taken had finished his exposition, he went away. The Rahans observed to each other that King Likkhavi's queen was by no means handsome, that she was very large and had big hands, but that she was certainly possessed of modesty. Parā Taken, overhearing their conversation, said:

"Rahans, my beloved sons, this is not so only now, but it was just the same in former times, when King Likkhavi was King Brahmadatta, ruling over the

---

[1] Divine law. [2] Modesty.

Benares country; at that time I was the king's minister. There was then residing in a village a young girl of an appearance not at all handsome, with a large body and big hands. This girl came on one occasion to Benares to see her relations. The king, happening to be looking out of his palace window as the girl passed by, saw her; and remarked that out of modesty, she was careful that her clothes should not fly open as she walked along.[1] Thinking that if he made so modest a woman his queen, she would not fail to present him with a son of great glory, he called to a nobleman who was near him, and told him to go and inquire whether she had a husband or not. The king, hearing that she was unmarried, took her and raised her to the rank of his queen, and always held her in the highest respect.

"The queen, before very long, fulfilled the king's expectations by giving birth to a son who had every sign of wisdom and glory. This son attained the rank of a Kakravarti king.

"This virtue of modesty is very rarely found. It has nothing to do with beauty or ugliness; let a person be as beautiful as you will, it is not worth talking about (in comparison).

"Rahans, my dear children, they who at that time were the king and queen of Benares are now King Likkhavi and his queen; and the nobleman is now I, the Parā."

End of the Story of the Modest Girl.

[1] The dress of the Burmese women is simply a square cloth, worn round the body, and tucked in at the waist and above the breast; in walking, if not careful, the women expose the leg.

CHAPTER XVII.

THE STORY ABOUT GRATITUDE.

In the Devadhamma verses, the person who was called Sabburisa was Katānukatavedi. Parā Taken, while he was in the *G*etavana monastery, related the circumstances connected with his receiving the name of Sabburisa.

In former times, I, then the Parālaun,[1] was the guardian Nat of a castor-oil[2] tree in the country of Benares. The people of the country used to make offerings to me of delicately flavoured dainties and flowers. At this time a poor man came and made an offering of a piece of bread and a cup of water. The Parālaun, the Nat of the castor-oil tree, appeared to him and said, "Ho! you poor man. Why do you make an offering to me?" He replied, "My lord Nat-King, I make an offering to you because I wish to be delivered from poverty." The Parālaun reflecting, "It is right that I should pay him the debt of gratitude I

---

[1] One who is to become a Parā.

[2] The castor-oil is only a plant; some other tree is probably meant, as Nats are always described as residing in large trees, not shrubs and plants. The Burmese text and manuscript, however, both distinctly say "castor-oil."

owe for his offering," said to him, "You poor man, at the foot of the castor-oil tree where I live, there is a number of pots of gold all close together; after having addressed the King of Benares about it, take them." With these words the Nat vanished.

The poor man, according to the Paralauṅ-Nat's instruction, addressed the king, and took the pots of gold. The king, moreover, on that very day made him a Thuthe, and presented him with all the appendages of that rank.

Hence, all who make offerings to the guardian-Nats of trees will be rewarded.

End of the Story about Gratitude.

CHAPTER XVIII.

THE STORY ABOUT COVETOUSNESS, GREEDINESS, AND ANGER.

Para Taken preached a discourse regarding those who from their covetousness became animals upon the spot where they had stored their treasures; and regarding death occasioned by not repressing anger under the influence of greediness.

At one time there lived a T*huthe* in the country of Kāsikarā*g*, who was excessively covetous. When he died he became a rat in the place where he had buried his treasures. At this time the Parālauṅ was engaged in excavating a stone temple. When the rat saw the Parālauṅ, he brought him two kahāpaṇas' worth of his treasure in a bundle, and said to him, "Young man, take one kahāpaṇa's worth, and buy me meat and curry-stuff, and keep the other yourself." The Parālauṅ in this way used every day to buy one kahāpaṇa's worth of meat and curry-stuff for the rat, and keep one kahāpaṇa for himself.

One day a cat caught the rat. The rat said to her, "Friend cat, I will give you meat and curry-stuff every day; do not kill me." The cat exacted from him a solemn promise to this effect, and let him go. From that day the rat divided his food into two parts, and gave one to the cat. Three other cats afterwards caught the rat, and he made them all the same promise as he had made to the first cat, so now he had to divide his food into five parts, and give four to the cats who, he was afraid, would take his life.

The Parālauṅ, who knew all this, when he had finished the rock temple, left a small hole in it only just large enough to admit the rat. "Friend rat," said he, "live inside the hollow of the rock, and do not give any food to the four cats; when they come, speak roughly to them." After a little while one of the cats came and said, "I am very hungry, give me some food."—"O you cat," said the rat, "why do you come and ask me for food?" The cat, being very greedy, flew into a violent passion, and made a spring at him with her outstretched claws; striking her chest against the stone cave, she was killed. In the same way the three other cats also met their death.

Wise men should reflect upon a man, through his covetousness, thus becoming an animal watching over his former wealth; upon excessive greediness, and upon death resulting from anger.

END OF THE STORY OF COVETOUSNESS, GREEDINESS, AND ANGER.

CHAPTER XIX.

THE STORY OF THE SENSE OF TOUCH.

Para Taken, when he was in the Getavana monastery, related a story regarding the sense of touch, one of the five senses:—

Whoever is possessed of an attribute of excellence, although he may be in poverty, will attain a lofty position. Here is a comparison: he is like a common piece of split bamboo, which, when wreathed with flowers, is set upon some noble head.

Rahans, my beloved children, in former times there lived in the city of Benares a very poor girl named Pañkapāpī. She was possessed of no beauty, but she was marvellously soft and delicate to the touch. In consequence of the extreme poverty of her parents no one ever noticed the girl.

About this time there was a great festival at Benares, which was kept up all through the night. The Parālaun, the King of Benares, who, in consequence of being versed in the eighteen sciences, trusted to himself, wandered out alone to look at the festival. The young girl Pañkapāpī also happened to be amusing herself there, and the king accidentally touched her with his hand. She felt as delicate as a piece of cotton wool which had been picked a hundred times, and then dropped in an oil-pot. The king was unable to contain himself, and said to her, "Lady, have you a husband?"—"I have not one yet, my lord," she replied. "If that be so," said the king, "come to your parents' house." They went there together, and he said to Pañkapāpī's parents, "I want to marry her." The girl's parents, who looked on her as a piece of unsaleable goods, were highly delighted, and gave her in marriage to the Parālauṅ.

The Parālauṅ, after consummating his marriage, reflected, "People who do not know the young girl's quality of excessive purity and delicacy will revile me." With these thoughts he began to feel a sense of shame. Then he went off to his palace, and bringing thence a golden basket, which he had filled with different kinds of dainties, presented it to the girl; after which he returned to his palace.

When it was daybreak, search was made for the missing golden basket. The king ordered his servants to go to such a place and such a house, and if they found it there, to bring it back with them together with the owner of the house. The king's messengers, searching as directed, found it, and brought the young girl, with the golden basket, before the king. The king, in the presence of all his nobles, said to her, "O you woman, why did you steal my golden basket?" The girl replied, "A young man brought it full of dainties to my house and gave it me, and then went away." The king, wishing to display to his nobles her quality of excessive delicacy, employing a king's stratagem, said to the girl, "O young girl, if you were to see this young man, would you know him?" The girl replied, "The young man brought it in the night, so I should not know him."

Now the king, when he was sleeping with the young girl, had purposely called her attention to a scar upon his hand, so now he said to her, "O girl, if you were to feel the hand of the young man who brought you the golden basket, would you know him?" She replied, "The young man when he came to my house made me notice a scar on his hand; therefore, if I felt his hand I should know him."

When the girl said this, the king, making use of a king's artifice, had her placed inside of a large coverlet, which was folded many times round her in such a way as to leave open only one small aperture. Then she was made to feel the hands of all the nobles as they came up to her one after the other, and inserted their arms in the aperture; but the girl said, "None of these is my husband's hand."

All the noblemen who had felt the touch of the girl's hand, seeing how fine and delicate she was, could not contain themselves, but were all like madmen. "My lord, your Majesty," they cried, "give me the young girl; let me pay the fine for the theft of the golden basket." The king would not agree to this, but went up to the girl in the coverlet and put his hand through the aperture that she might feel it, and so recognize him. Pañḍapāpī, directly she felt the scar, said, "This is my husband's hand; it was he who brought me the gold basket full of dainties." These words of the girl enlightened the noblemen on the state of affairs.

Then the king said to his nobles, "Fearing, lest not knowing the high quality of excessive purity and delicacy which this young girl possesses, you would impute blame to me, I have tested thus your sentiments. This young girl is already my wife."

On that very day the king had the ceremony of pouring water performed, and installed her in the position of head queen.

Hence those who, although they may have no beauty, are possessed of the attribute of extreme purity and delicacy will attain a lofty position.

END OF THE STORY OF THE SENSE OF TOUCH.

CHAPTER XX.

THE STORY ABOUT THE SENSE OF HEARING.

On one occasion Parā Taken, while residing in the Getavana monastery, preached a discourse regarding the sense of hearing, one of the five senses:—

Rahans, my beloved sons, when the King of Benares was enjoying himself one day in his garden, he heard the voice of a woman who was singing very sweetly while she was engaged in collecting fuel; on hearing the voice, desire for the woman seized the king, and he immediately gratified it, and the Parālaun became an embryo in the woman. On account of the great glory of the child that was to be born of her, the woman was immediately aware of it, and said to the king, "Your Majesty, I have conceived." The king took from his finger a ring worth a hundred thousand, and presented it to her, saying, "If your child prove a girl, sell this ring and live both of you on its proceeds; if it be a boy, bring him to me." After saying this, he returned to his palace, surrounded by all his nobles.

The woman, who gained her living by collecting fuel, when ten months had passed, gave birth to the Parālaun. When the child was somewhat grown, he asked his mother who his father was. She replied, "The great King of Benares." On hearing this, the Parālauṅ said, "If this be so, take me to my father." His mother accordingly took him, and presenting Parālauṅ, together with the ruby ring, to the king, she said, "My lord, your Majesty, this child is my lord your Majesty's honoured son." The king, although he knew it was so, felt ashamed in the midst of the assembly, and said, "It is not my son." Then the Parālauṅ's mother made this invocation in support of the truth of her assertion, "If this be not in truth your Majesty's son, may it fall to the ground and be killed! If it be your son, may it remain stationary in the air!" Saying these words she threw the child up in the air. The Parālauṅ, from his great glory, remained according to the invocation stationary in the air, seated in a cross-legged posture; in this position he remained while he expounded the law to his royal father, and explained to him the ten duties of kings, viz.: The making of offerings; the observance of the commandments; the giving of alms; upright conduct; meekness and gentleness; not to cause sorrow to his subjects; not to be angry with others; not to oppress others; forbearance; not to oppose the wishes of his people.

The King of Benares, when he saw this marvel, exclaimed, "This is truly my son! beloved son, deign to descend." The Parālauṅ descended on to his father's breast and remained there.

The king conferred upon the Parālauṅ the rank of heir-apparent, and gave his mother the position of queen.

He who was at that time the King of Benares is

now my father King Suddhodana, and the queen is my mother Queen Māyā. The little prince is I the Parā.

In this way Parā Taken related this *G*āt.[1]

Hence the possession of a pleasing voice conducts to a lofty position.

END OF THE STORY ABOUT THE SENSE OF HEARING.

---

[1] An account of some one or other of the different existences of Gotama; there are supposed to be 550 of them written.

CHAPTER XXI.

THE STORY ABOUT BRIBES.

PARA TAKEN preached a discourse about the evil consequences of taking bribes from a spirit of covetousness.

At one time there lived in the Sāvatthi country a Brahmin who addressed himself to King Kosala, stating that he was versed in the characteristic signs of daggers. The king made the smiths show all the daggers they offered him to the Brahmin, and if he approved of them, they were placed in the king's armoury. From that day the smiths used to bring bribes whenever they showed him the daggers. Of every dagger that the smiths who bribed him displayed, the Brahmin smelt the edge and said, "It is a good one;" then it was placed in the king's armoury, but all those which the smiths who did not bribe him brought, he would say were bad ones, although they were good.

One day a smith said to himself, "This Brahmin says that all our daggers are bad, and that all the daggers of those who bribe him are good; I will so contrive that he will not dare to say so in future." Accordingly he filled the scabbard of a dagger with very fine red pepper, and smeared the blade over with the same substance. He put the dagger in the sheath and presented it to the king. The king made him show it to the Brahmin. The Brahmin smelt the edge of the dagger as usual, the pepper got into the Brahmin's nose; unable to restrain himself, he sneezed violently and slit his nose completely against the edge of the dagger. The king and all his court, when they saw this, could not contain themselves, but roared with laughter.

Thus we see the evil consequences of an inclination to take bribes, without having any regard to good qualities.

END OF THE STORY ABOUT BRIBES.

CHAPTER XXII.

THE REWARD OF SARANAGAMANA.[1]

On one occasion, Parā Taken, when he was in the Getavana monastery, preached a discourse upon the greatness of the reward of Saranagamana.

One day the Brahmin Velāma completely filled with gold and silver a compartment of a rice-field, sufficient to sow ten baskets of seed-grain; and for the whole of seven years and seven months made offerings of eighty-four thousand golden cups, eighty-four thousand silver cups, eighty-four thousand copper cups; elephants, horses and carriages with ornamental trappings, milch cows, virgins, jewels, eighty-four thousand of each; besides these, food and sherbets of every kind.

Greater than the reward of such an offering as this is the reward of an offering made to a Sotāpan;[2] greater still to a Sakadāgāmi,[3] greater still to an Anāgāmi,[4] greater still to a Rahanda, greater still to a

---

[1] The formula, "I worship Buddha, the law, and the priesthood."
[2] First state of an Ariya.
[3] Second state of an Ariya.
[4] Third state of an Ariya.

Pa*kk*eka-buddha, greater still to a Parā Taken with his sacred assembly of Rahans, but greater than all these is the reward of a steadfast observance of the Sara*n*agamana.

End of the Reward of Sara*n*agamana.

CHAPTER XXIII.

THE FIVE COMMANDMENTS.

He preached as follows the consequences entailed by the five commandments:—

If a man have no teachers or priests, he should be constant in the practice of repeating each of the five commandments, beginning with Pāṇātipāta, with his hands raised in attitude of adoration in front of a sacred image of Parā Taken on a sacred pagoda.

1. Pāṇātipāta.—This law is broken by the killing of as much as a louse, a bug, or a tick.

2. Adinnādāna.—This law is broken by taking as much as a single thread of cotton which has not been given by another.

3. Kāmesumikkhākāra.—This law is broken by even looking at the wife of another with a lustful mind.

4. Musāvāda.—This law is broken by even jestingly uttering a falsehood which will affect the advantage and prosperity of another.

5. Surāmeraya.—This law is broken by even letting fall upon the tongue only such a drop of intoxicating liquor as would hang at the end of a blade of Thaman grass, if it is known to be intoxicating liquor.

He preached as follows regarding the great crime of Pāṇātipāta:—

King Kosala's wife, Queen Mallikā, while she was experiencing the three abodes,[1] having become a young girl, went into the bazaar to purchase some meat for a guest whom she had received at her house. Failing to procure any, she killed a goat to supply her guest with meat. For this evil deed, after completing her sufferings in the lowest hell, her neck was trodden on, and she was killed in her turn.

Again, Putigatta-Mahāthera, one of Parā Taken's holy disciples, suffered in hell for having been in one state of existence a fowler, and, until the time of his becoming a Rahanda, suffered the torture of having his bones broken into little pieces, after which he acquired Paranibbāna.

Again, the Rishi Paṇḍukabra, as a consequence of the sin of his having at the time when he was a carpenter pierced a fly with a splinter of wood, had, while engaged as a Rishi in the performance of good works, to suffer the torture of being impaled.

Again, in the time of Parā Taken, his sacred disciples, on account of having formerly been huntsmen, notwithstanding they had reached the state of holy disciples, fought among themselves, and all killed each other; and Parā Taken, who had no power to prevent them, was reduced to one solitary attendant.

Again, all the Sākiya kings, for having in a former existence caught fish in the Sansarāga tank by poisoning them, were every one killed by the Vidadūpa warriors, without Parā Taken having any power to prevent it.

[1] The abodes of Men, Nats, and Brahmas.

Parā Taken continued, "Rahans, my dear sons, whoever takes life, when he dies out of his present existence will appear again in hell, and afterwards in the state of an animal. After being freed from hell and the condition of an animal, even when he reaches the state of a man, he will have but a short life."

Such were the words of Parā Taken upon the subject of Pānātipāta.

Adinnādāna, or the taking of what has not been given by another.

A girl of the country of Benares suffered in hell for having stolen a putzo.[1] After she had left hell and had become a human being, she was excessively lovely and of an extremely delicate kind of beauty; her hair was (black and shining) like a humble-bee. All who saw her fell in love with her. Some women, however, who were envious of her, mixed some decapillatory drug in her hair-wash, and in consequence, all her hair came off just as if it had been pulled out by the roots; in fact, she looked like a plucked crow. Greatly ashamed at losing her hair, she went away to another place, where she employed herself in selling oil. While thus engaged, she made an offering to a Rahan of some food fried in oil, and prayed that, as a reward of the offering, in her future life she might have good hair. When she died out of that existence, as the reward of her offering, she became a Nat's daughter in a golden palace, which rose up from the midst of the sea; her hair was of immense length and beautifully fine, but as a punishment for her having in a former existence stolen a putzo, she had no clothes whatever, and was always quite naked. After she had been in this con-

[1] Waist-cloth of a man.

dition for a very long time, in the time of the most excellent Parā Gotama, there arrived at the island some sailor merchants, who, seeing her quite naked inside her palace, presented her with some clothes, but she could not put them on. The Nat's daughter said to them, "Brothers, if you wish to clothe me, make an offering to some one, and share the reward with me, saying, 'May the Nat's daughter obtain clothes!'" The sailors accordingly made an offering of a putzo to one of their companions who steadfastly observed the Saranagamana, and at the same time prayed, "May the Nat's daughter obtain clothes!" On the very day that the offering was made, the Nat's daughter, who had had to live naked in her palace, received for her apparel the garments of the Nats. Then the sailors said to the Nat's daughter, "In consequence of our having made an offering on your behalf, you are abundantly provided with clothes; make now an offering among us of clothes for an offering to Parā Taken; then, if you constantly reflect upon the virtues of Parā Taken, you will again become a Nat's daughter." The Nat's daughter did as the sailors directed, and made an offering of two putzos of the Nats. When Parā Taken received the putzos, he preached the Law, illustrating it by an account of the Nat's daughter; and she, when she died, became a Nat's daughter in the Tāvatinsa Nat-country, living in a golden palace, and surrounded by a thousand attendants.

Fixing your attention upon this sacred exposition of the Law, you must always shun the property which has not been given you by another.

Again Parā Taken preached, "Rahans, my beloved sons, whoever shall take what has not been given to him shall suffer the condition of a Hell-Preta, and even when delivered from this state of suffering he shall obtain again the condition of man, nothing that he possesses shall be permanent; it shall all be destroyed.

Such were the words of Parā Taken on the subject of theft.

Kāmesumi*kkhākāra*; transgression against a woman whom another possesses. Those who commit this crime will suffer in hell after they die. After completing their time in hell, even when they become human beings, they are the female servants of others. My lord Ānanda, Parā Taken's younger brother, after he had been completing the virtues during the whole of four Asaṅkhyas[1] and a hundred thousand cycles, when he had an existence among the race of blacksmiths, once committed adultery with the wife of another; for this he had to suffer hell, and after completing his time there, became a woman during fourteen existences. When he died out of the condition of a woman and became a man, he suffered mutilation during seven existences.

Again, the four *Thuthe's* sons in the Benares country, for committing adultery with the wives of others, had to suffer in the hell-pot; once every sixty thousand years they came to the surface, and, enduring dreadful torture, uttered the syllables, "du," "sa," "na," "so," after which they went back into the hell-pot. Besides this, every one who commits adultery with another man's wife, after death becomes a woman.

---

[1] According to Judson, a number expressed by a unit, followed by 140 cyphers.

Such were the words of Parā Taken on the subject of Kāmesumi*kkhākā*ra.

Musāvāda.—In consequence of King *K*etiya telling a falsehood, the carriage drawn by winged horses and the four Nat's sons guarding it with their daggers, all disappeared; the smell of his body, which was like that of sandal-wood, and the smell of his mouth, which was like that of a water-lily bud, became fetid, and the earth swallowed him up.

*K*iñ*k*amā*n*a also was swallowed up by the earth for telling a falsehood.

The huntsman who told a lie when he was under examination by the monkey-king, was swallowed up by the earth. They all had to suffer in the lowest hell.

Therefore, of all sins against the five commandments, the uttering of a falsehood is the greatest.

Parā Taken also said, "My beloved sons, whoever tells a falsehood, will after death suffer the condition of a Hell-Preta; when they are released from those states of suffering, and have become men, they will have to hear false accusations."

Such were the words of Parā Taken on the subject of Musāvāda.

Surāmeraya.—Whoever shall drink intoxicating liquor, when he dies out of his present existence, will suffer the condition of a Hell-Preta. Even when on release from that state of suffering he becomes a man, he will be insane.

Such were the words of Parā Taken on the subject of Surāmeraya.

The great rewards that those receive who shun these five actions are, an excellent condition of existence, a longer life than others, greater wealth and power than others, greater fame than others, existence in the country of the Nats more than others; these are the five great rewards which those will obtain who observe the five commandments. All those who keep the five commandments will reap much profit, and when they die will have an existence in the country of the Nats, and in the Uttarakuru Island. Every happiness which is to be attained in future existences is the result of observing the commandments.

I have concisely completed the subject of the five commandments, which have really and truly the power of procuring happiness, profit, and excellent virtues, for the use of my fellow-men who long for the results and advantages of those commandments, which the most excellent Parā, full of patience, has preached in a variety of different ways. If all my fellow-men who reverencing the Parā, the law, and the priesthood, desire the advantages which the commandments bring, shall at all times steadfastly observe them,—they will conduct them to the fulfilment of all their wishes, and give them peace and happiness in the church of Parā Taken.

END OF THE DISCOURSE UPON THE FIVE COMMANDMENTS.

CHAPTER XXIV.

ON DHAMMA-DANA.

Pará Taken, moreover, preached as follows, upon the measureless results and advantages derived from listening to the Law:—

"There were four questions which all the Nats in the Tāvatinsa Nat country had been considering for twelve years, and yet could not solve. At last they asked the four Katulokapāla Nat-Kings. These also said, 'We cannot solve them; our master, the Sakka-King, can answer at once the questions of a thousand people. Let us ask the Sakka-King.' So saying the four Katulokapāla Nat-Kings went with all the Nats to the Sakka-King, and asked him the questions. The Sakka-King in like manner said, 'I cannot solve them; it is only the omniscient Parā who is an Agga-puggalam who can solve them.' Accordingly, the Sakka-King and the four Katulokapāla Nat-Kings with all the Nats from the six stages of the Nat country went to Parā Taken and said to him, 'Parā, omniscient lord of the law, among offerings, which is the most excellent offering? Among the different kinds of food, which is the most excellent food? Among enjoyments, which is the most excellent enjoyment? Among all rests from the punishment of misery, which is the most excellent?' Parā Taken, in reply, preached as follows:—" Sakka-King, he who makes an offering of the Law makes an offering superior to all others. Of all foods, the food of the Law is the best. Of all enjoyments, the enjoyment of the Law is the highest. Nibbāna, which is the rest from the misery of lust and passion, is the head of all. The reason why Dhamma-dāna[1] is so excellent is this: Sakka-King! if any one should completely fill the whole of the Kakravāla kingdom, which is one million two hundred and three thousand four hundred and fifty yoganas in extent, with Parās, Pakkekabuddhas, Rahandas, and disciples, and should make offerings to them of thingans,[2] rice, milk, butter, and so forth; and if any one should repeat or listen to four feet of a sacred verse, and the four feet thus repeated or listened to, were divided into sixteen parts; the offerings I have mentioned would not be equal to one of these parts. It is on this account that the Dhamma-dāna is so excellent. Again, if any one does not listen to the Law, he must not make an offering of as much as a ladleful of milk-rice, or a single meal of plain rice. Thus it is that the offering of the Law and the hearing of the Law are so excellent. Putting aside Parās and Pakkekabuddhas, my lord Sāriputta, who could count the rain-drops that fall in the whole of the Kakravāla kingdom, could not of himself obtain the way of Sotāpatti, or any other; but when he heard four feet of the verses of the sacred Law recited by my lord Assagi, he was able to obtain the way of Sotāpatti. Therefore, excellent is Dhamma-dāna.

[1] The offering of the Law.   [2] Priests' garments.

"Although you eat the ambrosia of the Nats, which produces twelve effects, yet you have repeatedly to experience the three abodes;[1] but the food of the Law, if you listen to it but for a moment, can free you from the three abodes, and conduct you to Nibbāna. Therefore, excellent is the food of the Law.

"The enjoyment of the Nats lasts longer than that of men, but still only in the three abodes; while the excellent enjoyment of preaching and listening to the Law liberates from the three abodes, and conducts to Nibbāna. Therefore, excellent is the enjoyment of the Law."

When Parā Taken had thus solved the four questions which the Sakka-King had asked, and terminated his discourse upon the Law, eighty-four thousand Nats acquired the law of liberation.[2]

The Sakka-King said to Parā Taken, "If this be so, why do you not share with me the offering of the Law which is most excellent among offerings?" Thus he addressed the sacred ear. Parā Taken said, "Rahans, my dear sons, from this day forth do not say that the sacred Law which I preach, I preach only for the assembly of Rahans; but whenever I preach and discourse upon the Law in the assembly, say, 'May the Sakka-King receive a share!' and divide it with him."

Thus, because it can give rewards and advantages inestimable, those who recite or listen to the Law receive exceedingly great and most excellent rewards.

When Parā Taken thus, as it were, distributing the food of the sacred Law, preached the sacred Dhamma-

---

[1] *I. e.* of men, Nats, and Brahmas.
[2] *I. e.* had their salvation secured.

kakra Law in the Isipatana forest, Anyakoṇḍañña and eighty millions of Brahmas obtained the law of liberation. When he preached to the thirty Bhaddavaggis, the thousand Rishis, the hundred and ten thousand nobles of King Bimbisāra in the Laṭṭhi garden, and ten thousand congregations were liberated, and ten thousand congregations were firmly established in the observance of Saraṇagamana.[1]

END OF THE DISCOURSE UPON DHAMMA-DANA.

---

[1] In this last paragraph, the MS. differs considerably from the printed text; the latter has been followed.

CHAPTER XXV.

STORY OF THE PRIEST LOKATISSA.

PARA TAKEN, while he resided in the *Getavana* monastery, preached as follows the Vatthu[1] of Akusala[2] Upapi*l*itakam.

Lokatissa-Mahāthera, on account of an evil deed which he had committed in a previous state of existence, became an embryo in a village of a thousand fishermen, in the country of King Kosala. From the very day on which he was conceived, the thousand fishermen who were fishing with traps and nets, could not catch a single fish, and they consequently suffered from hunger. Moreover, from the day the child was conceived, their village was seven times burned down, and seven times had a fine imposed upon it by the king. The fishermen, who had been in misery ever since the child was conceived, began to reflect, "It was never like this with us before; it is only now that we have become poor and miserable, therefore, this state of things must have arisen from there being among us some degenerate being whose former deeds were bad." Accordingly, the thousand fishermen divided themselves into two parties of five hundred

---
[1] Sacred story.   [2] Guilt, evil deeds.

STORY OF THE PRIEST LOKATISSA.

each, which went out fishing separately. The fishermen who came from the quarter where the parents of the embryo Lokatissa resided, obtained nothing; but the other party of five hundred obtained abundance. The unsuccessful party of fishermen again divided themselves into two parties of two hundred and fifty each, and again the party to which the embryo child belonged obtained nothing. In this way they continued to subdivide, till at last the house of the parents of the embryo Lokatissa was alone in its misfortune; then the thousand fishermen, perceiving that the degenerate being must belong to that man's house, expelled the family from the village.

The parents of the child, who were in abject poverty at the time of its birth, had no love for it, for they said to themselves, "From the very day that the child was conceived, misfortunes befell the thousand fishermen, and we ourselves have been reduced to misery." Now, because the child was destined to become a Rahanda, they had no power to destroy it; the light of the reward of Arahatta was to shine in that child's heart like a lamp burning inside an earthen pot. When the child was big enough to walk alone, his parents gave him a piece of broken pot to serve as a cup; then inveigling him inside a house, they left him there and ran away to another place.

The child, thus left alone in the world, used to live by going about with his piece of broken pot in his hand, begging victuals from house to house; and this he continued to do till he was seven years of age. About this time, my lord Sāriputta came to receive alms in the Sāvatthi country. When he saw the child-beggar, he took compassion upon him, and calling him to him, said, "Who are your parents?" The child replied, "Lord and master, I have no one on whom to depend; my parents, in consequence of being in the greatest poverty ever since my birth, have deserted me." My lord Sāriputta took the child with him to the monastery, and made him a probationer for the priesthood. After some time had passed, and he was twenty years of age, he made him a Pañk̇aṅga. When he was advanced in years he became celebrated as Lokatissa. This Lokatissa had not the attribute of attracting offerings. At a time when unparalleled offerings were made, he could not obtain enough to fill his belly with; he procured just sufficient to sustain life. When any one put a single ladleful of yāgu[1] or rice into his thabet and was about to put more, the thabet always appeared to be full, so they poured it into the other thabets, and put no more in his. When the people, making offerings to all the priests in succession, came to this Lokatissa's thabet, all the food which they had in the yāgu-cup ready to offer to him, would disappear.

One day, Lokatissa having developed Vipassanā,[2] became a Rahanda. Notwithstanding that he had thus become a Rahanda, he could never obtain offerings. On the day when he was going to obtain Paranibbāna, my lord Sāriputta, who was aware of it, said to himself, "This Lokatissa-thera will obtain Paranibbāna to-day, therefore, I will give him as much food as will satisfy him." With this thought, he sent for Lokatissa-thera, and invited him to come and

---

[1] A particular preparation of rice made with a variety of ingredients.
[2] A kind of miraculous knowledge.

receive rice with him; but my lord Sāriputta, because Lokatissa was with him when he went to collect rice, did not obtain a single ladleful; the people did not even give him the usual respectful salutations. My lord Sāriputta, knowing that Lokatissa-thera had not the attribute of attracting offerings, then sent him away, saying, "Go and stay in my monastery." As soon as he had gone away, all the people cried, "Here comes my lord Sāriputta," and hastened to make him offerings of food. My lord Sāriputta sent a quantity of this food to Lokatissa-thera; but on the road to the monastery, the people who were taking it forgot all about Lokatissa, and ate it up themselves. When my lord Sāriputta returned to the monastery, Lokatissa made obeisance to him. Sāriputta said, "Lokatissa, have you eaten the food I sent you?" He replied, "I have had none to eat." Sāriputta, on hearing this, was startled; then looking at the sun and finding that it was not too late, he said to him, "Remain here," and having given him a place to stop in, he went off to the palace of King Kosala, and stood there ready to receive alms. King Kosala, directly he saw my lord Sāriputta, filled his thabet with rice and Katumadhu.[1] When Sāriputta arrived with the food at the monastery, he did not give him the thabet, but holding it against his breast said to him, "My lord Lokatissa, take the food out of the thabet which I am holding, and eat it;" but Lokatissa, out of respect to my lord Sāriputta, would not presume to eat it. Then my lord Sāriputta said, "I will stand up and hold the thabet, you also stand up and eat from it; if I let go the thabet, all the food will disappear, and you

[1] Food which a priest may eat after 12 o'clock; see page 120.

will have nothing to eat." Accordingly, Lokatissa stood up and ate the food out of the t*h*abet, while my lord Sāriputta stood up and held it with both hands. Lokatissa ate enough to fill his belly, and on that very day obtained Paranibbāna. Parā Taken performed Lokatissa's sepulture, and erected a Pagoda over his bones and other relics.

At this time the Rahans in the assembly of the law were saying to each other, "How was it that this Lokatissa-thera, who was so wanting in the attribute of attracting offerings, obtained the way, the reward, and Nibbāna?" Parā Taken, wishing to discourse upon the events of the past, preached as follows:—

"Rahans, my dear sons, it was because in a former state of existence this Lokatissa-thera destroyed the offerings of a Rahanda, that he himself received none. It is because he had formerly steadily practised the Vipassanā, 'instability, misery, unsubstantiality,' that he acquired the law of the way and the reward."

Then he proceeded to relate the events of times long past, as follows:—

"This Lokatissa-thera, in the time of the Parā Taken Kassapa, was a Rahan. A T*h*ugyuè built a monastery for him, and supplied all his wants. In this monastery of the T*h*ugyuè he strenuously exerted himself to acquire the Vipassanā. One day a Rahanda who had come from the Himavanta forest, arrived at this T*h*ugyuè's village. The T*h*ugyuè, inspired with affection for him as soon as he saw him, invited him into his house and set food before him. 'Deign to reside,' said he 'in my teacher's monastery, do not go anywhere else; as long as you remain here I will supply you with food.' So saying, he had him conducted to his teacher's monastery. The

STORY OF THE PRIEST LOKATISSA.

Rahan who resided in the monastery entered into conversation with his guest the Rahanda, 'My lord,' said he, 'Have you eaten food?' The guest, the Rahanda, replied, 'I have eaten.'—'Where did you eat,' the Rahan asked. 'In the T*h*ugyuè's house,' he replied. The Rahan who lived in the monastery was jealous at hearing that the Rahanda had been eating in the T*h*ugyuè's house, and maintained silence.

"In the cool of the evening the T*h*ugyuè went to the monastery, and invited his teacher and the Rahanda guest to come and receive rice. After reminding his teacher to bring his Rahanda guest with him [to his house to receive alms], the T*h*ugyuè went away.

"The occupier of the monastery, vexed with his Rahan guest, would not say a single word to him, but maintained complete silence, thinking that by doing so, the guest would not presume to remain in the monastery. The Rahanda guest, knowing the bad feeling of the Rahan who occupied the monastery, resolved to go elsewhere. Next morning the Rahan, who occupied the monastery, arose very early and put on his t*h*ingan; then, fearful of waking the Rahanda guest, in order to fulfil his duty he scratched with his finger-nail on the stone drum, and after rapping on the door with his nail, went out. When the T*h*ugyuè saw that the Rahanda guest had not accompanied him, he said, 'Lord and master, did you not invite your Rahan guest to come?' The Rahan replied, 'Tagā, in order to arouse the Rahan guest, I beat the stone drum at the entrance of the monastery, and, moreover, rapped at the door, but I could not wake him; it must be the food which the Tagā made an offering of to him yesterday, and of which he ate to satiety, that not being yet digested, makes him sleep so. Has the Tagā great affection for such a Rahan?'

"The Rahanda guest, when the time for collecting rice had arrived, put on his t*h*ingan, and carrying his t*h*abet at his breast, flew up into the sky and went away to another place to receive offerings.

"The T*h*ugyuè, after supplying his teacher with food, put a quantity into his t*h*abet, telling him to offer it to the Rahan guest. The Rahan, who was the occupier of the monastery, said to himself, 'If this Rahan guest were to eat this nice food, he would not go away even if I dragged him out;' and in his vexation he poured out all the rice, butter, and the rest of the food, in a place where the jungle was burning. On reaching the monastery he said, 'The Rahan guest must have been a Rahanda, who knowing my feelings to him, has gone elsewhere; and I in my jealousy have destroyed his offerings.' With these words he died of his own accord. He then went into hell, where he suffered for an immense length of time. When released from hell he was a Bilū[1] during the whole of five hundred existences, and never for a single day procured sufficient food to satisfy him. After completing five hundred existences as a Bilū, he was five hundred times a dog. When he died, after completing his five hundred existences as a dog, he became an embryo in the womb of a poor woman in a village of the Kāsikarā*g* country. From the very day of his conception, his parents became miserably poor. When he was born on the expiration of the ten months, they called the child Mittapindaka.[2] As soon as this Mittapindaka could walk alone, his parents, unable to bear hunger

---

[1] A species of Ghoul. [2] The MS. has *K*umittapindaka.

any longer, drove him away. The child, with no one to depend upon, went and found his way to Benares. At this time the Parālaun was the teacher Dīsāpamokkha at Benares, where he was giving instruction to five hundred young men who were his pupils. Mittapindaka also went and resided with the Parālaun, and was instructed in science and learning. From the very day that Mittapindaka came to receive instruction, the teacher Dīsāpamokkha was much concerned to find that no offerings were made to him. Mittapindaka, moreover, began to quarrel with the other pupils; at last, not heeding the admonitions of his teacher, and being always at variance with them, he ran away. Arriving at a village, he made his living there by labouring for hire. When he was grown up, he married a poor woman in that village, by whom he had two sons. On account of this Mittapindaka, the houses of the villagers were seven times burned down; and seven times a fine was imposed on them by the king; when they raised a dam for rice cultivation, it burst seven times. At last the villagers, seeing that all these misfortunes dated from the day when Mittapindaka came among them, drove him out of the village. As he was journeying to another place with his wife and children, he lost his way, and came into a forest where a Bilū lived. The Bilū devoured his wife and children. Mittapindaka, escaping, travelled to a great distance, and reached the harbour of Gambhīra; there he addressed himself to the captain of a ship, and asked to be allowed to work under him for hire; the sailors gave him employment and agreed to pay him wages.

"On the seventh day after setting sail, the vessel

remained stationary in the midst of the sea, just as if it were a fixture there. The sailors said, 'There must be some one on board our ship who ought not to be there.' So saying they cast lots, and Mittapindaka drew the lot seven times; they therefore gave him a bundle of bamboos which they made him take hold of with his hands, and throwing him overboard, sent him floating away in the midst of the sea. No sooner was he thrown overboard than the vessel started off like a flying horse.

"From the effect of his having in a previous state of existence, in the time of the Parā Taken Kassapa, practised the Vipassanā, 'instability, misery, unsubstantiality,' Mittapindaka, after floating about the sea on the bundle of bamboos, arrived at an island where there was a palace in which lived four Nats' daughters with whom he enjoyed himself for seven days. These, in consequence of their being the daughters of the Nat Vimānopeta, after enjoying seven days' happiness had to undergo seven days of misery. These Nats' daughters accordingly, after telling Mittapindaka to stay in the palace till they came back, went away to undergo their sufferings. Mittapindaka, as soon as the Nat's daughters were gone, mounted his bundle of bamboos, and floating away on the sea, arrived at an island where there was a silver palace in which were eight Nats' daughters with whom he enjoyed himself. Floating off again from the silver palace, he reached an island where there was a ruby palace in which were sixteen Nats' daughters with whom he enjoyed himself. Leaving this again, he arrived at a golden palace where there were thirty-two Nats' daughters with whom he enjoyed himself. All these Nats' daughters, being the daughters of the Nat Vimānopeta, after enjoying seven days' happiness had to suffer seven days' misery. Although all the Nats' daughters asked him to stay in their palace, he would not remain, but seating himself on the bundle of bamboos, floated off again. At last he arrived at an island in the midst of the sea where Bilūmas[1] lived.

"At this time one of the Bilūmas had assumed the appearance of a goat. Mittapindaka not knowing that it was a Bilūma, and thinking he would like to eat some goat's flesh, laid hold of it by the leg to kill it. The nature of the Bilūma being that of the Nat race, by means of her power and glory she seized Mittapindaka by the leg and hurled him away; and he fell down at the gate of the city of Benares. At the gate where he fell were some of the king's shepherds, who were in pursuit of some thieves who had stolen the king's goat. At this very moment Mittapindaka was pulling the leg of a goat, and the goat was making a great outcry. The shepherds, thinking that Mittapindaka was the thief, laid hold of him and gave him a beating, and then bound him and carried him off to take him before the king. At this juncture the Parālaun, the teacher Dīsāpamokkha, was coming out of the city with his five hundred pupils to bathe. When he saw Mittapindaka, he said, "This is my disciple; release him." The shepherds set him free and went away, and Mittapindaka remained with the Parālaun. The Parālaun asked him where he had been all this time, and he related all his adventures. The Parālaun recited this poetry: 'He who will not listen to the words of his well-wisher will come to misery.'

[1] A female Bilū.

"He who was then Mittapindaka is now the Rahanda Lokatissa. The teacher Dīsāpamokkha is now I, the Parā. Thus the Rahanda Lokatissa, because in a former state of existence he was jealous of the offerings and prosperity of another, had to suffer in hell; after this, even when he became a man, he could never obtain sufficient food for a full meal. Up to the very time when he became a Rahanda, owing to the effects of his evil deeds in a former existence, he never for one single day had sufficient food to satisfy him. It was only on the day of his obtaining Nibbāna that, through the power of my lord Sāriputta, he enjoyed a full meal just before entering Nibbāna.

"Therefore, neither men nor Rahans should ever be vexed with, or envious of, the offerings and prosperity of others."

END OF THE STORY TAKEN FROM THE KAMMAPABHEDA-
DIPA SCRIPTURE.

CHAPTER XXVI.

AN ACCOUNT OF GOTAMA'S FAMILY.

The Sākiya[1] kings of the family of Parā Taken were these: in the Kapilavatthu country there were eighty thousand, all of the royal race; those of the race of Kosala[2] and those of the race of Devadaha were all of the royal race of Sākiya. The way of it was this:—

The king who in due course reigned over the Kapilavatthu country was King Ukkākarāja.[3] This King Ukkākarāja had five daughters and four sons; the eldest son was King Ukkāmukkha.[4] When his queen died, he raised a princess to the rank of his queen. This queen gave birth to a prince named Gantu. When the queen gave birth to Prince Gantu, King Ukkākarāja made her very handsome presents. As soon as Prince Gantu came of age, the queen asked the king to make him king. Ukkākarāja said to her, "While there are my four elder sons, I cannot make him king." However, as the queen constantly repeated her request, King Ukkākarāja at last called his four

---

[1] The royal race from which Gotama descended.
[2] Manuscript has Kosiya.   [3] Okkāka, in the Suttanipāta.
[4] His five wives were called Hatthā, Kittā, Gantu, Gālinī, Visākhā; his four sons, Okkāmukha, Kavakandu, Hatthiniko, Nipuro; his four daughters, Piyā, Suppiyā, Ānandā, Vigitā, Vigitasenā.

sons, and said to them, "From the time the queen gave birth to my son *Gantu*, I have conferred continual benefits upon her; now she has asked me to give the royal place to *Gantu*. Since I cannot tell whether the queen has good or evil intentions towards my sons, take elephants, horses, and soldiers, as many as you wish, and settling in some suitable place, take up your residence there. When I am dead, assume the royal power by turns."[1]

The four princes made obeisance to their royal father, and set out on their journey; the five princesses also accompanied their brothers. The cavalcade of country people, elephants, horses, and soldiers that attended them, extended to the length of four yo*g*anas. The eldest son of King Ukkākarā*g*a, with his younger brothers, made search for a proper site for a city. At this time, my lord the Rishi Kapila, who was skilled in the characteristic signs of ground, in searching for a site for a monastery, had observed on a particular spot a deer pursuing a tiger. "This," said he, "is an auspicious spot," and he built a monastery there and took up his residence in it. The princes, while looking for a site for their city, fell in with the Rishi. My lord the Rishi asked the princes what they were doing, and they told him they were in search of a site for a city. "If this be so," said my lord the Rishi, "build a palace in the neighbourhood of my monastery, and erect your city in the vicinity; you have my permission." The princes, having received the permission of my lord the Rishi, erected a city and resided there. In consequence of the city having been built near the monastery of the Rishi Kapila, it was called the city of Kapilavatthu.

[1] Manuscript omits "by turns."

One day, some time after this, the four princes, placing their eldest sister in the position of mother, married each one, one of their younger sisters. When their royal father, King Ukkākarāja, heard of this, he said, "Most excellent are my sons and daughters," and highly applauded them.

In consequence of Prince Ukkāmukkha's eldest sister being afflicted with leprosy throughout all her body, her brothers one day dug a cave, and after stocking it with abundance of grain and other provisions of all kinds, shut her up in it, and closed the entrance.

At this time the great King Rāma, who ruled over the Benares country, being covered all over with leprosy, gave over charge of his dominions to his son, and went away to live in the forest. After eating the medicines and roots of the forest, he was cured of the leprosy, and his appearance became like gold. Freed from his disease, he travelled along, eating wild fruits and roots as he went, and arrived at the place where Prince Ukkāmukkha's sister had been shut up in the cave. Climbing into a tree, he went to sleep. A tiger, scratching at the cave with his claws, frightened the princess, and she began to scream, and the tiger ran away. King Rāma, hearing her cries, came down and dug open the cave; finding there was a human being there, he said, " Come out." The princess replied, " I am a king's daughter; I will not come out." King Rāma said, " I also am a king."—" If so," said the princess, " repeat the king's spell." [1] King Rāma recited the king's spell; when he had done so, the

---

[1] The word both in the text and manuscript is " māyā " " an artifice," but the correct word is probably " mantra," a " charm " or " spell."

N

princess said, "I am afflicted with leprosy."—"Do not be concerned about that," said the king, "for I also had leprosy, but by taking certain medicines, have completely cured myself." Hearing this, the princess came out, and after the king had given her the same medicines as he had himself used, she quite recovered from the leprosy, and her appearance became like gold. Remaining in that place, they married one another, and the princess gave birth to twin sons sixteen times, and all the thirty-two sons were like blocks of solid gold. These thirty-two royal sons married the daughters of their maternal uncles, in the country of Kapilavatthu. King Rāma, continuing to reside in the same place, erected a city there, which, in consequence of his having cleared away a Koli[1] tree, he called the city of Koliya.

The two cities of Kapilavatthu and Koliya having so much increased by constant intermarriage among the inhabitants of each, the name [of the latter] was changed to Devadaha.

Over this Devadaha country Prince Añkana was king. Thus, after there had been a succession of more than eighty-two thousand kings in the Kapilavatthu country, beginning from King Ukkāmukkha, King Gayasena, the great-grandfather of Parā Taken, reigned over the Kapilavatthu country in an unbroken line of succession. This King Gayasena had a son Sihanu,[2] and a daughter Yasodharā. The queen of this King Sihanu was Queen Kañkanā, the sister of King Añkana, who reigned over the Devadaha country. This King Sihanu's sister Yasodharā married King Añkana, and

---

[1] The jujube-tree.

[2] In Pali Sīhahanu, in Sanskrit Siṃhahanu, so called because his cheek-bones were like those of a lion.

became queen; each married the other's sister, and both the princesses became queens. Kañkanā, the queen of King Sihanu, gave birth to King Suddhodana the royal father of Parā Taken, King Dhotodana, King Sukkodana, King Amitodana, and King Ukyodana,[1] these five sons.[2] She had also two daughters, Princess Amitā and Princess Pālitā. King Añkana's wife, Queen Yasodharā, gave birth to two sons, Prince Suppabuddha and Prince Dandapāni; and two daughters, Sirimahāmāyā and Pagāpatigotamī. When the Brahmins interpreted the characteristics of these two princesses, Sirimahāmāyā and Pagāpatigotamī, they declared that they would give birth to a Kakravarti king. Accordingly the two sisters Sirimahāmāyā and Pagāpatigotamī were raised to the rank of queens of King Suddhodana. Sirimahāmāyā gave birth to Parā Taken,[3] and Pagāpatigotamī gave birth to Prince Nanda and Ganapadakalyāni. The Princess Amitā, the sister of King Suddhodana, married Prince Suppabuddha, and gave birth to Devadatta and Princess Bimbā; the Princess Bimbā's name was changed afterwards to Yasodharā, the name of the grandmother of Parā Taken; marrying the Parālaun my lord Siddhattha, she gave birth to Rāhula, and received the name of "the sacred mother of Rāhula."

At that time there were in the Kapilavatthu country eighty thousand, all of the sacred family of Parā Taken, and eighty thousand also in the country of Devadaha.

END OF THE GENEALOGY OF PARA TAKEN.

[1] Sukkhodana, in the com. to the Suttanipāta.
[2] Manuscript says "four sons," and omits Ukyodana.
[3] Manuscript has the "Parālaun Taken."

CHAPTER XXVII.

UPON THE TAKING OF CONSECRATED PROPERTY, AND THE TWENTY-ONE KINDS OF EVIL-DOERS.

No one must eat the food which belongs to Parā, the law, and the priests. Whoever eats of it shall suffer heavy punishment hereafter. In the time of the Parā Kassapa, a crow, because he had eaten some rice from a Rahan's t*h*abet, became a Preta-crow[1] on the Ki*kk*a-kut mountain. Whatever has been set aside for Parā, the law, and the priests, such as monasteries, fields, corn, water for cultivation, etc., no one from a king downwards must take; whoever takes or uses such, shall hereafter suffer for a long period in the lowest hell. Whatever has been offered and set aside as consecrated property for Parā, the law, and the priests, such as horses, gardens, fields, gold, silver, copper, slaves, etc., whoever shall take for his use shall become a Preta, and bear sufferings in hunger and thirst. The rewards of offering and setting aside property as consecrated, are great power and authority; but kings who make use of consecrated property shall be bereft of all power and authority, and shall become Pretas.

[1] A being in a state of punishment; of a lower kind than an animal.

Any Rahan who knows that property is consecrated, and shall not say so, shall suffer the punishment of the four hells; if he say so, he shall escape hell. Although any one shall give a substitute for a Pagoda-slave, he cannot liberate him; for the slaves set aside by kings as consecrated property for the five thousand years of the church, are fixed and settled for the five thousand years of the church.[1] Whoever from kings downwards shall break the continuity of the consecration for the five thousand years of the church, and resume the property, will pass into the lowest hell. If a king who has obtained the *K͡akra*[2] shall destroy any of the consecrated property belonging to the three jewels, his *K͡akra*-jewel shall disappear. Kings who repeatedly destroy consecrated property, shall not die in their own country, but in some other land.

I will give an instance. King Pasenadikosala, taking bribes from heretics, settled upon them a plot of consecrated ground to the west of the *G͡etavana* monastery of Parā Taken, as a site for a monastery; on account of this he was not able to stay in his own country, but died in a Zayat in a strange land. King Pasenadikosala, one of Parā Taken's Dārakas, who had made incomparable offerings, even he, for the sake of a bribe, settled upon others consecrated land; accordingly he did not die in his own country, but he had to wander in other lands, and ultimately perished in a ruined Zayat. The book Sutta says, "Kings who

---

[1] The dispensation of Gotama is supposed to last for five thousand years, when another Parā will appear. About one-half of this period has now elapsed.

[2] A fabulous weapon.

repeatedly destroy (the title of) consecrated land shall lose all their authority."

Slaves who have been offered to pagodas, can only be employed in cleaning pagodas. They must not wait upon kings or any one else. If those who have great power and authority employ pagoda-slaves, they will lose their power and die a frightful death; they will come to misery and destruction: so it is written in the book Sutta. No one must take as a bribe property which has been offered for the use of the priesthood; if they commit this offence, they will come to ruin. Slaves in the employ of Rahans, on the death of those Rahans become consecrated property. Those who offend by employing the slaves which belong to Rahans shall lose all they possess: so it is written in the book Sutta. Whoever shall take for himself or for another, any consecrated land, shall become a mite or a white ant upon that consecrated land for the whole of a hundred thousand cycles.

The sacred law, thus preached (by Parā Taken), is written in the book Āyu of the holy church.

After passing through the eight stages of the great hells, they shall have the condition of Pretas, from which twenty Parās cannot free them; after which they shall become insects and white ants in the consecrated monasteries and lands. Therefore kings, nobles, officers, poor people, every one, must take care not to take or injure lands for wet or dry cultivation, elephants, horses, slaves, bullocks, gold, silver, paddy, rice, clothes, utensils, or any description whatever of consecrated property. Those who take, or those who injure such property will have to suffer, as already stated, in hell and as Pretas.

Any one who kills a man.[1]
Any one who destroys cities and villages.
Any one who, possessed by a Nat,[2] steals the property of another.
Any one who works as a blacksmith.[3]
Any one who drinks[4] intoxicating liquors.
Any one who sells poison.
Any one who has a grant of the tolls at the barriers.
Any one employed as a general.
Any one who collects taxes.[5]
A hunter.
A fisherman.
A judge who takes bribes.
A Rahan who has committed an unpardonable sin.
A man who steals another's wife.
A woman who commits adultery.
Any one who gathers honey.
Any one who poisons or drugs fish.
Any one who offends against his parents.
Any one who ruins a female Rahan.
Any one who performs the process of castration.
Any one who injures the church of the Parā—

These twenty-one kinds of people, on account of their evil deeds, will fall into the lowest hell. In this way, Parā Taken preached the law, knowing all the people without exception who would fall into hell. Among the people who commit these twenty-one kinds of evil actions, there are nineteen who, if they see their

---

[1] Printed text says "a Rahan or a man."
[2] Thus in both text and manuscript.
[3] *I.e.* who makes weapons.
[4] Text says, "who sells intoxicating liquors."
[5] The text and manuscript differ here, the former says "a ploughman."

evil ways, perform good works, listen to the Law, steadfastly observe Saraṇagamana and the five commandments, and keep good watch over their bodies, shall be released from their sins; but the hunter and the fisherman, let them attend pagodas, listen to the Law, and keep the five commandments to the end of their lives, still they cannot be released from their sins. So it is laid down in the book Sutta.

CHAPTER XXVIII.

THE STORY OF KING KAKAVANNA.

A RAHANDA once preached the Law to King Kākavanna, his queen, and concubines, in the island of Ceylon. King Kākavanna, filled with love for the Law, resolved to make an offering of the putzo which he was wearing. In a spirit of niggardliness, however, he thought he would defer the offering till the next day. Two crows, a husband and wife, who were perched upon the tree, at the foot of which the Law had been preached, knowing what was passing in the king's mind, said to each other, "The king, from his niggardly spirit, excellent as the Law is, cannot make up his mind to make an offering of the putzo." Neither the queen, nor the concubines, nor the nobles, understood what the two crows were saying to each other; but the king, directly he heard the sound of the crows, knew what they said. "O you pair of crows," he exclaimed, "how dare you speak so of a king like me?" The crows replied, "Your Majesty, do not take the putzo you have at home, but make an offering of the one you are wearing, worth a hundred thousand (pieces of gold). In seven days hence, you will receive the five rewards." The king smiled at the crows' speech. My lord the Rahanda, who had been preaching the Law, said to the king, "Why does your Majesty smile at me?"—"I was not smiling at my lord Rahanda," replied the king, "I was smiling at what the two crows said." The Rahanda, who possessed the Nat's eye, which could behold eight past and eight future existences, and who saw the previous life of the king, said to him, "Great king, I will tell you something; will you be angry with me?"—"My lord," replied the king, "I shall not be angry with you; deign to tell it to me." My lord the Rahanda proceeded, "When your Majesty was a poor man in the Anurādha country, you used to collect firewood, and live by the sale of it. One day, when you went out to your work, you took with you a small cupful of boiled rice. Coming across a heap of white sand which looked like sheet silver, you reflected that your poverty must have been occasioned by your not possessing the merit of having made offerings, and accordingly you raised a pagoda of the white sand, placed in front of it, as an offering, one half of the rice you had with you, and gave the remaining half to the crows to eat, as an offering to the Rahans. These two crows, husband and wife, are the very same two crows who ate the rice of which you made the offering when a you were a poor man." When the king heard this, he exclaimed, "Oh, how unstable is prosperity! I have obtained the position of a king only from making offerings at a sand pagoda!" so saying, he made an offering to the Law of the putzo he was wearing, and which was worth a hundred thousand (pieces of gold). Seven days afterwards the five rewards came to the king. The five rewards were these:—

The Nats, wrapping up in a *t*hingan the relics of an excellent Rahanda who had obtained Paranibbāna, while he was up in the sky, and which were like a jasmine-bud, came and laid them down before the king. In front of his palace a mountain of gold arose. The Nats brought a virgin from the island of Uttarakuru. This woman was ten cubits in stature; she brought with her a kunsā[1] of rice, which, though one were to cook it and eat it during a whole lifetime, would never be exhausted. An elephant of priceless value, which could travel a hundred yoganas even before breakfast. Seven vessels arrived at the port completely filled with valuable putzos. In return for the offering the king had made to the law,.these five rewards came to him.

End of the Story of King Kakavanna.

[1] Name of a measure.

CHAPTER XXIX.

STORY OF THE RAHANDAMA UPPALAVA*NN*A.

I WILL now give an account of the reward of the offering of the crimson cloth:—

There lived in the city of Benares a poor man's daughter, who, being very desirous of having a crimson cloth to wear, in order to obtain one, went and remained in service with a T*h*ugyuè for three years. As soon as she had procured one, she went down to the river to bathe, and leaving the garment on the bank, went into the water. At this moment, one of Parā Taken's disciples, whose T*h*ingan and T*h*inbaing[1] had been stolen by thieves, made his appearance dressed in leaves. The young girl, when she saw him, said to herself, "Some thieves must have stolen this Taken's[2] T*h*ingan and T*h*inbaing; I too, from not having before made any offerings, have found it hard to procure any clothes." So saying, she cut off half of her crimson garment, and made an offering of it to him. The Taken, after going into a secluded place and putting on the half of the crimson cloth, came back to the Tagāma. When the poor Tagāma saw the handsome

---

[1] Articles of a priest's clothing.
[2] A title answering to "master," "lord."

appearance the Taken presented in the crimson garment, she said, "Just as Taken is handsome, may I also in all my future existences be possessed of beauty!" Then she continued in poetry, "Lord and master, even as my lord and master is beautiful in this garment, so also may I become an object of admiration, and be a gainer of hearts!" Such was her prayer. Then Taken preached to the poor woman the advantages to be derived from making offerings of clothing, as follows:—

"Sister, if any one be endowed with all the beauty of the Nats, and be decorated with gold and silver and all kinds of ornaments, yet if he be without a putzo, he would not present a comely appearance; therefore, excellent is the offering of garments. Whoever is always neat and seemly in his apparel meets with respect, and, with a soft and delicate complexion and handsome appearance, gains all hearts, and is beloved by all." The Taken, after thus preaching the Law, took his departure.

The poor woman who had made the offering of the crimson cloth, when she died out of the land of men, appeared in the Nat country, where she enjoyed all the luxury and splendour of the Nats. After completing her existence in the Nat country, she became the daughter of the Thuthe Sirivaddhana in the Arithapura country. The young girl, who was so beautiful that people went mad when they saw her, was called Unmādantī. When his daughter was sixteen years of age, the Thuthe Sirivaddhana went to the king of Arithapura and said, "In my house I have a jewel-daughter." The king ordered the Brahmins to go and interpret her characteristics. When the Brahmins went to the Thuthe's house for this purpose, Sirivad-

*dha*na set rice and dainty food before them; just then, Unmādantī appeared, dressed magnificently. The Brahmins, as soon as they saw her, went mad; one put a handful of rice on the top of his head, another made a mistake and put it into a hole in the floor, another put it inside his ear, another under his armpit. When Unmādantī saw the Brahmins behaving in this way, she ordered her slaves to turn them out of the house. The Brahmins, enraged at this, went and reported to the king that she was a very low kind of woman; and the king accordingly would not take her. The T*hu*t*he* Sirivad*dha*na then gave his daughter Unmādantī in marriage to the prime minister.

Unmādantī, dying out of that state of existence, appeared again in the Nat country; dying out of the Nat country, she became in the time of the Parā Gotama, a T*hu*t*he*'s daughter in the Sāvatthi country, as fair as a water-lily. She was called Uppalava*nn*ā. The beauty of the T*hu*t*he*'s daughter Uppalava*nn*ā was celebrated throughout the whole of the Island of *G*ambudvīpa. Every one of the kings of the island came with magnificent presents to induce the T*hu*t*he* to give him his lovely daughter, but Siriva*ddha*na, thinking that if he gave her to one, all the others would be angry, made her a Rahan. Reaching the stage of a Rahanda, she received the name of Uppalava*nn*ā Rahandama.

END OF THE STORY OF UPPALAVA*NN*A RAHANDAMA THERĪ.

CONCLUSION.

As a deposit of mud which is produced from water, may by water be washed away again; so sins which are produced by the mind, by the mind can be cleansed away.

SCHEME OF TRANSLITERATION.

CONSONANTS.

	PALI.	BURMESE.	
Gutturals ...	k kh g gh ṅ	k kh g gh ṅ	
Palatals	k kh g gh ñ	s hs z hz ñ	The first four letters pronounced by the Burmese as dental sibilants.
Linguals	t th d dh n	t th d dh n	Pronounced by the Burmese as dentals.
Dentals	t th d dh n	t th d dh n	
Labials	p ph b bh m	p ph b bh m	
Semivowels...	y r l v	y r l w	**r** pronounced indifferently by the Burmese as **y**.
Sibilant	s	th	pronounced by Burmese as **th** in Eng. "theatre."
Aspirate......	h	h	
Lingual	l	l	pronounced by Burmese as ordinary **l**.

SCHEME OF TRANSLITERATION.

VOWELS.

	PALI.		BURMESE.
a	as "a" in "America."	a	as "a" in French "patte."
ā	as "a" in "bar."	ā	as "a" in "bar."
i	as "i" in "pin."	i	as "i" in "pin."
ī	as "ee" in "feet."	ī	as "ee" in "feet."
u	as "u" in "put."	u	as "u" in "put."
ū	as "oo" in "boot."	ū	as "oo" in "boot."
e	as "a" in "pay."	e	as "a" in "pay."
o	as "o" in "hope."	o	as "o" in "hope."
		ai	as "i" in "light."
		au	as "o" in "how."
		ĕ	as "e" in "let."
		ó	as "é" in French "thé."
		è	as "ai" in "fairy."
		ȯ	as "o" in "nor."

N.B.—The anusvāra in the Pali forms is represented by the letter *m*. In Burmese it is impossible to distinguish it by any character as it takes the place of an "**m**" or "**n**;" all three characters being in a great measure used indifferently, without any fixed rule.

INDEX OF TECHNICAL TERMS IN THE PARABLES.

Pali.	Burmese.
a	**a**
Akusala	164.
Aggapuggalam	ĕggapoggalam, 160.
agapāla	idzapāla, 46.
adinnadāna	adinnadānā, 153, 155.
anāgāmi	anāgāmi, 44, 46, 47, 56, 57, 95, 123, 151.
anumodana	anumòdanā, 68, 76, 92.
arahatta	arahatta, 165.
ariya	ariyā, 4, 56.
arunavati	126.
asaṅkhya	athiṅkhye, 157.
ā	**ā**
āyu	āyu, 182.
āsivisut	āthiwithot, 106.
u	**u**
uddhamsota	oddhanthota, 123.
upapilitakam	upapilitakam, 164.
k	**k**
kamuttara	126.
kammaṭṭhāna	kammaṭhān, 4, 5, 27, 28, 29, 56, 63, 66, 74, 77, 94, 105, 174.
kammapabhedadīpa	kommapabhedadīpa, 174.
kammavākya	kammavā, 119.
kasina	kathon, 108.
kahāpana	athabyā, 47, 48, 140.
kāmesumikkhākārā	kāmethuméthsāsārā, 153, 157, 158.

o 2

INDEX OF TECHNICAL TERMS IN THE PARABLES.

PALI.	BURMESE.
g	**g**
gandha-dhūra	gandha-dhūra, 3, 4, 26.
gavyūti	gāwot, 82.
k	**s**
kakra	sĕkya, 181.
kakravarti	82, 136.
katumadhu	sadumadhu, 120, 167.
ketiya	sedi, 45.
g	**z**
gāt	148.
gātisāra	zātithara, 106.
t	**t**
	tagā, 28, 43, 169, 170, 189.
d	**d**
dāyaka (?)	dārakā, 5, 8, 27, 33, 66, 80, 87, 107, 109, 113, 181.
devakakkhu	déppasĕkkhu, 107, 108, 112, 113.
devadhamma	dewadhamma, 136, 138.
dh	**dh**
dhammakakra	dhammasĕkyā, 162.
dhammadāna	dhammadāna, 160, 161.
dhyāna	hzān, 105, 122, 123.
n	**n**
nat	2, 8, 14, 15, 32, 44, 46, 79, 93, 95, 108, 109, 111, 115, 120, 138, 160.
nāga	nagā, 127.
nibbāna	népbhān, 1, 102, 161, 162, 168, 174.
nirodhasamāpatti	niròdhathammābāt, 58, 59, 108, 110.
p	**p**
pakkekabuddha	pyitsekaboddhā, 43, 58, 59, 60, 78, 84, 108, 109, 110, 111, 112, 113, 152, 161.

INDEX OF TECHNICAL TERMS IN THE PARABLES. 197

Pali.	Burmese.
pañkānga	pyinsiń, 3, 26, 63, 117, 118, 119, 166.
paranibbāna	parinépbhān, 108, 123, 154, 166, 168, 187.
pavāranā	pawāranā, 4.
pānātipāta	pānātipātā, 153, 154, 155.
parā	parā, 1, 14, 38.
pāli	pāli, 3, 63.
pitaka	pitakat, 3, 49, 59, 60, 68.
puthuggana	pudhuziń, 117.
puluvakasañā	puluwakathiñā, 105.
prāsāda	pyathat, 34, 49, 53, 56, 57, 61.
preta	pyéttā, 157, 158, 180, 182.

b — **b**
brahmini . . . 44.

bh — **bh**
bhāvana . . . bhāwanā, 4.

m — **m**
mantra	177.
mahāthera	mathi, 1, 5, 8, 11, 154, 164.
musāvāda	muthāwādā, 153, 158.

y — **y**
yogana . . . yūzanā, 4, 42, 127, etc.

r — **r or y**
ragoharanam	razòharanam, 65.
rahanda	rahandā, 4, 6, 8, 9, 10, 26, 29, 47, 63, 66, 68, 77, 81, 84, 85, 86, 95, 96, 102, 106, 113, 116, 117, 123, 131, 151, 154, 161, 165, 166, 168, 169, 170, 174, 185, 186, 187, 190.
rishi	rithe, 20, 21, 22, 23, 24, 32, 33, 35, 36, 37, 154, 163, 176.

l — **l**
lohakumbhi . . . lòhakombhi, 132, 134.

198 INDEX OF TECHNICAL TERMS IN THE PARABLES.

PALI.	BURMESE.
v	**v**
vatthu	wutthu, 122, 164.
vipassanā	wipatthanā, 27, 29, 66, 105, 123, 166, 168, 172.
vipassanā-dhūra	wipatthanā-dhūra, 3, 4, 26.
veda	45, 129.
s	**th**
sakadāgāmi	thakadāgāmi, 56, 151.
satipatthāna	thatipathān, 106.
	thabét, 59.
samāpatti	thammābāt, 59, 73.
samvega	thanwega, 65, 106.
saranagamana	tharanāgon, 54, 104, 151, 152, 156, 163, 184.
	thingan, 73, 79.
	thugye, 1, 79.
	thuthe, 12.
sutta	thottan, 181, 182, 184.
susāna	thotthan, 26, 27, 28.
sūrameraya	thūrāmeriya, 153, 158.
sotāpatti	thòtāpatti, 16, 24, 31, 48, 56, 59, 60, 71, 83, 97, 101, 104, 106, 119, 134, 161.
sotāpan	thòtāpan, 14, 17, 48, 83, 85, 106, 151.
h	**h**
hatthikanta	hattikandhā, 33, 36, 37, 38.
hatthilinga	thihlaingā, 34.
hiri	hiri, 136.
z	**z**
	zayat, 18, 62.

INDEX OF PROPER NAMES IN THE PARABLES.

Pali.	Burmese.
A	**A**
Akani*th*a	Ëkkané*th*a, 123.
A*k*iravati	Asīrawadī, 103.
A*g*apāla	Idzapāla, 46.
Añ*k*ana	Iñsana, 178, 179.
Adinnapubbaka . .	Adénnapoppaka, 12, 14, 16, 17.
Anavatatta	Anawadat, 114, 115, 116, 117, 118.
Anurādha	Anurādha, 186.
Anuruddha	Anuroddhā, 107, 110, 111, 112, 113, 114, 115, 116, 117.
Anegava*nn*a . .	Anegawu*nn*a, 123.
Ano*g*ā	Anòzā, 80, 84, 85.
Annabhāra	Annabhāra, 108, 109, 110, 111, 112, 113.
Amitā	Améttā, 179.
Amitodana . . .	Améttòdana, 179.
Avriha . .	Awihā, 123.
Anyako*nd*añña . . .	Anyāku*nd*iña, 163.
Allakappa . . .	Alakappa, 32, 33, 34, 35, 36.
Assa*g*i	At*h*āzi, 161.
Avara*kkh*a	Awarithsa, 82.
Ari*th*apura . . .	Ari*th*apūra, 189.
Ā	**Ā**
Ānanda . .	Ānandā, 24, 50, 51, 55, 105, 117, 118, 157.
Ābhassara	Ābhatt*h*arā, 122.

INDEX OF PROPER NAMES IN THE PARABLES.

PALI.	BURMESE.
I	**I**
Isipatana . . .	It*h*ipadana, 163.
U	**U**
Ukkākarā*y*a .	Okkākarit, 175, 176, 177.
Ukkāmukkha	Okkāmokkha, 175, 177, 178.
Ukyodana . . .	Ukyòdana, 179.
U*gg*eni	Otseni, 38.
Uttarakuru . . .	Ottarakuru, 159, 187.
Udena	Udé*nn*a, 35, 36, 38, 39, 40, 41, 42, 43, 44, 47, 50, 51, 52, 53, 55, 56.
Upa*ggh*āya . . .	Upidhzè, 3,
Upadit*h*a	Upadit*h*a, 108, 109, 111, 112, 113.
Upari	Upari, 105, 106.
Uppalava*nn*ā . .	Oppalawu*n*, 86, 188, 190.
Unmādanti . .	Ommādandi, 189, 190.
K	**K**
Kakusandha . . .	Kaukkat*h*an, 105, 106.
Kañ*k*anā	Kiñsanā, 178, 179.
Katānukatavedi	Katiñukatawedhi, 138.
Kapila	Kappila, 176.
Kapilavatthu . .	Kappilawut, 110, 175, 176, 178, 179.
Kambalāra-Tissa .	Kambalāya-Tétt*h*a, 76.
Kamllakamahāvihāra .	Kamllākamahāwihāra, 106.
Kassapa	Katt*h*apa, 60, 64, 79, 80, 84, 87, 88, 121, 122, 125, 131, 135, 168, 172, 180.
Kāka	Kāla, 42.
Kākava*nn*a . . .	Kākawu*nn*a, 185.
Kāsikarā*y* . . .	Kāt*h*ikarit, 140, 170.
Ki*kk*akut	Kétsagot, 180.
Kimbila	Kimila, 112.
Kisāgotami . .	Kétt*h*agòtami, 98, 99, 100, 101, 102.
Kukkuvati . . .	Kokkuwadi, 80, 84.
Ku*t*i	Ku*t*i, 113.

INDEX OF PROPER NAMES IN THE PARABLES. 201

Pali.	Burmese.
Kururattha	Gururit, 44.
Koliyā	Kòliya, 178.
Kosambi	Kòthambhi, 32, 34, 36, 37, 38.
Kosala	Kòthala, 149, 154, 164, 167, 175.

Kh / Kh

Khuggúttarā . . . . Khodzottarā, 32, 47, 48, 49, 59, 60.

G / G

Gandhakuti . . . . Gandhakuti, 65, 89, 90, 101.
Gandhamādana . . . Gandamādana, 120, 121, 122.
Gandhā . . . . . Gandhā, 106.
Gambhira . . . . Gambhira, 171.
Gotama . . . . . Gòthama, 46, 49, 50, 51, 52, 80, 93,
106, 107, 110, 121, 125, 156, 175,
190.

Gh / Gh

Ghosita . . . . . Ghòthaka, 38.
Ghositārāma . . . . Ghòthidārom, 32.

K / S

Kakravartti . . . . Sĕkyawade, 82, 90, 136, 137, 179.
Kakravāla . . . . Sĕkyawalā, 161.
Kakkhupāla . . . . Sĕkkhupāla, 1, 6, 7, 8, 9, 10, 11.
Kandapaggota . . . Sandapitsòta, 38, 39, 40, 41, 42, 43.
Katumahārāja . . . Sadumahārit, 15, 122.
Katulokapāla . . . Sadulòkapāla, 95, 97, 160.
Kandapa . . . . . Sandapa, 82, 83.
Kiñkamāna . . . . Sĕñsamāna, 158.
Kullakāla . . . . Sūlakāla, 25, 26, 29, 30.
Kulla-Panthaka . . Sūla-Bandhaka, 61, 62, 63, 64, 65,
66, 67, 68, 71.
Kulla-Pāla . . . Sūla-Pāla, 2, 6, 7, 9.
Kulla-Māgandiya . Sūla-Māgandi, 11.

202 INDEX OF PROPER NAMES IN THE PARABLES.

PALI.	BURMESE.
Kullaratha	Sūlaratha, 123.
Kulla-Sumana	Sūla-Thumana, 107, 113, 117, 118, 119.
Ketiya	Setiya, 158.
Kelakanthi	Zethakuthi, 42.

G	Z
Ganapadakalyāni	Zanapadakalyāni, 179.
Gantu	Sanda, 175, 176.
Gambudvīpa	Zambūdipa, 22, 190.
Gīvaka	Ziwaka, 64, 65, 66, 67, 68.
Getavana	Zedawun, 1, 2, 9, 25, 72, 78, 87, 98, 104, 105, 117, 120, 122, 125, 138, 142, 146, 151, 164, 181.
Gayasena	Zeyathena, 178.

T	T
Takkasilā	Tĕkkatho, 68, 69.
Tāvatinsa	Tāwaténthā, 14, 15, 79, 156, 160.
Tissa	Téttha, 18, 19, 20, 24, 72, 74, 76.
Tissamahāvihāra	Tétthamahāwihāra, 106.

D	D
Dandapāni	Dantapāni, 179.
Disāpamokkha	Dithāpāmaukkha, 68, 71, 171, 173, 174.
Devadatta	Dewadat, 179.
Devadaha	Dewadaha, 175, 178, 179.
Devala	Dewīla, 20, 21, 22, 23, 24.

Dh	Dh
Dhanasethi	Dhanathethi, 61, 62.
Dhotodana	Dòdòdana, 179.

INDEX OF PROPER NAMES IN THE PARABLES.

PALI.	BURMESE.
N	**N**
Nanda	Nanda, 179.
Nandamūla	Nandamūla, 60.
Nāgadatta	Nāgadatta, 120, 121, 122, 123, 124, 125.
Nārada	Nārada, 20, 21, 22, 23, 24.
Nālāgiri	Nālāgiri, 42.
Nīlavāha	Nīlawāha, 82.
P	**P**
Pagāpatigotami	Pazāpatigòtamī, 179.
Pañkapathaka	Pyiñsapathaka, 106.
Pañkapāpi	Pyiñsapāpī, 142, 143, 144.
Pandapura	Pandapūra, 103.
Pandita	Pandita, 87, 94, 95, 96.
Padumuttara	Padommottora, 107, 112.
Pannaga	Pananda, 114, 115, 116, 117, 118.
Panthaka	Bandhaka, 62.
Pandukabra	Pandukabrā, 154.
ParanimmitaVasavartti	Paranémmitawatthawadī, 122.
Parantapa	Pŭrandappa, 34, 36, 37.
Pasenadīkosala	Patthenadikòthala, 125, 128, 133, 134, 181.
Pālita	Pālita, 7, 8.
Pālitā	Pālitā, 179.
Pindapātika-Tissa	Péndapātika-Téttha, 75.
Putigatta	Putigatta, 154.
Pubbārāma	Poppārom, 107.
Pūrika	Pūrika, 125.
B	**B**
	Benares, 10, 58, 69, 78, 87, 108, 136, 138, 171.
Bimbasāra	Pémpathāra, 163.
Bimbā	Pémpā, 179.

INDEX OF PROPER NAMES IN THE PARABLES.

PALI.	BURMESE.
Brahma	Brahmā, 105, 106, 115, 116, 123, 163.
Brahmadatta	Brahmadat, 58, 136.
Brihatphala	Wehappho, 123.

Bh	Bh
Bhaddavaggi	Bhadawĕggi, 163,
Bhaddavatī	Bhattawadī, 38, 42.
Bhaddi	Bhaddiya, 112.
	Bhurā T*h*akiṅ,[1] 2, 4, 5, 6, 9, 10, 12, 14, 15, 16, 18, 19, 20, 24, 25, 26, 29, 30, etc.

M	M
Maddhaku*nd*ali	Mat*h*ako*nd*ali, 12, 14, 15, 16.
Mallikā	Mallikā, 130, 131, 134, 154.
Mahākappina	Mahākapé*nn*a, 78, 80, 81, 82, 83, 84, 85.
Mahākāla	Mahākāla, 25, 26, 27, 28, 29, 30, 31.
Mahādūta	Mahādot, 88, 89, 90, 91, 92, 93.
Mahā-Panthaka	Mahā-Bandhaka, 62, 63, 64, 67, 68.
Mahā-Pāla	Mahā-Pāla, 2, 3, 4, 5, 6.
Mahāpunna	Mahāpo*nn*ā, 106.
Mahāmunda	Mahāmonta, 113.
Mahārat*h*a	Mahārat*h*a, 123.
Mahāsena	Mahāt*h*ena, 72, 73, 75.
Mahāsvanna	Mahāt*h*umana, 1.
Māgandiya	Māga*nd*ī, 44.
Māgandiyā	Māga*nd*ī, 32, 44, 46, 49, 50, 51, 52, 53, 54, 55, 57, 58.
	Mān-Nat, 46.
Māyā	Māyā, 148.
Mittapindaka	Méttapendaka, 171, 172, 173, 174.
Muñ*y*akesi	Moñsaket*h*i, 42.
Munda	Monta, 113, 114.
Meru	Myinmo, 22.
Moggalāna	Maukkalān, 6, 49.

[1] N.B.—Always pronounced Parā Takén.

INDEX OF PROPER NAMES IN THE PARABLES. 205

PALI.	BURMESE.
Y	Y
Yasodharā . .	. Yathòdharā, 178, 179.
R	R or Y
Rāgagaha	. . Rāzagyo, 61, 62, 72, 105.
Rāma	. . Rāma, 177, 178.
Rāhula . . .	. . Rāhulā, 179.
L	L
Latthi . . .	. Laddhi, 163.
Likkavi . . .	. . Léthsawi, 136, 137.
Lokatissa . . .	Lòkatettha, 164, 165, 166, 167, 168, 174.
V	W
Vanga . . .	. Winga, 72.
Vāsuladattā .	. Wāthuladatta, 38, 41, 43, 44.
Vidadūpa	. Widadūpa, 154.
Vimānopeta . .	. Wimānapeta, 172, 173.
Visākhā . . .	. Withākhā, 118, 123.
Vethadipaka	. . Wethadipa, 32, 33.
Velāma	. Welāma, 151.
Veluvana . . .	. Weluwun, 61.
Vesāli . .	. . Wethāli, 136.
S	Th
Samsarāka . . .	. Thantharāka, 154.
Sakka	. Thigyā, 8, 9, 15, 89, 90, 91, 92, 95, 97, 123, 160, 161, 162.
Sakkodana . . .	Thëkkòdana, 179.
Sabburisa . . .	Thabburitha, 138.
Sākiya . . .	Thāgiwiṅ, 110, 154, 175.
Sāketa	. Thāketa, 80.
Sāmavatī	. Thāmāwadī, 32, 38, 47, 48, 49, 50, 51, 52, 53, 54, 55, 56, 57, 58, 59.

206 INDEX OF PROPER NAMES IN THE PARABLES.

Pali.	Burmese.
Sāriputta	Thāripottarā, 49, 72, 73, 74, 75, 76, 94, 95, 96, 161, 165, 166, 167, 168.
Sāvatthi	Thāwatthi, 1, 4, 8, 9, 12, 14, 18, 25, 73, 75, 80, 81, 94, 98, 101, 103, 104, 149, 165, 174, 190.
Siddhattha	Théddhat, 179.
Sirimahāmāyā	Thirimahāmāyā, 179.
Sirivaddhana	Thiriwadhana, 189, 190.
Sivali	Thiwali, 120, 121.
Sīhanu	Thīhanu, 178, 179.
Sudatta	Thudatta, 123.
Sudassana	Thoddhāwātha, 123.
Suddhodana	Thuddhòdana, 18, 147, 179.
Suppabuddha	Thoppaboddha, 179.
Subhakritsna	Thubhakén, 122
Subhāga	Thòbhāga, 119.
Sumana	Thumana, 108, 109, 110, 112, 113, 119.
Sumanā	Thumana, 47, 48.
Setavya	Thetappa, 25.

H   II

Himavanta	Hémmawunta, 20, 32, 34, 78, 113, 118, 120, 122, 168.

www.ingramcontent.com/pod-product-compliance
Lightning Source LLC
Chambersburg PA
CBHW020300240426
43673CB00039B/657